Favorite Recipes
Of
Kentucky Celebrities

Compiled by Pamela Whinnery
Phone: 270-554-5332
e-mail: whinneryw@bellsouth.net

D0326154

Dedication

In appreciation for his willingness to courageously try any new dish I serve, I would like to dedicate this book to my wonderful husband, Walter.

Without his love, patience, and computer savvy, this book would have never come to completion. God truly blessed me when He sent you into my life.

In Memory of

Leo Burmester, 1944-2007, and Todd Williams, 1938-2007, who both graciously sent me recipes when I first started this project

&

Maria Sue Chapman, 2003-2008, daughter of Steve Curtis Chapman. Steve sent me a recipe a couple of years ago, which he stated was a favorite family recipe.

Expression
of Appreciation

In the spirit of Kentucky neighborliness, you are invited to take a lighthearted peek into the personal recipe files of celebrities from all across the state of Kentucky as well as those who have strong ties to the Bluegrass State.

It is with heartfelt appreciation that I express my gratitude to all the local and national personalities, highly-visible Kentucky businesses, artists, writers, athletes, sportsmen, actors, musicians, bed and breakfasts, restaurants, notable events and places for taking the time from their busy schedules to share their recipes.

It has been fun and exciting! Jeri Ryan and Christophe Eme sent their recipe for lamb, even though they had just had a new baby.

When sending his recipe, Academy Award Winner Bub Asman brought a smile to my face with the statement, "I knew that Oscar would finally pay off."

There are so many wonderful people and places in Kentucky! Time kept me from contacting more people. If you do not find your favorite celebrity, please forgive me.

This cookbook and each recipe is a gift to be shared as a fundraiser for nonprofit organizations all across Kentucky. May God bless those who sent recipes and those who use it as a fundraiser.

Pam Whinnery

Duplicate Recipes

There are certain recipes that are traditional Kentucky recipes. As might be expected, I received duplicates of some of these extremely popular recipes. I listed the recipe only once, but wished to include information on all the great people and places that also submitted these recipes.

Burgoo – The Heartland Dulcimer Club located in Elizabethtown endeavors to share and preserve the music of the mountain dulcimer, hammered dulcimer and other historical instruments.

Burgoo – The Honorable Order of the Kentucky Colonels was established in 1813 just after the War of 1812. They serve as both Kentucky Ambassadors and a charitable foundation.

Kentucky Hot Brown – Magician Lance Burton, Louisville. He has performed for 26 years in Las Vegas. He is at the Monte Carlo in the Lance Burton Theatre, which he helped design.

Kentucky Hot Brown – Kentucky born Paul Cross has starred in Broadway, television, and produced and directed numerous feature films including Westend Story starring Petula Clark, Lucie Arnaz, and Andrew Lloyd Weber.

Sausage & Egg Casserole – Teresa A. Barton is the County Judge Executive for Franklin County. The county was formed in 1795 and named after Benjamin Franklin. The county seat, Frankfort, is also the capital of Kentucky.

Sausage & Egg Casserole – Kentucky Derby Festival held two weeks immediately preceding the Derby has more than 70 events and attracts crowds in excess of 1.5 million people.

Table of Contents

Appetizers, Relishes, and Pickles

Spinach Dip
1 c. mayonnaise
1 c. sour cream
1 pkg. good Seasons
   Italian dressing mix
tsp. lemon juice
   onion, diced
   powder to taste
   spinach, thawed
   ...ained

...ents well. Refrigerate
   the vegetables'
   ...brown br...

Recipe Favorites

Page No.

Recipe Title:_____ _____

_____ _____

_____ _____

_____ _____

_____ _____

_____ _____

_____ _____

_____ _____

_____ _____

_____ _____

Family Favorites

Page No.

Recipe Title:_____ _____

_____ _____

_____ _____

_____ _____

_____ _____

_____ _____

Notes:_____

_____

_____

_____

Appetizers, Relishes & Pickles

❧ Benedict's Restaurant ❧ Spread

Benedict's Restaurant

This spread can be used as a dip or a sandwich and canape ingredient. It was made popular at Louisville's Benedict's Restaurant earlier in this century.

1 large cucumber
8 oz. cream cheese, softened
2 Tbsp. grated onion
¼ tsp. salt

1 Tbsp. mayonnaise
dash green food coloring
(optional)

Pare, grate and drain cucumber. Combine with remaining ingredients in food processor. Serve as is or as a sandwich or canape spread. Thin with sour cream to make a dip for vegetables.

Jennie Carter Benedict was born in Harrods Creek, Kentucky, on March 25, 1860. She founded Benedict's Restaurant and Tearoom, Louisville, Kentucky, in 1900. Her classic recipe for Benedictine sandwich spread is a traditional recipe served at Kentucky Derby parties.

❧ Patti's Chicken Spread ❧

Carson Center

1 large can white meat
chicken, drained

1 envelope Ranch dressing
mix
2 blocks cream cheese

Let the cream cheese sit out and soften. Mix all together and refrigerate overnight. Serve with crackers and veggies or as a sandwich on a toasted bagel.

Chicken Ranch Roll-Ups:

large flour tortillas
Patti's Chicken Spread

tomatoes or cucumbers (or
  both)
spinach or leaf lettuce

Spread the tortillas with Chicken Spread. Top with tomatoes and fresh spinach. Roll up. Cut in ½-inch slices and arrange on a tray.

The Luther F. Carson Four Rivers Center opened February 2004 and is an 1806-seat regional performing arts center in Paducah. In addition to a Broadway series, it hosts nationally acclaimed artists and is home of the Paducah Symphony Orchestra.

Cheese Ball

Christian Way Farms

2 ½ c. (10 oz.) shredded
  sharp Cheddar cheese
1 (8 oz.) jar process cheese
  spread
1 (8 oz.) pkg. cream cheese,
  softened
1 Tbsp. mayonnaise

1 Tbsp. Worcestershire sauce
1 Tbsp. frozen chopped
  chives, thawed
⅛ tsp. garlic powder
⅛ tsp. onion powder
½ c. chopped pecans

Combine all ingredients except pecans; beat on medium speed of electric mixer until smooth. Chill 2 hours. Shape into a ball, and roll in pecans. Serve with crackers. Yield: 1 cheese ball.

Christian Way Farm in Hopkinsville opened in 1998. The primary purpose was to have a farm that would be open to the public teaching and providing a "farm" experience. Visitors participate in planting, tending or harvesting crops, and feeding animals.

Red Pepper Pickle

Julia Dinsmore Homestead

½ bushel ripe mango peppers
3 oz. white mustard seed
1 pt. salt

1 gal. water
4 lb. brown sugar
1 qt. vinegar

Take the stems and seeds out and chop fine, and mix with white mustard seed. Put salt in water and bring it to the boiling

Appetizers, Relishes & Pickles

point and pour over the pepper(s) and mustard and let it stand over-night. Then pour off the brine. Put brown sugar in vinegar; put pepper(s) in; let it comes to a boil and can. Delicious.

Julia Dinsmore ran the family's 700 acre farm from 1876 until her death in 1926 at age 93. A published poet, she kept a journal of her life on the farm. Located near Burlington, Dinsmore farm is now an educational resource for artists, naturalists, students and scholars.

Doodle's Munchy Yummies
Doodles Studio

2 c. flour	**½ lb. extra-sharp Cheddar**
2 c. Rice Krispies	**½ lb. butter, softened (but**
¼ tsp. cayenne pepper	**not melted)**

Preheat oven to 350°. Grate up the cheese well and add to softened butter. Cream well. Add the flour and mix well. Add the cayenne pepper and Rice Krispies. Mix, but don't crunch up the Rice Krispies too much. Drop on an ungreased cookie sheet and flatten with a fork. Bake for 10 to 15 minutes, or until the crackers are slightly browned.

Doodles Studio and Gallery in Flemingsburg is located in a restored 1840's three-story building which housed a former Masonic Lodge and Mercantile Store. The working studio and gallery, which represents over 27 artists, is owned by artist Brenda Flynn.

Baked Brie
Amy Dudgeon

1 wheel Brie cheese	**1 sheet puff pastry**
6 oz. ruby port wine (or your	**1 whole egg, beaten**
favorite preserves in a	**1 loaf sliced French bread**
pinch)	**1 box variety of crackers**
1 c. dried cranberries or	**1 to 2 Granny Smith and/or**
other dried berries	**Fiji apples, sliced (optional)**
(blueberries, cherries, etc.)	**1 c. walnuts (optional)**

Place Brie wheel in freezer for about 30 minutes to harden. This makes the Brie easier to cut later on. Defrost puff pastry according to package. Preheat oven to 350°.

In a saucepan, simmer port and berries until slightly thickened, stirring constantly. Remove from heat and let sit for a minute until it thickens a little more. Remove Brie from freezer. Using a knife, scrape the rind off the Brie. Using a larger knife or floss, yes floss, slice the Brie in half horizontally. Flip the top part of the Brie over like bread to make a sandwich. Scoop the port sauce onto the bottom half of the Brie. Don't use all the sauce. Take the top piece of Brie and place it on the bottom like a sandwich. Place Brie and port onto the puff pastry sheet and wrap the sheet around it. Brush the bottom with the beaten egg to seal. Flip over so all you see is the smooth pastry. Brush with the egg. Place on cookie sheet and place in oven. Bake for about 20 minutes. It's normal for some of the Brie and port to seep out. Bake until the pastry has puffed and is golden. Remove from oven and place on platter with crackers or sliced French bread, and sliced apples. Top the Brie with the remaining port sauce and walnuts and serve. Serves 1 to 8.

Actress Amy Dudgeon is from Elizabethtown. She has performed in various television programs including ER, Desperate Housewives, House and Street King with Keanu Reeves. She also worked as assistant director for "The David Letterman Show."

BBQ Boiled Eggs

Frances BBQ Restaurant

enough hard-boiled eggs to fill a jar

enough vinegar-based BBQ sauce to cover the eggs in the jar

This recipe couldn't be easier. Place hard-boiled eggs in the jar, cover with sauce, refrigerate for a week and eat!

Frances BBQ in Hestand is owned by David and Jennifer Arms and has been in business for over 30 years. BBQ is in big demand in Monroe County, with 10 BBQ restaurants. Even with all the competition, Frances serves 11,000 pounds a week along with the BBQ boiled eggs.

❧ *Appetizer On Garlic Toast* ❧

Ferd Grisanti's Restaurant

2 lb. tomatoes, chopped
fresh in ½-inch cubes
1 Tbsp. garlic, ground
1 Tbsp. salt
1 Tbsp. black pepper, ground
1 c. fresh basil, chopped
fresh

½ lb. red onions, chopped
fine (⅛ to ¼-inch)
1 c. olive oil (virgin or 100%
pure)
½ c. balsamic vinegar
¼ c. red wine vinegar

Chop, dice or grind as indicated. Mix. Spoon on hot garlic toast.

Ferd Grisanti's has been a Louisville tradition for years. The warm personality of the founder, Ferd Grisanti, has been a hallmark of the restaurant from the beginning in 1972. The dishes reflect the cuisine that emerged in Florence and surrounding areas during the Renaissance.

❧ *Apple and Blue Cheese* ❧ *Pita*

Hollie Hummel

1 to 1 ¼ c. Blue cheese
crumbles
¼ c. mayonnaise

4 pita bread pockets or naan
bread
1 apple
½ c. chopped walnuts

Preheat oven to 425°.
In small bowl, combine 3 tablespoons Blue cheese crumbles and mayonnaise; mix well. Place naan bread (or pita bread) on baking stone; spread one side of each bread with 2 tablespoons of cheese mixture. Top bread evenly with 1 cored thinly sliced red apple, 2 tablespoons chopped walnuts and 2 tablespoons additional Blue cheese crumbles. Bake 10 to 12 minutes or until cheese is melted.

Hollie Hummel was born in Lexington and won a beauty contest as a baby in Paris, Kentucky. The television and film star is best known for her roles on Days of Our Lives, General Hospital, Stories from the ER, and The Bold and The Beautiful.

Loyal's Barbecue Sauce

Loyal Jones

1 c. apple cider vinegar
1 c. water
1 (15 oz.) can tomato sauce
2 cloves garlic or generous
powdered garlic
1 medium onion, minced

1 pod red pepper (or to
taste)
1 tsp. black pepper (or to
taste)
1 Tbsp. salt (or to taste)
no sugar (for Heaven's sake!)

Cook for a few minutes. Good for chicken or pork, such as country ribs. Put meat in with the sauce and cook for about 20 minutes. Then put meat over a charcoal fire and cook until good and brown, or black. When turning the meat, dip it in the sauce.

Loyal Jones has authored seven books, dozens of articles and short stories on Appalachian culture. After twenty-three years as Founding Director of the Berea College's Appalachian Center, he is now retired, but still writing.

Vivian Bradley and Mom's Cheese Wafers

Naomi Judd

(Makes about 6 dozen.)

1 lb. grated sharp Cheddar
cheese
2 sticks butter (room
temperature)
2 c. all-purpose flour
1 tsp. salt

½ tsp. ground hot-red pepper
(cayenne; or less if you like
your food less spicy)
pecan halves (1 for each
wafer)

Mix cheese and butter. Add flour, salt and pepper until smooth dough is formed. Shape into 2 logs, 9 ½ x 1 ½-inches. Place in refrigerator until well chilled, about 2 hours.

Preheat oven to 350°. Cut log into ¼-inch slices and place on ungreased baking sheet. Place a pecan half on top of each. Bake until lightly colored, about 12 minutes. Transfer the baking sheet to wire rack to cool slightly. Transfer the wafers to the rack to cool.

Naomi Judd from Ashland helped The Judds (with daughter Wynona) set new standards of excellence and ushered in the resurgence of country music's popularity. They received 6

Appetizers, Relishes & Pickles

Grammys and their 2000 "Power to Change Tour" was the top grossing tour of the year.

❧ Corn Relish ❧

Labrot and Graham

12 ears of corn
2 c. chopped red bell peppers
2 c. chopped green bell peppers
2 c. chopped celery
1 c. chopped onion
3 ¼ c. vinegar

1 ⅓ c. sugar
2 Tbsp. pickling or canning salt
2 tsp. celery seeds
2 Tbsp. dry mustard
1 tsp. turmeric
⅓ c. Woodford Reserve bourbon

Boil the corn in a generous amount of water in a stock-pot for 5 minutes. Drain and plunge into a large bowl of cold water to stop the cooking process; drain. Cut the tops of the corn kernels with a sharp knife into a bowl.

Bring the bell peppers, celery, onion, vinegar, sugar, salt and celery seeds to a boil in a saucepan, stirring occasionally. Reduce the heat to low and simmer for 5 minutes, stirring occasionally. Mix the dry mustard and turmeric in a bowl. Stir ½ cup of the bell pepper mixture into the dry mustard mixture. Stir the dry mustard mixture, bourbon and corn into the hot bell pepper mixture and mix well. Simmer for 5 minutes, stirring occasionally. Serve at room temperature or chilled.

Woodford Reserve Distillery, a historic landmark in Versailles, is a division of Labrot and Graham. The name "Bourbon" comes from Bourbon County, Kentucky, which, in the 1700's, covered a large portion of Kentucky. This recipe used by permission, David Larson, distillery Chef in Residence.

❧ La Donna's Fruit Dip ❧

Maple Hill Bed and Breakfast

8 oz. cream cheese
1 small jar marshmallow cream

1 c. heavy whipping cream

Blend with mixer and refrigerate. Serve with fresh fruit.

Maple Hill Bed and Breakfast is a historic home that dates back to the 1850's, located in Eddyville, perched high atop a hill overlooking Lake Barkley. Enjoy a relaxing sunset over the lake or fishing, golfing, hiking and boating, which are just moments away.

❧ Mom's Spicy Kentucky Beer Cheese ❧

J. Richey Nash

8 oz. sharp Cheddar cheese
4 tsp. finely minced or grated
  onion and juice
1 tsp. Tabasco sauce
1 tsp. ground red pepper

1 ½ tsp. garlic powder
½ tsp. salt
½ tsp. sugar
4 to 6 oz. beer

Allow cheese and opened beer to reach room temperature. Beer should be flat. With hand-mixer or food processor, blend all ingredients except beer. Gradually add beer, blending until creamy. Refrigerate both remaining beer and cheese overnight. Cheese may have stiffened. Gradually work more of the beer into the chilled cheese until smooth and shiny. Enjoy as a snack or appetizer with fresh vegetables or your favorite chips and crackers.

Award winning actor and writer J. Richey Nash from Lexington graduated from Princeton University, was a minor league outfielder, and now resides in Los Angeles where he has starred in numerous films and network television shows such as George Lopez and Criminal Minds.

❧ Black Bean Salsa ❧

Old Governor's Mansion

3 (15 oz.) cans black beans
1 (15 oz.) can corn
⅓ bunch cilantro, chopped
½ onion, minced
1 medium tomato, chopped

1 to 2 Tbsp. jalapeno
  peppers, chopped
1 (2 ¼ oz.) can sliced black
  olives
⅛ tsp. cumin (sprinkle)

Appetizers, Relishes & Pickles

Stir together and serve with tortilla chips.

The Old Governor's Mansion, Frankfort, was built in 1798 and is the oldest official executive residence officially still in use in the United States, as the mansion is the official residence of the Lieutenant Governor of Kentucky.

Country Ham Balls

Old Kentucky Dinner Train

2 lb. ground or finely
  chopped country ham (use
  a food processor)
1 medium onion, processed
1 red bell pepper, processed

cayenne and black pepper to
  taste
½ lb. Gruyere or white
  Cheddar cheese, shredded
3 eggs
bread crumbs

Process onion and pepper separately, and drain off juices in a fine screen strainer. Mix onion, pepper, ham and cheese until well combined. Season with black and cayenne pepper and mix in eggs. Add bread crumbs a little at a time until mixture forms firm balls. Place on a sheet pan sprayed with nonstick spray and bake at 350° until lightly browned and cheese is melted, 15 to 20 minutes. Serve warm or room temperature.

I came up with this recipe as a way to use country ham as an appetizer other than the traditional ham biscuits. They freeze well after cooking for a couple of weeks. I also enjoy them with an alfredo sauce over pasta, a "Spaghetti and Meatballs Kentucky Style".

The Old Kentucky Dinner Train is located in Bardstown. The depot was constructed in 1860. The dinner excursion passes through the Berheim Forest and crosses Jackson Hollow Trestle, a totally timber structure 310 feet across and 60 feet above the hollow floor.

Perfectly Decadent Cream Cheese Spread

Joanne Rock

16 oz. cream cheese
1 small can crushed
  pineapple, drained
¼ to ½ c. green pepper,
  chopped fine

¼ c. onion, chopped fine
1 to 2 Tbsp. seasoned salt (to
  taste)
½ c. chopped walnuts

Stir cream cheese to soften. Add remaining ingredients. Chill for two hours to allow flavors to blend. Scrumptious with Triscuits or your favorite crackers.

Author Joanne Rock has written more than 30 contemporary romances and medieval historicals that have been printed in 24 countries and translated into 19 different languages by Harlequin Romances. This University of Louisville graduate is a Romance Writers of America Golden Heart winner.

—•*Extra Recipes*•—

Soups,
Salads,
and Sauces

Recipe Favorites

Page No.

Recipe Title:_____

_____   _____

_____   _____

_____   _____

_____   _____

_____   _____

_____   _____

_____   _____

_____   _____

_____   _____

Family Favorites

Page No.

Recipe Title:_____

_____   _____

_____   _____

_____   _____

_____   _____

_____   _____

Notes:_____

_____

_____

_____

Soups, Salads & Sauces

Louise Castleman Hoffman Coleman's Frozen Fruit Salad

Ashland, KY

| 4 egg yolks, beaten well | 2 Tbsp. vinegar |
| 2 Tbsp. water | 4 Tbsp. sugar |

Cook in double-boiler, stirring constantly, until thickness of custard.

When cool, add:

1 pt. whipping cream	1 can diced pineapple
1 can Queen Anne cherries	¾ c. miniature marshmallows
small bottle maraschino cherries	1 c. chopped pecans

Freeze at least 4 hours. Serves 6 to 8.

The city of Ashland founded in 1854 was named for Henry Clay's estate in Lexington. Located in Eastern Kentucky, it has long been the home of Ashland Oil Company. Recipe is from City Commissioner Russ Powell and came from his grandmother.

Curried Seafood Salad

Pat Banks

2 lb. lobster or crabmeat	1 jalapeno
1 bunch green onions	2 grated carrots
1 red pepper	fresh cilantro (is a great
1 green pepper	addition!)

Break up or slightly shred the seafood by hand. Chop the peppers and onions. Add the carrot and lightly mix together.

Sauce:

1 c. yogurt (plain)
1 to 2 tsp. curry

juice of 1 lemon or lime
salt and pepper to taste

Pat Banks is an artist who works primarily in watercolor. She lives and works in northern Madison County, Kentucky. She and her husband Alan built their home and studio on a ridge overlooking the Kentucky River Valley near Richmond, KY.

Ramen Noodle Coleslaw

Bell of Louisville

1 lb. pkg. coleslaw
1 bunch green onions,
  chopped
1 c. sunflower seeds

½ c. slivered almonds
2 pkg. Ramen noodle soup
  and seasoning packets

Crunch up noodles and add the rest of the ingredients.

Add:

1 c. oil
⅓ c. vinegar

⅔ c. sugar
1 tsp. soy sauce

Stir until well blended. Let set in refrigerator overnight, then serve.

The steamboat Belle of Louisville was built in 1914 and is now recognized as the oldest river steamboat still in operation providing dinner cruises. The Belle and the Delta Queen steamboats traditionally race annually Wednesday before the Derby.

Cynthia and Son, Keven's Seafood Bisque

Bell Sisters

1 lb. salted butter
8 large onions, chopped
1 ½ bunches celery, chopped
4 (46 oz.) cans clam juice
1 (46 oz.) can cream of
  mushroom soup
2 (46 oz.) cans clams
2 Tbsp. black pepper
1 Tbsp. white pepper
2 Tbsp. garlic powder

2 bay leaves
12 large potatoes, peeled and
  chopped
8 large carrots, chopped
2 large pkg. (large) scallops
2 pkg. each: shark, cod,
  scrod, red snapper and
  roughy
1 qt. half and half cream
1 gal. whole milk

Soups, Salads & Sauces

Roux:

1 lb. salted butter	**1 ½ lb. unbleached flour**

Into 32-quart pan, with large, long handle ladle (scoop) or spoon, saute and put aside 1 pound salted butter, onions (chopped bite size), and celery (chopped bite size). Bring to boil: clam juice, cream of mushroom soup, clams (drained juice only). Add and stir black pepper, white pepper, garlic powder and bay leaves. Now add large cut-up chunks of potatoes, carrots, sauteed onions and celery, and clams from cans. Add seafood: shrimp, (large) scallops, shark, cod, scrod, red snapper, roughy, etc. Cut up bite size.

In separate pan, make Roux. Mix 1 pound salted butter and unbleached flour. Bubble butter in pan while stirring in flour until golden brown. Carefully stirring, add soup mixture to Roux, 1 cup at a time, then add back into soup; be sure no lumps. Add ½ and ½ cream and whole milk.

Cynthia (16) and sister Kay Bell (11) from Kentucky had several radio and jukebox hits including "Bermuda", which reached #7 in 1952. The Bell Sisters were in radio, movies and television with Bing Crosby, Bob Hope, Dinah Shore, Nat King Cole and Frank Sinatra.

❧ *Margarita Coleslaw* ❧

Stephen D. Boyd

½ c. olive oil	1 large onion, sliced into thin rings
1 c. white balsamic vinegar	12 pkg. sweetener (such as Equal)
1 heaping Tbsp. dry mustard	2 Tbsp. tequila (optional)
2 bags shredded cabbage or 1 large head cabbage, shredded	1 Tbsp. lime juice

Whisk together in 2-cup glass measuring cup the first 3 ingredients. Heat 2 minutes on High in microwave.

Meanwhile, mix together next 3 ingredients. Add to oil/vinegar mixture the tequila (optional) and lime juice. Pour over cabbage mixture and toss. Serves 8 to 10.

Stephen Boyd is a professional speaker, seminar leader and communication consultant. He received his Ph.D. from the University of Illinois and is on the faculty of Northern Kentucky University and author of From Dull to Dynamic: Transforming Your Presentations.

Anna Mae's Bone Soup

Ray Brune

soup bone	pepper
water	tomato juice
salt	noodles

Ask your neighborhood butcher for a soup bone. (Prices range from free to free, slightly higher in a supermarket.) Cook in a large pot with lots of water for 2 hours. Salt and pepper to taste. Remove bone from the pot; add one large can of tomato juice. Bring to a boil and add a package of "fat" noodles. Cook for the number of minutes recommended on the package of noodles!

Emmy and Peabody Award winner Ray Brune is from Covington. He was executive producer of Good Morning America/Sunday, E Network, and is owner of Kimco Jagger Productions, which heads the TV division of Merv Griffin Entertainment.

Chilled Avocado Soup

Lonnie Burr

(Serves 4 to 8 depending on portion size.)

4 ripe (but not overripe) avocados	3 tsp. freshly grated onion
2 ¾ c. vegetable stock or water	½ tsp. white pepper
1 ½ c. heavy cream	1 tsp. salt
½ tsp. "Mexican spice" or chili powder	1 tsp. lemon juice
	garnish: sour cream (or ½ low-fat sour cream and ½ plain low-fat yogurt)

Cut 3 avocados in half; remove the skin and the pit. Put the 4th avocado in the refrigerator. Slice avocados roughly. Put half of avocado and half of stock in blender; blend on high 2 minutes or until smooth. Pour into large glass bowl, then repeat with second half, adding chili powder, onion and lemon juice before blending. Once avocado/stock mixture is smooth, stir in 1 ½ cups heavy cream, salt and white pepper until thoroughly blended. Leave in bowl and wipe down the inside of the container with a damp paper towel so no splashes of the soup remain on the sides. Cut a piece of plastic wrap large enough to place directly onto the surface of the soup. Make sure the plastic is in contact with the soup all the way to the sides of the container, then run the plastic wrap up the inside of the container. The point of this is to keep out any air that will change the color of the top of the mixture from avocado green to brown-gray. Can chill overnight up to 24 hours. Thirty minutes prior to serving, place your bowls or cups in the freezer to chill. Cut 4th avocado in half, peel and remove pit and cut into small bite-sized cubes. Remove plastic wrap from soup; if any of the top bits have oxidized (turned brown-gray), mix it into the rest. Add cubes of avocado to soup. Stir. Remove bowls/cups from freezer and ladle soup into them, being sure to get some of the cubes in each serving. Add garnish.

Mouseketeer Lonnie Burr is from Dayton. He is one of the nine original cast members of "The Mickey Mouse Club" which aired from 1955-59. Lonnie has performed in film, television and stage both before and after MMC. He is a professional actor and choreographer.

❧ *Brandywine-Black Bean* ❧ *Soup*

Jeff Chapman-Crane

2 qt. fresh brandywine
   tomatoes, peeled and
   chopped
3 c. dried black beans
8 plus c. water
5 to 6 bay leaves
1 Tbsp. salt
2 large onions, chopped
1 large garlic clove, minced
1 lb. Jimmy Dean sausage
3 Bulgarian Shipka peppers,
   seeded and chopped

1 medium green bell pepper,
   roasted, peeled, seeded and
   chopped
approximately 1 Tbsp. salt*
2 to 3 leaves fresh basil,
   minced
½ tsp. dried French tarragon
½ tsp. dried lovage leaves or
   celery seed
1 tsp. paprika

In large soup pot, cook beans with bay leaves and 1 tablespoon salt in water until tender; add water as necessary (2 to 4 cups). In skillet, cook onions, garlic, peppers and sausage together until vegetables are tender. In medium pot, cook tomatoes, 1 tablespoon salt and herbs until tender. Add ingredients to large pot as they get done. Simmer for 30 minutes to one hour.

Jeff Chapman-Crane is a professional and award winning painter, artist, and book illustrator from Eolia, in the Appalachian

Mountains, where he has lived for the last 26 years. His portraits of mountain people show their character and souls.

Fruit Salad With Glaze

Creekside Treasures

1 can fruit cocktail
1 can chunk pineapple
3 bananas
fresh strawberries

3 Tbsp. Tang (instant breakfast drink)
1 box instant vanilla pudding

Drain fruit cocktail and dispose of juice. Drain pineapple, reserving juice. Combine all fruit in large bowl and stir. Take reserved pineapple juice and mix with Tang and vanilla pudding. Pour the glaze over the fruit.

Creekside Treasures is a photography studio located in Ravenna near Richmond. Owner Linda Durham specializes in environmental portraiture, photographed on property, which has been in her family for over 100 years, using the creek and natural surroundings.

Not Your Mom's Chicken Soup

Daniel Boone Outdoor Drama

1 chicken breast, diced
1 can chicken broth
½ lime
1 clove minced garlic
¼ c. diced onion
1 can each veggies (add your favorites, corn, beans, potatoes, carrots)
1 can diced flavored tomatoes (undrained)

½ c. rice
diced avocado
⅛ tsp. thyme
½ tsp. parsley
1 tsp. cilantro (also known as coriander)
salt and pepper to taste
water (keep the water level above the food; this isn't good as a stew)

Warm the already diced chicken and garlic in a skillet or a pan. To keep it from sticking and to bring out more flavor, squeeze the lime over it. Then you'll throw everything into a stockpot to cook slowly and add enough water to cover ingredients. Put in more of your family's favorite vegetables. Let the soup cook slowly for at least 1 ½ hours. Do NOT add the avocado immediately. Wait

Soups, Salads & Sauces

about 45 minutes into the cooking time, or it will simply turn to mush. The lime juice and the cilantro are the key ingredients to this soup.

"Daniel Boone, the Man and the Legend" is performed at the outdoor amphitheater at Old Fort Harrod State Park, Harrodsburg. The historical based script and production that keeps the audience on the edge of their seats has held summer performances for over 40 years.

❧ *Salad Recipe* ❧

Kassie DePaiva

1 head romaine lettuce
1 Granny Smith apple
Blue cheese, crumpled

crushed bagel chips
poppy seed dressing (I like Brianna's)

Chop and serve.

Actress Kassie De Paiva is from Morganfield. She has starred in numerous television roles, including Chelsea Reardon on "The Guiding Light", Melrose Place and Baywatch. She presently has a leading role as Blair Cramer on "One Life to Live."

❧ *Gramma Burr's Vegetable Chowder* ❧

Dot and Dash

(Serves 8, with leftovers.)

6 Tbsp. shortening
2 large onions, peeled and sliced
5 cloves garlic, peeled, roughly chopped and flattened
4 bay leaves
10 carrots, peeled and sliced into ¾-inch
2 parsnips, peeled and sliced into ¾-inch rounds
6 potatoes, peeled and quartered
16 small (boiler size) onions, peeled and left whole, or 8 medium onions, peeled and cut in half
3 turnips, peeled and cut into ⅛ths

1 ½ c. fresh green beans (with ends removed), cut into 1-inch pieces
1 (15 oz.) can chopped tomatoes
2 c. chopped broccoli or cauliflower or a mixture
2 zucchini, sliced into 1-inch rounds
1 (15 oz.) or so can of cooked corn (preferably without added sugar)
1 green or red bell pepper, seeded and cut into ⅛ths
1 c. chopped celery (1-inch pieces, NOT diced)
salt and pepper

Optional:

8 oz. mushrooms, quartered or sliced
1 diced mashed garlic clove
1 Tbsp. cooking oil
1 bunch spinach or 12 kale leaves, washed and dried well (with stems and big veins removed)

fresh herbs (if you have them), rinsed well and patted dry: chives cut into ½-inch pieces, sage leaves removed from stems and chopped, oregano leaves removed from woody stem, and a good-sized sprig of rosemary left whole

Melt shortening in soup pot; add onions, garlic and a small handful of each of the carrots, parsnips and celery. Cook, stirring often, just until soft. Do not brown. Add flour and stir. Remove from heat and stir in 8 ounces warm water, until smooth. Replace on stove over medium-low to medium heat; add 48 ounces water. Stir until blended. Add bay leaves, carrots and parsnips; stir several times and cook 20 minutes. Add potatoes, onions, turnips and green beans; stir several times and cook for 20 more minutes; keep on simmer or very slow boil. Do not let it come to a full boil or you will bruise the vegetables. Add chopped tomatoes, broccoli/ cauliflower and cook for 20 more minutes. (If you want to add a sprig of fresh rosemary, do so now, but remember to remove it later.) Add zucchini, corn, bell pepper and chopped celery. Stir. Increase heat slightly and cook for 20 more minutes. When chowder has cooked gently for 80 minutes total, turn off heat, partially cover and let sit for 20 minutes. Remove lid and add salt and pepper, stirring after each addition. Let sit without lid for an additional 20 minutes. Ladle into wide bowls, making sure every serving has a good variety of vegetables. Serve with freshly baked biscuits or garlic bread.

Gramma Burr lived to be 105 years old. She was the mother of Dorothy Burr. Dorothy and her husband Howard Babin were a vaudeville dance team that performed in film and on stage as "Dot and Dash." They were from the Covington-Newport area and the parents of Mouseketeer Lonnie Burr.

Ellis Park Meatball Soup

(Recipe makes a large quantity of soup!)

Soup Base:

8 c. chopped onions
8 c. chopped celery
8 c. chopped carrots
2 (16 oz.) tubs chicken base
2 (No. 10) cans crushed or
  chopped tomatoes
2 (No. 10) cans water
4 minced garlic cloves
3 fresh chopped zucchini

2 Tbsp. dried basil
2 Tbsp. dried thyme
2 Tbsp. dried oregano
1 Tbsp. cayenne pepper
1 c. sugar
4 Tbsp. dried parsley
black pepper (to taste)
5 lb. elbow macaroni or any
  pasta, cooked

Meatballs:

10 lb. ground beef
10 eggs
20 Tbsp. Parmesan cheese

10 tsp. garlic salt
5 tsp. black pepper

Make meatballs; shape into desired size. Bake in 350° oven for 20 to 30 minutes or until done. Set aside.

Cook first seven soup stock ingredients until vegetables just start to become tender. Add zucchini and all spices. While this is cooking, prepare pasta. Once vegetables are tender, add meatballs and cooked pasta. Simmer together for 20 to 30 minutes. (Recipe makes a large quantity of soup!) Serve with pride!

Ellis Park is a thoroughbred racetrack located in Henderson, Kentucky and was built in 1922. Although it is in Kentucky, it is located north of the Ohio River near Evansville, Indiana due to the fact that the Ohio's flow was changed when the New Madrid earthquake occurred.

Chicken Stew

Fordsville Days

1 large stewing chicken
salt and pepper to taste
½ c. cream
1 diced celery stalk
1 sliced medium carrot

½ to 1 c. milk
1 tsp. parsley and sage (to
  taste)
chopped onions (to taste)

Cut up chicken. Season. Roll in flour and brown in hot fat. Put in a baking pan and add the remaining ingredients. Cover and bake in hot oven for about 2 hours or until tender. When the chicken is done, take off cover and brown the top of the bird. Add milk during cooking if needed. Serve in pan.

Fordsville was known prior to 1833 as "Kelly's Precinct." Benjamin Kelly came to the area with Daniel Boone, whose nephew married Sallie Ford. This recipe was Daniel's favorite. Fordville Days is celebrated the 3rd weekend in September at the Depot Museum.

Chili Tex

Dale Evans

(From the Kitchen of Grandma Dale.)

1 large can chili with beans	chopped onions
1 medium can white or yellow hominy	grated cheese

Turn oven on to 350°. Alternate layers of chili, cheese, onions and hominy in baking dish. Top with more grated cheese and bake until onions are tender and cheese is thoroughly melted. Main Dish: Serves 4 to 6.

American leading lady of musical westerns of the 1940's, Dale Evans began her career in Louisville where she became a popular singer on a local radio station. In the 1940's she was cast as leading lady to rising cowboy star Roy Rogers and the rest is history.

Sausage Rendezvous Stew

Frontier Christmas Ball

1 lb. Italian sausage	2 (14 oz.) cans Italian tomatoes
1 chopped onion	1 (14 oz.) can red beans
¼ tsp. garlic powder	1 (14 oz.) can whole kernel corn
2 Tbsp. flour	1 (14 oz.) can butter beans
1 (10 oz.) can broth	

In a cast-iron skillet, brown and break up Italian sausage with chopped onion and garlic to taste. When sausage is done, onion will be done. Drain off any grease.

Put in flour and stir. Then add broth, Italian tomatoes (not drained), red beans (drained), corn (drained) and butter beans (drained). Bring all to a boil and let simmer, usually 30 minutes max. Serve with some good cornbread or biscuits to get any remaining juice. If you have a beverage in your hand, you might add some of it to the stew.

Scott Ware: Frontier Christmas Ball is held annually in Augusta, at the Beehive Tavern, a historic building on the Ohio River built in 1794. It is a pre-1800's celebration complete with costumes, food and music. (Hometown of George Clooney. His parents still live there.)

❧ *General William Orlando* ❧ *Butler's Chili*

General Butler State Park

3 lb. lean ground beef
2 large cans hot chili beans
spaghetti (break up into small pieces)
1 large bell pepper, diced (put in a skillet to simmer with a bit of oil)

3 stalks celery, diced (put in same skillet)
1 yellow onion, coarsely chopped (also in the skillet)
1 clove garlic, crushed or minced (yes, same skillet)

Seasoning Mix:

2 medium cans tomato sauce
2 Tbsp. salt
1 Tbsp. black pepper
5 Tbsp. Italian seasoning (very important)

2 whole bay leaves
1 Tbsp. basil
chili powder (as much as you can take)

Brown ground beef over low to medium heat. Drain and rinse with water. Put in a large cooking vessel with 1 cup of water. Add seasoning mix, chili beans and skillet stuff. Simmer for 30 minutes, so all the flavors get mixed together. Add water (what you think is right), then put a fist full of raw broken spaghetti in pot. Bring heat up to cook spaghetti until tender but firm. Add more chili powder as you cook and taste. Don't be afraid of the chili powder. Choose beans with little to no sugar.

General Butler State Park, Carrolton, is the site of the Turpin home built in 1859 and a place of remembrance to one of Kentucky's foremost military families from Colonial times through the American Revolution, the War of 1812, the Mexican War and the Civil War.

Famous quote from the Marquis De Lafayette: "When I wanted a thing done well, I had a "Butler" do it."

Grandma's Sweet Chili

Georgetown College

2 lb. ground beef	2 cans tomato soup
olive oil	1 large can V-8 juice
1 large onion	$^1/_3$ c. dark brown sugar
2 (16 oz.) cans dark red beans	salt and pepper

Brown beef in olive oil. Cut onion into thin slices. Cook the slices in additional olive oil until they become tender and straw-colored. Separate into ringlets. Drain beef. Add salt and pepper, onion ringlets, beans, soup, 1 soup can of water, V-8 juice and brown sugar. Simmer until seasoning and sugar are blended.

Georgetown College, Georgetown, Kentucky, was the 1st Baptist College west of the Allegheny Mountains. It was founded in 1829 by Silas Noel, a Frankfort lawyer, jurist and minister. This recipe was graciously provided by Dr. Sonny Burnette, Music Department Chair.

Summer Salad

Cindy Holder

1 head lettuce	red onion
fresh strawberries	poppy seed dressing

Cut lettuce in small pieces. Slice about 6 strawberries (longways) in fine pieces. Slice red onion (just enough to give it good color). Mix together with poppy seed dressing and chill.
This salad is good served any time of year!

Cindy Holder, Florence, is one of Nashville's most exciting, new gospel-recording artists. She has performed with such well known artists as the Crossman and comedian Carl Hurley. Cindy also performs in churches across the state to benefit The Christian Church Homes of Kentucky.

Soups, Salads & Sauces

Kentucky Vege-Chili Recipe

Jenifour Jones

1 c. vegetarian broth
2 (40 oz.) large cans diced tomatoes
2 (40 oz.) large cans Brook's chili beans
1 large can kidney beans
1 ½ c. chopped onions
2 green peppers, diced
1 red pepper, diced

1 can corn
1 bag Morningstar ground beef substitute
1 Tbsp. cumin
salt
pepper
Bloemer's Original chili base
½ box spaghetti

Saute onions and peppers in olive oil. Add the vegetarian meat. Saute for 5 minutes. Add the vegetable broth, tomatoes, beans, corn and cumin. Cut Bloemer's chili base into thin slices and add to pot. Cook on low heat for 1 to 1 ½ hours. Add water as needed. Add salt and pepper to taste.

Cook spaghetti and add to chili pot when finished. Serve hot!

Actress and former film producer Jennifour Jones from Louisville is founder of Go Get It Events, which custom designs once-in-a-lifetime events and special occasions, including everything from celebrity A-list Kentucky Derby parties to carefully choreographed proposals.

Kentucky Cove Potato Salad

Kentucky Cove Restaurant

7 lb. red potatoes
½ lb. country bacon
1 bunch green onion

½ lb. sour cream
3 oz. whole grain mustard
6 oz. aioli

Blanch potatoes until slightly soft. Cool immediately. (Do not cool in ice water.) Cut potatoes in quarters when cooled. Chop crispy bacon and green onions and add all other ingredients. Mix well. Season with salt and pepper. Yields 7 ¾ pounds.

This great recipe for potato salad was submitted by Leslie Frye, executive chef of Kentucky Cove. The restaurant is located in downtown Louisville in the Kentucky Center for the Arts. For real Kentucky flavor, she recommends substituting country ham for bacon.

Southwestern Chicken Tortilla Soup

Kentucky HeadHunters

(In a Crock-Pot)

2 (10 oz.) cans (or 2 ½ c.)
  shredded chicken
3 cans chicken broth
1 can (or 2 c.) corn
2 cans (or 4 c.) kidney beans
½ onion, chopped (or ¼
  to ½ c.)
1 c. carrots, chopped

2 to 3 stalks celery, chopped
  or sliced
1 can (or 2 c.) diced
  tomatoes
2 Tbsp. Southwestern chili
  powder (adjust to taste)
1 Tbsp. crushed red pepper
1 Tbsp. cilantro
tortilla chip strips

Pour all ingredients in crock-pot and mix well. Let cook overnight on low. Serve in bowl and add chip strips on top. You can add shredded cheese and sour cream if it suits you. It's that easy! It makes a bunch, so what you don't eat the first time, you can put the rest in the fridge and reheat and eat! It gets better the longer it sets!

In the spring of 1985 in the south central region of Kentucky, Richard and Fred Young, Greg Martin, Ricky Lee and Doug Phelps joined forces to create the Kentucky Headhunters. They have won a Grammy, an Academy of Country Music Award, and Country Music Association Awards.

Italian Chili

Kentucky Soybean Association

cooked pasta or rice (enough
  for 4 to 6 people)
1 c. chopped onion
1 clove garlic, pressed
1 (15 oz.) can tomato sauce
1 (15 oz.) can black beans,
  rinsed and drained
1 (15 oz.) can Great
  Northern beans, rinsed and
  drained

1 (14 ½ oz.) can diced
  mushrooms
1 (4 ½ oz.) can diced
  tomatoes
1 c. frozen soybeans
1 (4 ½ oz.) can chopped
  green chili peppers
½ c. water
1 Tbsp. apple vinegar
⅓ c. sliced olives, pitted
2 Tbsp. cilantro

In a large skillet, cook onions and garlic until tender in small amount of water. Add tomato sauce, black beans, Great Northern beans, diced tomatoes, frozen soybeans, green chilies, water and vinegar. Bring to boil, reduce heat, and simmer. Uncover for 20 minutes, stirring occasionally. Stir in olives and cilantro. Simmer covered for 5 minutes. Ladle into bowls over hot cooked rice or pasta. Makes 5 servings.

Kentucky Soybean Association's focus is to promote soybeans, which are used for biodiesel fuel, candles, food, even environmentally safe polyurethane foam. This recipe comes from Lindsay Bramlage, who was a finalist in the KSA's Kentucky State Fair Cookoff.

❧ *Black Bean Venison Soup* ❧

Mantle Rock

½ c. corn oil
1 lb. chorizo sausage, chopped into bite size pieces
1 lb. venison back roast, chopped into bite size pieces
1 tsp. salt, divided
2 medium onions, chopped

4 cloves garlic, roasted and chopped
1 Tbsp. celery seeds
6 c. water
2 c. black turtle beans, cooked
2 c. tomatoes, cooked and chopped
2 bay leaves

Any of the following or combination of the following:

1 small Nero, Anco or Pasilla pepper, roasted and chopped
2 medium Poblano or Mulato peppers, roasted and chopped
1 small jalapeno pepper, roasted and chopped

2 Tbsp. ground cumin
1 Tbsp. chili powder, roasted
½ Tbsp. freshly ground pepper
2 Tbsp. epazote or oregano, chopped

Heat the oil in a large skillet over medium-high heat. Add the chorizo, cooking and stirring quickly to sear in the juices. Spoon the chorizo over to one edge of the skillet and add the venison bits, stirring and cooking quickly. Add half of the salt to the cooking meat; stir well, and spoon to one side. Add the onions, garlic and celery seeds. Cook thoroughly, stirring well. Cover and set aside.

In a deep soup or stockpot, place the water, beans, tomatoes and bay leaves. Cook over medium heat, covered, moderating it to a slow, bubbling boil for about 20 minutes. Stir occasionally. Add the hot meat mixture to the vegetable and bean pot, stirring thoroughly. Add all the remaining ingredients, blending carefully, and simmer for 15 minutes.

This recipe is from the cookbooks Momfeather Cooks Native American and Buffalo Cooking by Momfeather Erickson, Director of Mantle Rock Native Education Cultural Center in Marion. Mantle Rock is part of the Cherokee Trail of Tears.

❧ *Asparagus Potato Soup* ❧

Mason County

1 (14 oz.) can chicken broth
⅓ c. chopped onion
1 ½ c. milk
¾ c. Velveeta cheese, cubed
2 Tbsp. butter
3 medium potatoes, pared and cubed

⅓ c. diced carrots
1 ½ c. chopped fresh asparagus
2 Tbsp. flour or cornstarch
1 tsp. salt

Combine broth, potatoes, carrots and onions and cook for approximately 10 minutes, then add the asparagus and cook until all vegetables are tender. Add the butter and Velveeta until it is melted. Take a small portion of the milk and mix with the cornstarch or flour. Mix the remaining milk with the vegetalbes and broth. Next, add the flour/cornstarch mix and stir until the soup is thickened.

Mason County, tucked away in a sweeping arm of the Ohio River, is rich in heritage with such famous pioneers as Simon Kenton and Daniel Boone. It is also home to actor George Clooney, TV personality Nick Clooney, singer and actress Rosemary Clooney.

❧ *Senate Bean Soup* ❧

Mitch McConnell

2 lb. small Michigan navy beans
4 qt. water
1 ½ lb. smoked ham hocks

1 onion, chopped
2 Tbsp. butter
salt and pepper to taste

Take beans; wash and run through hot water until beans are white. Put on fire with water and ham hock. Boil slowly, approximately 3 ½ hours in covered pot. Braise onion in butter until lightly brown. Add to bean soup. Season with salt and pepper, then serve. Do not add salt until ready to serve.

Senator Mitch McConnell has served Kentucky 24 years, served as Majority Whip and Chairman of the National Republican Senatorial Committee. He is married to U.S. Secretary of Labor Elaine Chao. This traditional soup is served daily in the Senate Restaurant since the early 1900's.

❦ *Grandmother Terri's Pretzel* ❦ *Salad*

Matthew Mosher

2 c. crushed (NOT in blender or food processor) pretzels
1 ¼ c. sugar
1 ½ sticks melted butter
1 (8 oz.) cream cheese, softened
1 c. (or less) sugar
2 c. (or a little more) Cool Whip
20 oz. frozen, thawed, unsweetened and mashed strawberries
2 c. pineapple juice
1 (6 oz.) large strawberry Jell-O

Mix pretzels, ¼ cup sugar and butter and place in a greased or sprayed 9 x 13 baking dish. Bake for 10 minutes at 350°. Cool. Mix cream cheese, remaining sugar and Cool Whip and spread over cooled pretzel mixture. Heat pineapple juice. Mix in Jell-O (do not add water). Add strawberries. Mix well and allow to cool. Pour over cream cheese mixture. Refrigerate until firm.

Matthew Mosher, an award winning cinematographer, currently resides in Hollywood, a transplant from Louisville. With 13 years in the biz, he has shot feature films, television shows, both episodic and reality, documentaries, and national commercials.

Nine Bean Soup

Anne Murray

2 c. nine bean soup mix*
2 qt. water
1 lb. diced ham (preferably
  smoked, or if possible,
  Kentucky country ham!)
1 large onion, chopped
1 clove garlic, minced

¾ tsp. salt
1 (8 oz.) can tomato sauce
16 oz. can chopped tomatoes
  with juice
10 oz. can chopped tomatoes
  and green chilies (with
  juice)

Sort and wash bean mix. Place in a Dutch oven. Cover with water about 2 inches above beans. Soak overnight.

Drain beans. Add water and next four ingredients. Cover and bring to a boil. Reduce heat and simmer 1 ½ hours or until beans are tender.

Add remaining ingredients. Simmer 30 minutes, stirring occasionally. Makes 8 cups of delicious, high fiber, low-fat hearty soup. Serve with cheese bread.

Nine Bean Soup Mix*:

barley pearls
dried black beans
dried red beans
dried pinto beans
dried navy beans

dried Great Northern beans
dried lentils
dried split peas
dried black-eyed peas

Combine one small package of each variety and store in airtight container.

President of Kentucky Speakers Association, Anne Murray, Bowling Green, connects with audiences to entertain, inform, inspire and is a resource for Organizations, Companies, Institutions and Associations who need to focus on interpersonal and organizational communications.

Cornbread Dressing Salad

Natural Bridge State Park

3 c. self-rising flour
⅓ c. sugar
6 eggs
1 ½ c. vegetable oil

3 c. sour cream
2 ⅔ c. cream-style corn
1 ¼ c. butter
½ c. honey

For cornbread, combine first 6 ingredients in order listed; mix in greased 9 x 13-inch pan; bake for 30 minutes. This will make 12 cornbread squares. For honey butter, mix softened butter and honey together.

1 sheetpan cornbread	½ c. pimentos
1 doz. diced eggs	12 oz. crumbled bacon
2 diced green peppers	white pepper to taste
2 diced red onions	mayonnaise (to bind mixture)

Combine all ingredients together, adding the honey butter and mayo last.

Natural Bridge State Park, Slade, was founded by the L&E Railroad Company in 1895. In 1926, the Kentucky Department of Parks formed and purchased the park for $1. With its great natural sandstone arch (78 feet wide x 65 feet high), it was one of the state's first 4 original parks.

Spinach, Strawberry and Almond Salad

Becca Owsley

fresh leafy spinach	white vinegar
strawberries	sugar
sliced almonds	

Salad: Wash the spinach and put into a bowl. Slice the strawberries lengthwise, saving 6 to 10 for the vinaigrette. Add the sliced almonds.

Vinaigrette: Squeeze the juice out of the strawberries (a ricer works well for this); add vinegar and at least 2 teaspoons of sugar. (Usually match the amount of vinegar with the amount of strawberry juice.) Toss the vinaigrette into the salad and enjoy.

Becca Owsley is a feature writer for the Elizabethtown News-Enterprise. The News Enterprise was established in Hardin County in 1974. Cameron Crowe helped promote his hometown when he wrote and directed the Orlando Bloom movie "Elizabethtown."

Soup Beans

Julie Parrish

2 c. dry pinto beans
a piece of salt pork (about 2 x 3-inches), cut in about 3 sections to the rind (but do not separate pieces from rind)

1 tsp. salt
some chopped raw white onion

Night Before: Cover pinto beans with water and soak overnight.

Rinse soaked beans and cover with fresh water to about 1 inch above. Add the piece of salt pork. Bring to a boil, then cook over medium heat until done. Beans should hold together but be quite soft. Serve with chopped onion sprinkled over top, and a couple big slices of hot cornbread and butter.

Julie Parrish was born in Middlesboro. She has been involved in such television as Gunsmoke, Ben Casey, Star Trek, and Murder She Wrote. Movies to her credit are "Greatest Heroes of the Bible", "Devil and Max Devlin" and "Politics of Desire."

Easy Crab Bisque

Monica Pearson

2 (10 ¾ oz.) cans cream of mushroom soup
2 (10 ¾ oz.) cans cream of asparagus or cream of broccoli soup
4 c. whole milk
2 c. half and half (or if you really want it rich, use cream)

1 lb. lump crabmeat
½ c. sherry or dry white wine
2 dashes Worcestershire sauce (you can add more for taste, if you'd like)

Combine first four ingredients in a saucepan; heat thoroughly over a medium-low heat, stirring occasionally so as not to burn or scorch. Add crabmeat and wine; heat thoroughly. I cook it a day ahead, so the spices go through it overnight and really make it more flavorful.

Emmy award winner and Louisville native Monica Pearson graduated from U of L and worked as a reporter and anchor for WHAS-TV in Louisville. She has been Atlanta's WSBTV's anchor for

33 years. In 2001 she was selected to Kentucky Journalist Hall of Fame.

❧ *Black-Eyed Peas Salad* ❧

Pennyroyal Area Museum

1 (10 oz.) pkg. frozen black-eyed peas	4 tsp. thinly sliced green onions
1 (7 to 10 oz.) pkg. garlic salad dressing mix	2/3 c. salad oil
1/4 c. cider vinegar	1 tsp. sugar
	1/4 tsp. salt and pepper

Cook peas as label directs, omitting bacon; drain. Prepare salad dressing mix as directed, using vinegar, oil and amount of water specified on the package. Add 2/3 cup of dressing to peas along with sugar and salt. Mix well. Refrigerate, covered, overnight. Add pepper and onions just before serving.

Pennyroyal Area Museum in downtown Hopkinsville features exhibits on Hopkins County natives; psychic counselor and clairvoyant Edgar Cayce, author Robert Penn Warren, who wrote "All the Kings Men" and Confederate President Jefferson Davis.

❧ *White Chili* ❧

Kelly Perdew

1 lb. white beans, soaked overnight in cold water	2 tsp. ground cumin
8 to 10 c. chicken broth	1 1/2 tsp. dried oregano
2 cloves garlic, minced (or 1 tsp. garlic powder)	1/4 tsp. ground cloves
2 medium onions, chopped	1/2 tsp. red cayenne pepper
1 Tbsp. oil	4 c. cooked chicken or turkey breast, diced
2 (4 oz.) cans green chilies, chopped	3 c. Monterey Jack cheese
	sour cream (optional)

Combine white beans, chicken broth, garlic and one onion in a big soup pot (can be made in the crock-pot). Bring to a boil. Simmer until onions are very soft (usually about three beers or more). Add more broth, if necessary. Sauté remaining onion in oil until tender. Add green chilies and seasonings to onion and oil; mix thoroughly. Add seasoning mixture to beans. Add chicken or turkey; mix well, and continue to cook for one hour. Serve with grated Monterey Jack cheese and sour cream on top. Tortilla chips, salsa and guacamole are great accompaniments. Also very good with corn bread.

Louisville native Kelly Perdew was the 2004 winner of Donald Trump's Apprentice 2. He graduated from West Point and holds both an MBA and a JD (law degree) from the University of California. This recipe was his grandmother's from Murray, Kentucky.

❧ *Marinated Cucumbers* ❧

Quail Hollow Candle Factory and Gift Shop

1 large cucumber	⅓ c. vinegar
1 tsp. salt	½ tsp. celery seed
3 Tbsp. sugar (or Splenda for diabetics)	several thin slices of onions

Slice cucumber paper thin. Sprinkle with salt and sugar; add vinegar and celery seed. Mix thoroughly; fold in onions. Chill until ready to serve. The longer it sits, the better it tastes. Keep refrigerated.

Quail Hollow Candle Company is located in Adolphus and was founded in 1985 by Tee Kurelic. The company now has locations in Ohio as well as Kentucky and offers factory tours and candle carving demonstrations.

❧ *Red Potato Salad* ❧

The Red Mile

16 medium red potatoes, washed and chopped	1 Tbsp. mustard
1 c. green onions, chopped	½ c. Zesty Italian salad dressing
1 c. celery, chopped	1 tsp. celery seed
6 hard-boiled eggs (whites and yolks separated)	½ tsp. salt
1 ½ c. sour cream	¼ tsp. pepper
1 ½ c. mayo	1 jar bacon bits (or to taste)

Boil potatoes in salted water until tender, approximately 15 to 20 minutes. Drain and allow to cool. In a large bowl, mix potatoes, onions, celery, chopped egg whites and zesty Italian dressing; set aside.

In a smaller mixing bowl, mix mashed egg yolks, mayo, sour cream, mustard, celery seed, salt and pepper. When well mixed, pour into potato mixture and mix together. Pour and mix in bacon bits to taste. Refrigerate until cold. (Note: The recipe calls for the entire jar of bacon bits, but I don't usually prefer that much in my potato salad so I use about ½ a jar.)

Known for its red clay, one-mile track, The Red Mile is the 2nd oldest harness track in the world. For over 130 years, harness racing's elite have converged on The Red Mile. Located in Lexington, it also hosts Quarter Horse meets and numerous horse sales.

❦ *Sausage Bean Chowder* ❦

Kenneth Rollins

3 lb. bulk sausage	2 ¼ tsp. salt
4 (8 oz.) cans beans (kidney, pinto or navy)	¾ tsp. garlic salt
	¾ tsp. thyme
4 ½ c. canned tomatoes	⅜ tsp. pepper
6 c. water	1 ½ c. diced potatoes (4 to 6
3 small onions, chopped	potatoes)
1 or 2 bay leaves	¾ c. chopped green pepper

Cook sausage until brown. Drain off ingredients. Simmer covered for 1 hour and 15 minutes. Remove bay leaf. Will serve 12 to 16. Freeze leftovers.

Kenneth Rollins, from Wickliffe, played basketball for the University of Kentucky's 1948 NCAA Championship Team. He was 1 of the 5 Kentucky players to compete and win a Gold Medal in the 1948 Olympics. This is his favorite recipe made by his wife.

❦ *Spicy Turkey Chili* ❦

R.M. Rollins

1 lb. 97% lean ground turkey	28 oz. can diced tomatoes
8 oz. multi-grain spaghetti	16 oz. can chili beans
16 oz. can low-sodium V8 juice	16 oz. can kidney beans
	1 packet chili seasoning mix
1 large diced yellow onion	1 Tbsp. cayenne pepper

Cook spaghetti according to directions on the box; drain and set aside. Put turkey and onions in a skillet; cover and cook over medium heat until the turkey is brown and the onions are translucent. Drain and rinse the kidney beans to eliminate the excess salt. In a 6-quart stockpot, combine all of the ingredients. Cook over medium heat for 45 minutes, stirring as needed. Add a little water if necessary. Taste and add more cayenne pepper if desired.

This is an original recipe by Kentucky artist, R.M. Rollins, who creates abstract paintings, folk art-style wood carvings and gourds. His work can be found at the Chestnut Tree Gallery in Richmond.

Ground Ham Salad

Scott Hams

1 lb. Scott Country ham, ground
$^1/_3$ c. chopped sweet pickle

$^1/_3$ c. Kraft salad dressing or mayonnaise

Add sweet pickle and salad dressing or mayonnaise to ham. Mix together. Store in refrigerator. Spread on your favorite bread for a delicious sandwich, or serve on beaten biscuits.

Leslie and June Scott own Scott Hams, which is located on a 3rd generation family-owned farm in Greenville, Kentucky, in Muhlenberg County. They have been in business over 40 years. They were selected the Grand Champion at the Kentucky State Fair 2 times and U.S. National Champion 16 times.

Cucumber Salad

Shaker Museum at South Union

2 cucumbers
$^1/_2$ onion
$^1/_2$ c. sour cream
$^1/_2$ c. Shaker Mint Vinegar

$^1/_2$ tsp. salt
$^1/_4$ tsp. pepper
2 Tbsp. sugar
$^1/_4$ tsp. mustard

Make sure your cucumbers are fresh and tender. Slice very fine. Sprinkle with salt and let stand 3 minutes. This removes any bitter taste of the skin. Mix dressing of sour cream, vinegar and seasonings together. Combine well. Pour over cucumbers and serve at once.

This Shaker community at South Union near Auburn was established in 1807 and closed in 1922. The museum consisted of several buildings built in the 1800's, including the 40 room Centre

House and Shaker Tavern, which continues to serve today as a restaurant and lodging facility. The Shakers were a religious group that believed in a simple way of life and strong work ethics.

Oyster Soup

John Stephenson

5 lb. fresh oysters
4 Tbsp. butter
gal. milk
2 sticks butter
1 tsp. Old Bay spice

2 tsp. Mrs. Dash
½ tsp. salt
3 Tbsp. parsley
3 Tbsp. chives
¼ tsp. black pepper

Sauté oysters in butter just until they curl on the ends a little. Mix milk, butter, Old Bay spice, Mrs. Dash, salt, parsley, chives and black pepper. Stir all this up and bring milk to almost a boil, but do not scorch the milk. Then add the oysters, which you have just sautéed, to the milk and let set until cool enough to eat.

John Stephenson was Kentucky's last elected Superintendent of Public Instruction, who holds the claim as the only living person who has traveled into each of Kentucky's 120 counties at least five times and filmed the history of each on location.

Low-Fat Alfredo Sauce

Bob Tools

8 oz. fettuccine
3 c. low-fat cottage cheese
½ c. Parmesan cheese
¼ c. cornstarch

2 Tbsp. butter sprinkles
1 tsp. garlic powder
black pepper to taste

Cook fettuccine. While pasta is cooking, process the rest of the ingredients in a blender. Drain fettuccine. Mix with sauce in a serving bowl. Serve immediately. If deired, add shrimp, vegetables, etc. to your fettuccine alfredo. Serves 6 to 8.

This recipe comes from Carol Tools. Her husband, Bob Tools, was the 1st person in the world to receive an artificial heart implant, performed by Jewish Hospital/University of Louisville team led by surgeons Laman Gray, M.D., and Rob Dowling, M.D., July 2, 2001.

Savory Red Pepper Soup

Toyota Motors Manufacturing, Kentucky

½ c. unsalted butter (1 stick)
2 large onions, chopped
2 cloves garlic, minced
4 large carrots, peeled and
  chopped
1 large Russet potato, peeled
  and chopped
6 red bell peppers, roasted,
  peeled, seeded and
  chopped

2 pears (firm), peeled, cored
  and chopped
5 c. chicken stock
1 Tbsp. parsley (fresh),
  chopped
salt (to taste)
pepper (to taste)
sour cream (garnish)
Italian parsley sprigs
  (garnish)

Melt butter in a large saucepan. Add onion and garlic and sauté 10 minutes. Add carrots and sauté 10 minutes. Add potatoes and peppers and sauté 10 minutes. Add pears, stock and parsley. Bring to boil. Reduce heat. Simmer uncovered 20 minutes, or until vegetables are tender. Season with salt and pepper. Transfer in batches to food processor or blender. Process until smooth. Re-heat. Garnish with sour cream and sprigs of parsley.

To roast peppers, place on broiler rack in oven, 6 to 8 inches from heat. Blacken without burning. Rotate peppers to roast even-ly. Immediately place peppers in plastic bag to steam. When cool, peel off skin. (Makes 8 servings.)

Toyota Motor Manufacturing, Georgetown, is the largest Toyota plant outside of Japan, covering 7.5 million square feet. The 7,000 team members produce more than 2,000 vehicles per day, including the award-winning Toyota Camry. Special thanks to Plant Manager Gary Convis and wife Debbie.

Kentucky Burgoo

Wolf Creek Dam

650 lb. ground beef
88 hens
8 bushels onions

16 bushels potatoes
80 doz. ears of corn

Just add water to make 900 gallons. Simmer several hours, and eat with 50 cases of bread. Serves 7,000 to 10,000 people.

Wolf Creek Dam in Russell County formed the 6,089,000 acre Lake Cumberland. This recipe was served at the groundbreaking ceremony in 1941. It was made in galvanized washtubs, stirred with boat paddles, and served 7,000 to 10,000 people.

Tomato Bisque

Woody's On Main

1 (16 oz.) can diced
  tomatoes
2 large white onions

1 qt. heavy whipping cream
4 Tbsp. dill weed
½ c. chicken stock

Dice onions and sauté in oil until translucent. Add other ingredients. Stir together well. Simmer for 20 minutes. Number of servings: 4.

Woody's on Main is located in downtown Richmond next to the historical Glyndon Hotel. With an eye for detail, the ambience is delightfully exquisite in this friendly intimate restaurant. Owner and Executive Chef Andrew Jones provided this recipe.

—•Extra Recipes•—

Meats

and

Main Dishes

Recipe Favorites

Page No.

Recipe Title:_____ _____

_____ _____

_____ _____

_____ _____

_____ _____

_____ _____

_____ _____

_____ _____

_____ _____

Family Favorites

Page No.

Recipe Title:_____ _____

_____ _____

_____ _____

_____ _____

_____ _____

Notes:_____

_____

_____

_____

Meats & Main Dishes

Mexican Chicken

A Personal Touch

2 pkg. chicken strips
  (pre-cook in water)
1 can refried beans

2 pkg. Spanish rice, cooked
1 can nacho cheese
2 c. Mexican cheese

In a 9 x 12 pan, layer as follows: refried beans, Spanish rice, chicken and nacho cheese. Top with Mexican cheese and bake at 350° until cheese is melted and golden, about 45 minutes.

This recipe was shared by artist Sue Michael. She is the owner of A Personal Touch Studio in Lousia, Kentucky. Sue specializes in all types of unique handmade ceramics, wood products, needlework and quilts.

Granny's Meat Balls

American Quilter's Society

1 lb. pork sausage
1 lb. ground beef
1 egg
2 ½ c. bread crumbs

1 medium onion, chopped
1 tsp. chili powder
1 Tbsp. salt

Mix together and form into balls about the size of an egg. Drop in the following sauce:

1 can tomato soup
2 c. water
1 tsp. chili powder
1 tsp. salt (you can omit if
  desired; there is enough
  salt in soup)

1 medium onion
½ green pepper, chopped
  fine

Bake 1 hour in a moderate oven of 350°. Serve with your favorite pasta!

In 1984 Meredith and Bill Schroeder founded the American Quilter's Society with 1500 charter members. Today 37,000 members converge annually on Paducah for the four-day AQS Quilt Show and Contest, which is considered the premier international quilting event.

❧ *Pepperoni Pork Loin* ❧

Bub Asman

pork loin
bacon strips
dried pepperoni slices

1 packet Good Seasons
Italian dressing

Line the bottom of a 2-inch deep glass baking dish with the bacon strips. Place the pork loin on top of the bacon. Sprinkle the Italian dressing across the top of the pork loin, and then top with the dried pepperoni slices. Wrap the bacon strips up and around the pork loin and use colorless toothpicks to hold the bacon in place. Bake at 350° for one hour per pound.

Academy Award Winner Bub Asman is from Louisville, Kentucky. He won the Academy Award for Best Sound Effects Editing on Letters from Iwo Jima (2006) and was nominated 3 other times. He also was nominated and won the Golden Reel Award.

❧ *Kentucky Bourbon Barrel Ale Braised Beef Short Ribs* ❧

Azur Restaurant

8 beef short ribs
2 c. flour
½ c. olive oil
4 carrots, peeled and roughly
  chopped
4 stalks celery, roughly
  chopped
2 white onions, quartered

1 c. soy sauce
½ gal. Kentucky Bourbon
  Barrel Ale
1 small can tomato paste
2 heads garlic, halved
4 sprigs fresh thyme
4 bay leaves
salt and pepper

Heat a very large skillet over high heat. Season the short ribs liberally with salt and pepper and then dredge them in the flour, patting off the excess. Add olive oil to the hot pan and sear, or brown the short ribs, 2 or 3 at a time, on all sides. Remove the short ribs from the pan and let them rest on a large tray. Add the celery, onion, carrot and garlic to the pan and, stirring frequently, caramelize the vegetables over medium-high heat for 10 minutes. Reduce the heat to medium; add the can of tomato paste. Stir to coat the vegetables. Cook 3 minutes longer. Deglaze the pan with the red wine and the Kentucky Bourbon Ale. Add the bay leaves and thyme and heat the braising liquid to a boil. Remove from heat and place the short ribs in the pan with the braising liquid. Make sure the short ribs are submerged. Cover the pan and bake in the oven for 3 hours, or until the meat is falling off the bone. Season the braising liquid to taste and serve it with the short ribs as a sauce. Serves 8.

Azur Restaurant and Patio is located at 3070 Lakecrest Circle, Suite 550, Lexington, Kentucky, where they have music on the patio. Co-owner Fred Wohlstein indicated they utilize local ingredients whenever possible. This recipe is from Executive Chef Jeremy Ashby.

❧ *Baked Roast Chicken* ❧

BB Riverboats

4 boneless chicken breasts　　**2 tsp. garlic powder**
bottle Italian dressing　　　　**2 Tbsp. soy sauce**

Wash and dry chicken breasts. Set aside. Mix next three ingredients. Pour over chicken breasts and let marinate for 1 hour up to overnight. Bake, broil or grill to likeness.

In Covington, Kentucky, BB Riverboats offers year-round entertainment with everything from hour-long sightseeing cruises to overnight vacations on several boats, such as the steamboat-era River Queen and the authentic sternwheeler Mark Twain.

❧ *Capellini Con Aglio Olio & Peperoncino* ❧

Adrian Belew

(Angel Hair Spaghetti with Garlic, Oil and Chile)

1 lb. angel hair pasta　　　　**2 Tbsp. finely chopped**
4 cloves garlic, finely　　　　　**parsley**
**　chopped**　　　　　　　　　　**1 dried red chili, crumbled**
　　　　　　　　　　　　　　　　½ c. extra-virgin olive oil

Cook pasta in a large pot of salted, boiling water for 3 minutes until al dente. While the pasta is cooking, saute the garlic, parsley and chili in the oil in a medium skillet over medium heat until the garlic begins to darken. Remove from heat and add 2 tablespoons of the cooking water from the pasta pot. Drain the pasta. Stir the pasta in the skillet with the garlic, parsley and chile. Toss well. Serve hot. Serves 4.

Adrian Belew, from Covington, is an amazing guitarist who has performed with David Bowie, Talking Heads, Joe Cocker, Paul Simon, Robert Palmer, Cyndi Lauper, Herbie Hancock and Peter Gabriel. He also produces and writes for Jars of Clay and tours with "Tool."

❧ *Penne Kalamata* ❧

Bella Notte

8 oz. penna pasta, cooked al dente in salted water
4 oz. grilled chicken breast, sliced
¼ c. Kalamata olives, pitted and chopped
¼ c. chicken stock*

2 oz. butter (unsalted)
1 Tbsp. chives (fresh), chopped
2 Tbsp. pine nuts, toasted
2 Tbsp. extra-virgin olive oil
kosher salt and fresh ground black pepper to taste

*If you do not have fresh chicken stock available, substitute a high quality, low-sodium canned chicken broth.

Heat 10-inch sauté pan over medium-high heat with olive oil for 30 seconds. Add chicken and sauté for 2 minutes, or until chicken has lightly browned and a "fond" (the part that sticks to the bottom of the pan) has formed.

Add the olives and "de-glaze" (adding a liquid and scraping with a wooden spoon to release all the rich flavorings that have stuck to the bottom of the pan) the pan with chicken stock.

Add cooked penne (cook penne ahead of time and "shock" in ice water, then refresh penne in hot water when ready to eat) and butter; remove the pan from heat and gently stir with a wooden spoon until the butter has emulsified and formed a creamy sauce. Season with chives, pine nuts, kosher salt and fresh ground black pepper.

For the Chicken: Marinate fresh chicken breast for 12 hours. Remove from marinade and season heavily with kosher salt and fresh ground black pepper. Grill (Bella Notte uses a wood-burning grill) evenly on both sides until cooked all the way through. Allow cooked chicken breasts to "rest" for 10 minutes before cutting "julienne"-style ¼-inch thick.

For the Marinade:

3 c. olive oil
1 c. balsamic vinegar
2 Tbsp. oregano (dry)
2 Tbsp. basil (dry)

4 garlic cloves (fresh)
1 Tbsp. black pepper (fresh ground)
3 lemons, juiced (fresh)

Combine all ingredients in a standard blender and blend on high for 30 seconds, or until completely emulsified.

For the Pine Nuts: Using a flat baking pan lined with parchment paper, distribute pine nuts evenly so there is a single layer. Roast at 325° for 10 minutes or until pine nuts are golden brown. Remove and allow to cool before storing in an airtight container.

International Chef, Kevin Toyoda, is the Executive Chef for Bella Notte (The Beautiful Night), 3715 Nicholasville Road, Lexington, Kentucky. Penne Kalamata is one of the Italian restaurant's most requested recipes.

Diane's Breakfast Casserole

Berea's Shady Lane Bed and Breakfast

¼ c. flour
¼ tsp. salt
¼ c. melted butter
4 eggs, beaten

1 c. cottage cheese
2 c. Monterey Jack cheese, grated

Combine first 3 ingredients and add next 3 ingredients.

Optional Additions at the Discretion of the Cook:

¼ c. piquant sauce (hot or mild)
¼ c. chopped green peppers
¼ c. chopped onions

¼ c. chopped ham (without this, it is an excellent vegetarian casserole)

Pour into 6 x 10-inch pan at 375° about 45 minutes. Serves 6 to 8.

Individual crocks an option but these need only 20 minutes of baking time.

Fried green tomatoes or a grits casserole is a nice accompaniment.

This can be prepared the night before. Just put in the oven in the morning, but for best results, serve immediately as this is similar to a souffle.

Shady Lane Bed and Breakfast, 123 Mt. Vernon Road, named because of the many beautiful trees on the property. It is a "Bird Lovers'" paradise. The house is of Southern Colonial design and was the official residence of Mayor Hensley, the 2nd Mayor of Berea.

Reaper's Pigs In The Meadow

Ron Blair

6 boneless, skinless pork loins
a bowl of Kentucky Kernal flour
canola oil
2 c. Minute rice
3 c. water

1 tsp. salt
1 tsp. garlic salt
1 tsp. lemon pepper
1 Tbsp. butter
1 can Campbell's mushroom soup

Preheat the oven to 425°.

Pour desired amount of oil in frying pan and let heat on medium-high for three minutes. Coat the pork chops in Kentucky Kernal flour. Fry up meat. Once the pork chops are nice and brown, take them out and let them sit for a moment. It's important that you don't cook them all the way through.

While the chops are sitting, mix 2 cups of water and the garlic salt, salt, butter and lemon pepper into a saucepan and bring it to a boil. Remove from the burner and pour in the rice, making sure it's covered in the water before covering it and letting it sit for five minutes.

While the rice is sitting, mix one cup of water with the mushroom soup mix. In a large baking dish (I use glass, but metal will work just as well), pour in the rice. Place the pork chops over the rice. Then pour the mushroom soup mix over the pork chops and rice, making sure to cover all of the rice. Place the baking dish in the oven for twenty minutes or so. After it's done, I reckon you should eat it.

Ron Blair, better known as Reaper M. Jones, is from Rineyville, Kentucky. Blair, who attended Western Kentucky University, is co-founder of Dark Winter Studios, which produces and specializes in Horror and Mystery Films with emphasis on the dark side.

Simple Salmon ❧

Broad Run Vineyards

1 salmon filet
Kikkoman soy sauce

1 to 2 tsp. minced garlic

Place a salmon filet on a large piece of heavy-duty aluminum foil. Douse with Kikkoman soy sauce and spread with lots of minced garlic (the prepared kind, not fresh, no substitutions). Draw up the ends of the foil loosely; do not seal tightly. Bake on grill or in 350° oven until firm and slightly browned. Open the foil during the last few minutes. Chill for several hours or overnight. When ready to serve, set on platter and gently tear away the foil and remove. For impressive presentation, garnish with lemon slices or cucumber slices or fresh herbs. Let your creative juices flow! Serve cold with chilled Broad Run Vineyards dry Gewurztraminer. No substitutions. Enjoy!

Broad Run Vineyards is located near Louisville in Jefferson County. It was started in 1983 and consist of almost 100 acres, with an 8000 square foot winery and tasting room. Kentucky was site of America's first commercial vineyard, planted in 1798 by Marquis de Lafayette.

Country Ham With Croquettes ❧

Broadbent Country Hams

2 Tbsp. butter
4 Tbsp. flour
1 c. milk

½ tsp. lemon juice
1 c. ground Broadbent
Country Ham

Melt butter and blend with flour; stir milk in gradually. Cook until thick. Add ham and lemon juice; cool thoroughly. Shape into croquettes. Roll in bread crumbs. Dip in beaten egg. Roll again in bread crumbs. Fry in deep fat.

Cream Sauce for Croquettes:

1 Tbsp. butter
1 Tbsp. flour
¼ tsp. salt

$\frac{1}{16}$ tsp. pepper
1 c. milk

Melt butter. Add flour, salt and pepper. Add milk slowly, stirring constantly. Cook slowly to desired thickness, preferably in a double boiler.

Broadbent Hams was founded by Smith Broadbent II and his sons over 80 years ago. Ronny and Beth Drennan purchased the Cadiz, Kentucky business in 1999. Broadbent Hams have been selected as the Kentucky State Fair Grand Champion 5 of the last 8 years.

❧ *Chicken Enchiladas* ❧

Buffalo Trace Distillery

4 chicken breasts
½ tsp. lemon pepper
1 pkg. 10 tortilla shells

1 ½ c. grated Cheddar
cheese

Boil chicken breasts with lemon pepper until done, approximately 45 minutes. Save the broth after cooking and keep it heated on low. Chop chicken up into bite size pieces.

In separate pan, combine filling:

1 can cream of mushroom
soup
1 (16 oz.) container sour
cream

1 can green chilies
lemon pepper to taste
garlic powder to taste

Heat.

Dip your soft taco size flour tortillas in the broth until soft. Fill your tortillas with approximately 2 spoonfuls of filling. Cover the top of the filled tortilla rolls with the leftover filling and cover with grated Cheddar cheese. Cook in oven at 350° for 30 minutes.

Buffalo Trace Distillery, located in Franklin County, has a history (started in 1787) of finely crafted, award-winning spirits. They have won more international awards in the last decade than any other North American distillery, including 85 distinctions in national and international competitions.

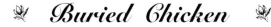

Buried Chicken

Leo Burmester

1 whole chicken	butter
2 apples, chopped	sage
2 c. fresh cranberries	mint
1 c. chopped nuts	salt
1 onion, chopped	pepper
1 tsp. garlic powder	Cajun seasoning
olive oil	

Make stuffing out of apples, cranberries and nuts. Stuff in chicken. Place on large sheet of aluminum foil. Spread olive oil on outside of chicken. Place onion over top of chicken, then season liberally with rest of seasonings. Place pads of butter wherever they will fit. Then wrap foil around chicken. Do five layers. Dig a hole in your backyard or your neighbor's. Get a good fire going using hard wood. Let burn until wood has turned to red coals. Put layer of dirt over coals. Then bury chicken completely for 1 ½ hours. When you dig the chicken up, remove foil except last layer. Open and dig in. Chicken will fall off bone.

Actor Leo Burmester from Louisville, has been featured in many films including Broadcast News, Devil's Advocate, The Abyss, Gangs of New York, and Monday Night Mayhem and in TV with regular roles on Them, Flo, and Arresting Behavior. He starred on Broadway in Les Miserables, Big River and Buried Child.

Greek Pizza

Dr. Sonny Burnette

pizza crust (Chef Boyardee)	½ tsp. oregano
¼ lb. ground lamb	½ medium onion
¼ lb. ground beef	¼ medium eggplant
1 Tbsp. lemon juice	vegetable oil
garlic salt	Feta cheese
pepper	Greek olives

Follow instructions on pizza crust box, with one exception. Add the Parmesan cheese to the pizza dough, not as a topping. Spread dough evenly on pizza pan, creating a lip at the rim to contain sauce. Pour tomato sauce (from mix) onto crust and spread evenly. Brown meat. Drain. Add lemon juice, garlic salt, pepper and oregano and stir.

Dice onion and eggplant and toss with vegetable oil. Drain liquid from Feta cheese. Crumble evenly over crust. Distribute ground meat, diced onion and eggplant evenly. Cut olives, removing seeds, and add to pizza. Bake at 425° for 16 to 20 minutes.

Dr. Sonny Burnette is the Music Department Chair at Georgetown College. This talented musician has performed with: Bob Hope, Red Skelton, Jerry Lewis, Rich Little, Lou Rawls, Four Tops, Lettermen, Temptations, Crystal Gale, Jimmy Dorsey, Amy Grant.

❧ Lasagna ❧

Cabin Creek Band

1 carton cottage cheese
¼ to ½ c. Parmesan cheese
medium pkg. grated
  Mozzarella cheese
1 onion (medium)
about ½ can Sloppy Joe
  sauce or Manwich sauce

about 9 lasagna noodles
1 lb. pork sausage, torn up in
  pieces
2 cloves garlic
1 (14.5 oz. approximately)
  can tomatoes (Italian)

Cook noodles and drain. Cut up and brown pork sausage (I use mild). Add garlic. Pour off grease. Add onion, tomatoes and Sloppy Joe sauce.

Oil a 9 x 13 or larger baking dish. Layer ingredients starting with the noodles, then adding the cheese and sauce (after sauce has been cooked in a skillet for 15 to 20 minutes). Bake in 350° oven for approximately 30 minutes.

Homer Ledford and Cabin Creek Band are dedicated to performing good ole traditional Bluegrass and Gospel Music. Homer plays the Fiddlefone (a novel instrument he invented), the musical saw, the autoharp and sometimes the mountain dulcimer, which he makes.

❧ Dad's Meat Loaf ❧

Trent Carr

2 lb. beef
2 eggs
2 cans tomato paste (flavored
  if you like)
4 large carrots

1 whole onion
1 whole (sweet) apple
1 pepper (green, red, orange
  or any combination)
2 cloves garlic

Put the meat in a cooking pan. Dice all the vegetables; mix it all up. Add a glaze of ketchup, then cook at 450° for about 1 hour.

Trent Carr is from Lexington, Kentucky, but has lived most of his life in Toronto. He now performs as guitarist with the Canadian Rock Band Headstones. They are presently touring Canada with their 6th latest release "Oracle of Hi-Fi" produced by Maple Music.

❧ Baked Chicken Crostina ❧

Carter Cave State Resort Park

3 boneless, skinless chicken breasts	2 cloves roasted garlic, minced
2 c. and 1 Tbsp. flour	1 ½ c. cream
2 Tbsp. salt	6 Tbsp. olive oil
2 Tbsp. pepper	1 lb. linguine
1 Tbsp. Italian seasoning	1 c. Parmesan cheese
	1 c. tomatoes, diced

Crust:

1 ½ c. bread crumbs	¼ c. parsley, chopped
¼ c. butter	¼ c. Parmesan cheese
½ tsp. garlic powder	salt and pepper to taste

Mix crust. Set aside. Then mix 1 ½ cups flour, salt, pepper and Italian seasoning in a dish. Dip chicken into Italian mixture. Dust off excess. Heat skillet with 3 or 4 tablespoons of oil. Cook chicken until golden brown on both sides or 170°. Place chicken on cooking sheet. Top with crumb mixture. Stick in broiler 2 to 3 minutes.

Cook pasta; set aside.

Heat 3 to 4 tablespoons oil in skillet. Add flour, cream, garlic and Parmesan cheese. Cook for 1 to 2 minutes, then add parsley and tomatoes. Put on top of chicken and pasta.

Carter Caves State Resort Park, Olive Hill, is home to more than 20 caverns. Among the better known is Cascade Cave, with its 30-foot underground waterfall and X-cave with its unique formations. This recipe was submitted by Executive Chef Terry Poppywell.

Roasted Cornish Hens With Lemon Mushroom Sauté

Cave Run Muskie Guide Service

Mixed Mushroom Sauté:

1 ½ lb. fresh portabella mushrooms
1 lb. small button mushrooms
½ c. butter
1 Tbsp. olive oil
3 Tbsp. minced garlic
⅛ c. basil
⅛ c. oregano
⅛ c. parsley

Cut portabellas into rough chunks about the size of the button mushrooms; leave button mushrooms whole. Heat butter and olive oil in a large skillet over low heat. Add garlic and sauté one minute, stirring; do not allow garlic to color. Raise heat to high; add mushrooms and toss to coat with butter. Sauté quickly until mushrooms have softened, about 2 minutes. Season to taste with salt and pepper. In last 30 seconds, add herbs and then remove from heat.

4 Cornish hens
1 large lemon
3 Tbsp. olive oil
½ c. chicken broth

Heat oven to 375°. Season cavities of hens with salt and pepper. Remove rind from lemon; cut into julienne strips. Gently lift breast skin away from meat by slipping your fingers between skin and meat of hens. Divide lemon strips among hens and place under skin. Lightly grease the bottom of a shallow roasting pan. Place hens breast side up; brush with olive oil on all sides. Fill with mushroom sauté. Roast at 375°, basting every 15 minutes with chicken broth.

Cave Run Musky Guide Service is owned by Professional Guides Tony Grant and Gregg Thomas. Two Kentucky locations (Frenchburg and Wellington) in the heart of Midwest musky country. It was ranked in the top 10 guide services by Fisherman and Field and Stream.

Salmon Cakes

Center for Appalachian Studies

2 lb. grilled fresh salmon	½ c. breadcrumbs (season
1 red onion	the breadcrumbs with a
1 stalk celery	combination of herbs and
1 green pepper	spices to taste, such as: ¼
1 red pepper	tsp. paprika, dash of
1 jalapeno	cayenne, ½ tsp. oregano
2 to 3 cloves garlic	and basil and salt and
1 egg	pepper)

Grill the salmon; set aside. Chop the onions, celery and peppers; sauté until translucent. Gently break apart the salmon and add the sautéed vegetables, breadcrumbs and egg. Let sit and rest for about 30 minutes. Preheat a griddle or heavy pan to medium-high, then coat with olive oil. Form the Salmon Cakes into patties and place on grill/pan; sauté until golden brown, then turn over to the other side. Salt and pepper to taste.

Serve plain, with sauce or herbed mayonnaise. Suggestions include Hollandaise, dill (or cilantro) sauce, or herbed mayonnaise with garlic.

This recipe comes from Alan Banks, who is the director of The Center for Appalachian Studies at Eastern Kentucky University. The center was created to coordinate and promote a multi-disciplinary approach toward teaching, research and service on issues pertaining to Appalachia.

Ginny Rollins Sweet Cranberry Ham

Chestnut Tree Gallery

1 (5 lb.) canned boneless	2 c. brown sugar
precooked ham	2 Tbsp. prepared mustard
1 (16 oz.) can whole	optional garnish
cranberry sauce	

Empty the can of cranberry sauce into a saucepan. Add brown sugar and mustard; stir until blended. Cook over medium-high heat until mixture begins to bubble and thicken a bit. Remove the ham from the can and place in a heavy-duty aluminum foil lined-roasting pan. Pierce the top of the ham in several places with a knife down about ¾ of the way through the ham. This will allow the sauce to seep into the interior of the ham. Pour about ½ of the cranberry sauce mixture slowly over the top of the ham. It will run down the sides, but the top of the ham should remain covered in the berries and sauce. Using another piece of heavy-duty aluminum foil, create a cover for the ham, taking care not to touch the top of the ham with the foil. Press the foil over all the edges of the pan to seal it. Insert a meat thermometer through the foil and into the center of the ham. Place in oven and bake at 375° until the thermometer reaches about 130°. Remove pan from oven; remove foil covering; pour remaining sauce over the ham. Recover and place back in oven. Cook until thermometer reaches 170°. Remove from oven and place ham on a platter. If the top of the ham needs more sauce, spoon any sauce remaining in the pan over the top. For garnish, use slices of whole oranges with peeling left on which creates a bright contrasting color and compliments the taste. Slices of jellied cranberry sauce or fresh parsley also work well.

This original recipe comes from Ginny Rollins, owner of the Chestnut Tree Gallery, a fine art and craft gallery in Richmond, Kentucky. It has been a "must have" Christmas dinner favorite at the Rollins and Bertram family Christmas dinners for over 25 years.

❧ *Bed and Breakfast* ❧ *Casserole*

Columbus-Belmont State Park

3 Tbsp. melted butter	1 c. grated Cheddar cheese
½ c. Bisquick	2 green onions, finely
½ c. milk	chopped
2 eggs, slightly beaten	1 (8 oz.) can crushed
2 c. cooked ham, diced	pineapple, drained

Pour all ingredients together and bake at 350° until set or lightly browned.

Columbus-Belmont State Park is located in Columbus, Kentucky. The Confederate fortification sits high on the bluffs overlooking the Mississippi River. At the park you will see a Civil War Hospital Museum, six-ton anchor and great chain that stretched across the Mississippi River.

❧ Meat Loaf ❧

Completely Kentucky

1 jar Rebekah Grace sweet pepper relish	2 eggs
2 lb. ground beef	¾ c. bread crumbs
	salt and pepper

Preheat oven to 350°. Mix all ingredients and form in bread pan. Cook for 40 minutes.

Located in a restored 150-year old building in Frankfort, Completely Kentucky is proud to offer work of over 500 of Kentucky's best artisans through catalog and internet sales. They buy from small family businesses with generations of family traditions in their crafts.

❧ Chicken and Dumplings ❧

Julian Cook

1 (2 lb.) chicken	2 chicken bouillon cubes
2 ribs celery	1 can cream of chicken soup
3 bay leaves	4 qt. water
1 large onion	

Cut up the chicken but make sure you leave the skin on. Place chicken, celery, onion, bay leaves and bouillon in the water and cook to a rolling boil. Cook for 45 minutes. Take out the chicken pieces and remove the skin and bones. It will fall right off. Remove the bay leaves. Now make the dumplings (recipe follows) and set the dough aside for a few minutes. Add the soup and the chicken to the water and bring back to a boil. Drop the dumplings into the boiling stock. Don't stir them, just drop them in. Cook for a few minutes and turn off.

Dumplings:

2 c. all-purpose flour	¾ c. water

Drip a small amount of water into the center of the flour and start working the flour into the water from the edges. Continue adding small amounts of water and keep kneading. It's going to feel tough. Dust some flour onto your rolling surface and roll out the dumplings to about ⅛-inch thick. Cut into 1-inch strips or hand tear them before dropping them into the chicken soup.

Julian Cook from Louisville is an accomplished digital artist and senior audio commentator for Travel Radio International that syndicates half hour audio travel essays to NPR, CBC, Armed Forces

Radio and international markets, which are heard by over 12 million people worldwide.

Beef On The Run

Drawing Board Farm

2 to 2 ½ lb. boneless round steak

1 envelope dry onion soup mix
1 jar alfredo sauce

Cut steak into serving size pieces; place in slow cooker. Combine soup mix and alfredo sauce. Pour over beef. Cover and cook on low for 7 to 8 hours or until meat is tender. Yields 6 servings.

Drawing Board Farm, Crestwood, is a working horse farm and artist studio specializing in equine art. This recipe is perfect for owners Joseph and Janet Burch, who keep busy schedules as artists and teaching, training and show judging in the equine industry.

Duncan House Breakfast Casserole

Duncan House Bed and Breakfast

3 c. frozen shredded hash brown potatoes
¾ c. shredded Cheddar cheese
½ to 1 lb. pork sausage, cooked and crumbled

1 to 2 chopped green onions
6 eggs
12 oz. evaporated milk
¼ tsp. black pepper
⅛ tsp. salt

Place potatoes in an 8-inch square baking dish. Sprinkle with sausage, cheese and green onions. Beat eggs; add milk, pepper and salt. Pour over potatoes and sausage, etc. Cover and refrigerate several hours or bake immediately. If refrigerated, allow casserole to come to room temperature for 30 minutes. Bake, uncovered, in a 350° oven for 55 to 60 minutes.

In 1783, Benjamin Blackford built a home on original land grants which became Nicholasville. The estate was passed to his daughter, Nancy, who married William Duncan. The home has been in the Duncan Family for over 200 years and on Kentucky Heritage Council and Bluegrass Trust.

Marvin's Rice Hot Dish

Justin R. Durban

1 lb. hamburger
2 medium-sized onions, chopped
1 c. celery, diced
1 c. rice (regular)
2 c. water
1 can mushroom soup

1 can chicken rice soup
4 Tbsp. bean sprouts (optional)
2 c. chow mein noodles
2 Tbsp. Worcestershire sauce (optional)
4 Tbsp. soy sauce

Brown hamburger, onion and celery. Mix together soups, water, rice, Worcestershire sauce, soy sauce and salt and pepper to taste. Mix all ingredients in casserole dish, well-greased. Bake at 350° for 1 hour. Remove from oven; spread on chow mein noodles and bake another 15 to 20 minutes.

Justin Durbin is from Madisonville. Now living in Los Angeles, he is a cinematic composer and digital artist for the motion picture industry. He was the composer for Star Trek: Of Gods and Men, Beauty and the Beast: A Latter-Day Tale, and Inalienable.

The Count's Stroganoff

Dick Dyszel

1 lb. very lean ground beef (80 or 90% lean)
1 medium onion
½ green bell pepper
½ red bell pepper
½ lb. white mushrooms
1 can mushroom soup
11 oz. hearty red wine
6 to 8 cloves garlic (shocking isn't it!)

olive oil
Pickapeppa or Worcestershire sauce
coarse ground pepper
1 bag yolk-free broad ribbon noodles
1 (16 oz.) container fat-free sour cream

Coarsely dice the onion, peppers and mushrooms. Pour enough olive oil to barely cover the bottom of your large skillet. Gently sauté the onions and pepper for a couple of minutes, adding in 3 crushed cloves of garlic and mushrooms in the last minute or so. Then remove them onto a preparation plate. Now, gently brown the ground beef, adding the remaining garlic, and a generous amount of ground pepper. Carefully pour off any remaining fat. Add the onions and peppers back in with the meat on a medium heat. Stir it all together. Pour in the cream of mushroom soup that has been whisked together with the red wine. (I usually keep a jug or box of inexpensive Burgundy on hand for cooking, saving the good stuff to drink!) Stir together over a medium heat.

In a separate pot of boiling water (unsalted), prepare a couple of cups of yolk-free broad ribbon noodles. This usually takes about 3 or 4 minutes. As the noodles are draining, add about 8 ounces (half a container) of the fat-free sour cream (I personally like "Naturally Yours" brand).

Stir the sour cream in over a medium heat until it's completely mixed.

Put the stroganoff and the noodles into serving dishes and enjoy!

Dick Dyszel started his career hosting horror movies on WDXR-TV 29 in Paducah. He later when to Washington, DC, won an Emmy and started the television series "Creature Feature". Living in Chicago, he hosts the Creature Feature website as Count Gor De Vol.

Valerie's Chicken and Dumplings

Eighth of August Homecoming
Valerie Newsome

1 larger fryer or hen, seasoned to taste

Wash chicken in water and place in a large pot. Cover with water and seasoning (celery, chicken bouillon cubes) and cook on top of the stove until chicken is tender. Remove from broth and let cool. De-bone the chicken to be placed back in the pot with the dumplings after the dumplings have cooked. (Save chicken broth in pot to cook dumplings.)

Dumplings:

2 c. all-purpose flour	**1 egg**
1 Tbsp. shortening	**¾ c. water**
1 tsp. salt	

In a large mixing bowl, add flour, salt and shortening. In a separate bowl, beat the egg and add ¾ cups of water to the egg. Slowly add the egg and water a little at a time to the flour, salt and shortening. Shape the mixture into a ball and place on a floured board. Knead slightly, then roll very thin and cut in 2-inch strips. Bring the chicken broth to boil and drop the dumplings in one at a time. Cover and cook about 20 or 30 minutes (reduce heat).

Eighth of August Homecoming, Paducah, is a chance for African Americans to pay tribute to their heritage and roots, with a memorial service, picnic and salute to black music. It would not be complete without the recipes shared by 82 year-old family matriarch Valerie Newsome.

❧ *Chef Jerry's Dressing* ❧

Executive West Hotel

½ loaf bread, diced
1 box cornbread mix, cooked as on pkg.
1 medium onion, chopped fine

3 pieces celery, chopped fine
¼ lb. pork sausage
2 Tbsp. ground sage
24 oz. chicken broth
2 eggs

Cook off sausage and vegetable and sage. Put bread and cornbread in large bowl. Add meat and vegetables and eggs; mix. Add stock. Bake in pan at 350° about 30 to 45 minutes (until golden brown).

Executive West Hotel, Louisville, delivers a unique combination of old-fashioned Southern hospitality, world-class facilities and creative cuisine from their Executive Chef, Jerry and his culinary staff at the restaurant Golden Targe Tearoom. This is his Grandma's recipe.

❧ *Tortilla Chicken Casserole* ❧

Farewell Drifters

¼ c. margarine, melted
small chopped onion
1 can mushroom soup
2 c. cubed chicken

1 can Ro-Tel tomatoes
12 corn tortillas, torn to bite size pieces
2 c. sharp Cheddar cheese

Mix first 5 ingredients. Butter 9 x 9-inch glass baking dish. Then layer tortillas, soup mixture and cheese. Then repeat 2 times. Bake at 325° for 40 minutes.

Several members of the bluegrass and folk band Farewell Drifters are Kentucky natives. Banjo player Trevor Brandt is from Paducah. Brothers Clayton and Josh Britt are from Franklin. Their concert tours have taken them all over the United States and Canada.

❧ Kentucky Proud Country Ham ❧

Richie Farmer

1 (16 to 20 lb.) Kentucky
 Proud country ham
2 c. vinegar
1 c. orange juice
1 c. packed brown sugar
5 to 8 whole cloves

1 Tbsp. allspice
1 Tbsp. nutmeg
⅓ c. prepared mustard
½ c. packed brown sugar
½ c. carbonated beverage

Scrub the ham. Soak in cold water to cover in a large pan for 8 to 10 hours. Drain. Place the ham in a 3 to 4-gallon stockpot and add enough water to cover. Add the vinegar, orange juice, 1 cup brown sugar, cloves, allspice and nutmeg. Bring to a boil and reduce the heat. Let stand until cool. Discard the bones. Place on a large baking sheet. Mix the mustard, ½ cup brown sugar and carbonated beverage in a bowl. Spread over the ham. Bake at 400° for 20 minutes. Cool completely before slicing. Yields 35 servings.

Commissioner of Agriculture Richie Farmer submitted this recipe from the Kentucky Department of Ag. and UK Cooperative Extension Service. From Clay County, he was a standout player for the UK basketball Wildcats from 1989 to 1992 and now resides in Frankfort.

❧ First Farm Inn Breakfast Pasta Carbonara ❧

First Farm Inn

1 lb. bacon
1 lb. extra-thin spaghetti or
 vermicelli
several c. whole milk
8 oz. Neufchatel (low-fat
 cream cheese) cheese
½ tsp. garlic salt

1 tsp. each: dried basil,
 parsley, oregano and/or
 Italian seasoning mix
½ to 1 c. fresh grated or
 shredded Parmesan cheese
8 eggs

Meats & Main Dishes

Brown bacon; drain on paper towels on paper plate and drain skillet (save drippings in skillet). Cook spaghetti or vermicelli for 10 minutes. Drain the water and add several cups of whole milk to prevent it from sticking to the pan. (You may use cream if you want a higher calorie dish or skim milk for less fat.) Add Neufchatel (low-fat cream cheese) cheese; cover and replace the pot on the burner; now set to low. Add garlic salt, dried basil, parsley and oregano and/or Italian seasoning mix. (Use about 2 teaspoons if herbs are fresh.) Add fresh grated or shredded Parmesan cheese. Stir to distribute cheese. Add more milk if needed.

In the bacon fryings in the skillet, scramble roughly 2 eggs per person, stirring so they are separated into fine crumbs. Crunch bacon inside paper towel into fine crumbs and replace on paper plate. Place pasta in serving bowl; top with scrambled eggs and crumbled bacon. Serve with pepper grater and more grated Parmesan if desired.

First Farm Inn is an elegant, updated 1870's farmhouse on 20 acres of rolling hills in Idlewild, just across the Ohio River from Cincinnati. They offer horseback riding, a fish pond, hiking and rocking chairs. Owner Jennifer Warner is also author of Boone County's history book.

❧ *World's Greatest Meat Loaf Recipe* ❧

Clint Ford

6 oz. garlic-flavored croutons
½ tsp. ground black pepper
½ tsp. cayenne pepper
1 tsp. chili powder
1 tsp. dried thyme
⅓ onion, roughly chopped
1 carrot, peeled and broken
3 whole cloves garlic
¼ red bell pepper
¼ green bell pepper

2 lb. ground beef (preferably 1 lb. sirloin, 1 lb. chuck)
1 ½ tsp. kosher salt
2 eggs
¼ c. lemon juice, divided (minus 2 Tbsp. for glaze, see following)
½ tsp. fennel seed
1 tsp. beef bouillon granules

For the Glaze:

1 c. ketchup
⅔ c. brown sugar
2 Tbsp. lemon juice
1 tsp. mustard powder
2 Tbsp. ground cumin

2 dashes Worcestershire sauce
2 dashes hot pepper sauce
2 Tbsp. honey

Preheat oven to 325°.

Combine croutons, black pepper, cayenne pepper, chili powder and thyme in a food processor and pulse until the contents are well blended. Place into a large bowl and set aside.

Combine the onion, carrot, garlic and red pepper in the food processor and pulse until the mixture is roughly chopped. Combine this mixture with the ground beef in the large bowl with the bread crumb mixture. Season the meat with the kosher salt to taste. Add the eggs, lemon juice, fennel seed and bouillon and combine thoroughly.

With your hands, mold the meat loaf into a football shape. Place the meat loaf onto the center of a parchment paper-lined baking sheet. Insert a temperature probe at a 45° angle into the top of the meat loaf, but try not to touch the bottom of the tray with the probe, as this could give false readings. Set the probe for 155°.

Combine the ketchup, brown sugar, lemon juice, mustard powder, cumin, Worcestershire sauce, hot pepper sauce and honey. Separate equally into two small bowls. After the meat loaf has been cooking for about 15 minutes, open the oven and carefully slide the rack it sits on partially out so that you may work on the meat loaf. Brush one entire bowlful of the glaze onto the meat loaf, and return to the oven. Then, when the temperature probe reads around 125° to 130°, check the meat loaf. The original glaze should be firmer and a bit sticky. Brush the entire remaining bowl of glaze onto the meat loaf, and return to the oven. When the internal temperature reaches 155°, remove from oven and allow to cool for at least ten minutes before serving.

Clint Ford graduated from Western Kentucky University, Bowling Green. He is CEO of Ford Creative Media, which provides professional character, commercial, announcer, industrial narration and promotional voiceovers: Disney characters and Japanese anime.

❧ *Patti Jarvis' Goetta* ❧

Glier's Goettafest

2 ½ to 3 lb. pork	**3 tsp. salt**
1 onion	**3 c. pinhead oatmeal**
8 c. water	**pinch of pepper**

Boil meat in water for 2 hours until tender. Let cool. Grind meat up and then place back in the water along with all other ingredients. Cook on low for 1 to 2 hours, stirring often. It will get very thick. Let cool and pour into loaf pans. Refrigerate until cold and then cut into blocks. Cut slices from blocks and cook as you would Glier's famous Goetta. (Brown both sides nice and crispy!)

Glier's Goetta is the world's largest producer of Goetta, a German breakfast sausage. Glier's hosts the annual Glier's Goettafest held the first weekend of August at Newport on the Levee. The festival attracts over 40,000 visitors for the 3-day weekend.

❧ *Dijon Shrimp* ❧

Tom T. Hall

1 lb. large shrimp, cleaned
  and deveined
1 clove garlic, crushed
2 Tbsp. margarine or butter
⅓ c. Grey Poupon Country
  Dijon mustard

¼ c. lemon juice
¼ c. chopped parsley
hot cooked Minute premium
  white rice (optional)

Cook and stir shrimp and garlic in margarine in large skillet on medium-high heat, until shrimp are pink and cooked through.

Blend in mustard, lemon juice and parsley; heat thoroughly. Serve over rice, if desired. Makes 4 servings.

Country music singer and songwriter Tom T. Hall from Olive Hill scored seven No. 1 hits on Billboard magazine's country singles chart and wrote No. 1 song "Harper Valley PTA." He and Miss Dixie have been selected as SPBGMA "Songwriter of the Year" 2006-08.

❧ *Mom Gorbandt's Noodle* ❧ *Ravioli*

Harrods Creek Baptist Church

1 ½ lb. ground beef
1 medium onion, chopped
2 to 4 stalks celery, chopped
1 large can diced tomatoes

¼ c. sugar (more or less for
  taste)
1 small pkg. wavy noodles
¼ c. tomato juice
pepper and salt to taste

Cook noodles as directed. Also cook beef and season with the salt and pepper. Drain beef. Place in 9 x 13 pan. Cook onions and celery together in a small amount of butter or olive oil. Add to the beef mixture. Add diced tomatoes and sugar. Mix all together.

Last, add cooked noodles with all other ingredients. If you need more juice, you can add it at this time. Bake at 350° for about 30 to 40 minutes, until noodles start to get crisp.

Harrods Creek Baptist Church, Brownsboro, was started in 1797. The old stone church built in 1822 is used today as a chapel for weddings and special church services. Mildred Parrish Gorbandt was a cherished member of the church until she went to be with the Lord in 2002.

🌿 *Racing Chicken Tetrazzini* 🌿

Nick Hayden

1 large chicken (or 5 breasts)	salt and pepper to taste
1 (10 oz.) pkg. thin spaghetti, broken	1 (4 oz.) jar diced pimentos
	1 small onion, chopped
1 lb. Velveeta cheese, cut in small slices	2 (10 oz.) cans cream of chicken soup

Boil chicken until tender. Then set out and let cool. Cook spaghetti, pimentos and onions until spaghetti is finished. Add cheese and soup until cheese is melted. Cut chicken into small pieces, then add chicken to spaghetti and cheese. Put all of that into an 11 x 13 baking dish and bake at 370° for 30 to 40 minutes. Yields 8 servings.

Nick Hayden, Owensboro, has been racing for 6 seasons in the world renowned Moto GP racing series. In 2006 at age 25, he made motorcycle racing history; winning the overall series and title of Moto GP Champion.

🌿 *Sausage and Egg Casserole* 🌿

Harper's Country Hams

6 to 8 slices bread, torn into pieces	½ c. grated cheese (your choice)
1 lb. sausage or 1 pkg. ham pieces	2 c. milk
	6 to 8 eggs, beaten
	salt and pepper

Cook ham by stir-frying in skillet on medium heat for 1 to 2 minutes per side. In large baking dish, layer torn bread, ham and cheese. Add milk to beaten eggs and season with salt and pepper.

Pour egg mixture over meat, cheese and bread. Refrigerate over-night. Bake at 350° for 35 minutes prior to serving.

Harper's Country Hams located in Clinton, has been a Kentucky Tradition for over 55 years. Winner of the Kentucky State Fair Grand Champion Country Ham competition on numerous occasions. They have gone from whole country hams in 1952 to over 100 different products.

Southern Fried Wild Turkey

Tim Herald

1 turkey breast	1 Tbsp. black pepper
1 egg	2 Tbsp. seasoned salt
3 to 4 c. Kentucky Seasoned Flour (available at most grocery stores)	2 Tbsp. your favorite Cajun seasoning powder
	1 tsp. red pepper (optional)

Cut wild turkey breast into bite-sized cubes. Dip in beaten egg. Mix remaining ingredients. Roll turkey cubes in flour mixture. Deep-fry in peanut oil at 375° to 400° until golden brown. Drain and serve.

Tim Herald, Lexington, is on Journal Television Show (Outdoor Channel), Whitetail Country (ESPN2), Limb Saver Outdoors (Men's Channel), and hosts the award winning Outdoor America (Outdoor Channel). He has written several books and owns a professional hunt consulting firm, Grand Slam Hunts, and is on the pro-staff of Knight and Hale located in Cadiz.

Quail Medallions With Raspberry/Cranberry Marsala Sauce

Heather French Henry

12 oz. bag fresh or thawed frozen raspberries (about 3 ¼ c.), and add some dried cranberries
⅔ c. firmly packed dark brown sugar
½ c. apple juice
½ c. cranberry juice
⅓ c. Marsala
¼ tsp. allspice
¼ tsp. ground ginger
¼ tsp. dry mustard
1 c. chicken broth
½ stick (¼ c.) unsalted butter
zest of 1 orange, removed with a vegetable peeler
18 (2 to 3 oz.) quail medallions, rinsed and patted dry
wild rice with dried cranberries

In a saucepan, combine raspberries, brown sugar, apple juice, cranberry juice, Marsala, allspice, ginger, mustard, ½ cup of the broth, 2 tablespoons of the butter, zest and salt and pepper to taste; bring the liquid to a boil, and simmer the mixture, stirring occasionally for 25 minutes, until it is thickened and the berries have burst. Strain the glaze through a fine sieve into a bowl, pressing hard on the solids and discarding them. The glaze may be made 1 day in advance, kept covered, and chilled, and reheated.

Transfer ½ cup of the glaze to a small bowl and reserve it. In a large ovenproof skillet, heat remaining 2 tablespoons butter over moderately high heat until the foam subsides; in it, brown the quail medallions, turning them, for 4 minutes. Baste the medallions generously with some of the remaining glaze and roast them in the top third of a preheated 450° oven, basting them with some of the remaining glaze every 5 minutes, for 15 minutes more, or until the meat is no longer pink. Transfer the quail to a plate, and pour off the fat in the skillet.

Deglaze the skillet with the remaining ½ cup broth over moderately high heat, scraping up the brown bits; stir in the reserved ½ cup glaze, and boil the mixture, whisking, until it is thickened. Strain the sauce through a fine sieve into a heated sauceboat and season it with salt and pepper. Serve the sauce with the quail. (Serves 6.)

Heather French Henry, Augusta, won the title of Miss America in 2000. Her husband is Lt. Gov. Steve Henry. This recipe was prepared for them while they lived at the Old Governor's Mansion (official home of the Lt. Gov.) by the Executive Chef Angie Vives.

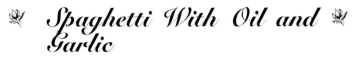

Spaghetti With Oil and Garlic

Mayor Sandy Jones

12 cloves garlic
¼ c. olive oil
4 qt. water
1 ½ Tbsp. salt
1 lb. spaghetti

1 ½ c. chicken stock
1 c. finely chopped Italian
  parsley
freshly ground black pepper
grated Parmesan cheese

Peel garlic. Mince 6 of them and set aside. Slice remaining garlic. Heat oil in skillet. Add sliced garlic and cook over medium heat, stirring occasionally, until golden brown. Bring water to boil. Add salt and spaghetti and cook until tender, but still firm. Do not overcook. Drain pasta. Add chicken broth and simmer until most of broth has been absorbed. Add olive oil/garlic mixture, minced garlic and parsley. Toss thoroughly. Top with freshly ground black pepper and grated Parmesan cheese.

Bowling Green Mayor Sandy Jones is President, CEO and Founder of Quality Personnel, an independent regional temporary service. Founded in 1977, the company's locations are in Bowling Green, Glasgow, Franklin, Russellville, Hopkinsville and Columbia, Kentucky.

French Fried Shrimp

Kentucky Aquaculture

2 eggs, beaten
1 tsp. salt
½ c. all-purpose flour
½ c. dry bread crumbs
½ tsp. paprika

oil (for deep frying)
peppy or tartar sauce
1 ½ lb. raw peeled
  freshwater shrimp

Thaw and shell shrimp if frozen. Combine eggs and salt. Combine flour, dry breadcrumbs and paprika. Dip each shrimp in egg, and then roll in bread mixture. Fry in a basket in deep, hot oil,

350°, for 2 to 3 minutes or until golden brown. Drain on absorbent paper. Serve with peppy or tartar sauce. Makes 6 servings.

Kentucky Aquaculture Marketing group supplies high quality Kentucky aquaculture products, like caviar, shrimp and smoked fish! They offer the opportunity to serve Kentucky grown products in your home, restaurant or grocery store.

Kentucky Hot Browns

Kentucky History Center

8 thick white bread slices
1 c. Parmesan cheese
2 large tomatoes, sliced and halved

1 lb. roasted turkey slices
8 bacon slices, cooked

Trim crust from bread and discard. Place bread on a baking sheet and broil 3 inches from heat, until toasted, turning once. Arrange 2 slices in each of 4 lightly greased individual baking dishes. Place turkey on top. Pour Cheese Sauce evenly over turkey and sprinkle with Parmesan cheese. Broil 6 inches from heat 4 minutes or until bubbly and lightly browned. Top with bacon and tomato. Serve immediately.

Cheese Sauce:

½ c. butter or margarine
3 ½ c. milk
¼ tsp. salt
⅓ c. all-purpose flour

½ c. shredded Parmesan cheese
¼ tsp. pepper

Melt butter in a 3-quart saucepan over medium-high heat. Stir in flour and gradually add milk. Bring to boil, stirring constantly, 1 to 2 minutes. Add cheese, salt and pepper.

Dr. J. Kevin Graffagnino is the Executive Director of the Kentucky Historical Society and The Kentucky History Center, the Old State Capitol and the Kentucky Military History Museum, all of which are located in Kentucky's state capital, Frankfort.

Crunchy Sausage Casserole

Jim Klotter

1 pkg. Uncle Ben's long-grain and wild rice (original recipe)
1 pkg. Uncle Ben's brown and wild rice (mushroom recipe)
1 lb. each sausage and ground beef
1 large onion, chopped
1 (8 oz.) can sliced mushrooms, drained
2 (8 oz.) cans sliced water chestnuts, drained
3 to 6 Tbsp. soy sauce
1 (2 ¼ oz.) pkg. sliced almonds

Cook rice mix according to package directions; set aside. Brown sausage, ground beef and onion; drain. Mix rice, mushrooms, water chestnuts, soy sauce, and meat mixture together; stir well. Spoon into ungreased 2-quart casserole. Cover and refrigerate overnight. Remove from refrigerator and allow to sit at room temperature 30 minutes. Sprinkle almonds over top. Bake, uncovered, at 325° for 50 minutes or until thoroughly heated.

Kentucky State Historian, Jim Klotter, Georgetown. He likes this recipe because "the sausage part reminds me, as a historian, of an earlier time when people killed hogs and made their own sausage. Such ties to the past always help us remember who we are."

Mamaw Henderson's Meat Loaf

Shannon Lawson

1 lb. ground chuck
½ lb. sausage (mom likes to use hot sausage)
1 chopped onion
2 to 3 eggs
⅓ c. unsweetened condensed milk or half and half
14 oz. can whole tomatoes (not crushed; she says the crushed canned tomatoes are not the same variety, so it's important)
1 Tbsp. Worcestershire
salt and pepper to taste
2 cloves garlic (dad likes 3 to 4, but he really likes garlic)
corn flakes (enough to absorb liquid)

Mix all ingredients together, crushing tomatoes as you mix. Form into 3 loaves. Bake at 375° until done (45 minutes to an hour).

Country rock and bluegrass singer Shannon Lawson was raised in Taylorsville, a tiny town 40 miles southwest of Louisville that has been home to his family for generations. Lawson, who is a prolific songwriter, is now based in Nashville, Tennessee.

❧ *Apple-Glazed Pork* ❧ *Tenderloin*

Lebanon Tourist Commission

2 whole pork tenderloins (each about ¾ lb.)

Marinade:

½ c. Maker's Mark bourbon	¼ c. brown sugar, packed
¾ c. apple cider	¼ tsp. ground cinnamon

Bourbon Applesauce:

3 Red Delicious apples, diced	1 c. beef broth
1 onion, diced	3 oz. heavy cream
3 oz. Maker's Mark	¼ c. walnuts, chopped
1 c. chicken broth	

Place pork tenderloin in glass baking dish. Thoroughly mix bourbon, cider, brown sugar and cinnamon and pour over tenderloin. Cover dish with plastic wrap and refrigerate 8 hours or more, turning meat several times.

Heat oven to 325°. Place marinated tenderloin in oven and cook 1 hour 15 minutes or until internal temperature of meat is 170°. Brush meat with marinade every 15 to 20 minutes. Once meat is done, let it stand out of oven 10 to 15 minutes before carving.

To prepare bourbon applesauce, sauté apples and onions for 5 minutes until soft. Add bourbon; flambé, being careful not to have bourbon near flame when pouring.

Add broths to other ingredients and simmer for 5 minutes. Then add cream and reduce sauce until it begins to thicken; whirl in blender to make smooth, if desired. Add walnuts to sauce and serve with tenderloin.

True heart of Kentucky is Lebanon, the geographic center of the state. Founded 1789 by a group of Catholic families, it was the site of several Civil War raids by General John Hunt Morgan

(Morgan's Raiders). Marion County is also the home of Maker's Mark Distillery.

🌺 *Maple Hill Manor Sunrise* 🌺

Maple Hill Manor

eggs	**grated Cheddar cheese**
whipping cream or half and half	**Parmesan**
	paprika
salt and pepper	**fresh parsley**

Preheat oven to 375°. Spray large muffin pan with nonstick spray. Two eggs per person: muffin pan for twelve will feed six. (Multiply number of people by two and use the appropriate number of pans.) Line each slot with a foil muffin cup. Spray once again with nonstick spray. Break open an egg in each cup. Pour a teaspoon of whipping cream or half and half over each egg. Sprinkle with salt and pepper (additional herbs may be used to add extra flavor, such as basil and thyme). Cover each egg with grated Cheddar cheese. Add Parmesan for an extra burst of cheese flavor.

Bake for about 15 minutes (until yolk is hard). Arrange two per plate; sprinkle with paprika and a sprig of fresh parsley.

Maple Hill Manor B&B (circa 1851), located in Springfield, only minutes from Historic Bardstown, is listed on the National Register of Historic Places and designated a Kentucky Landmark Home. The antebellum mansion took 3 years to construct and features 13 rooms.

🌺 *Grilled Pork Tenderloin With Bourbon Sauce* 🌺

Catherine McCord

(Serves 6)

2 (1 lb.) pork tenderloins	**1 Tbsp. (or 1-inch piece) fresh ginger, shaved on a microplane or minced**
¼ c. Kentucky bourbon	
¼ c. Dijon mustard	
¼ c. brown sugar (light or dark)	**3 cloves garlic, minced**
	2 Tbsp. vegetable oil
¼ c. soy sauce	

Trim pork tenderloin. Whisk all ingredients except pork in a bowl.

In a large Ziploc bag, add all ingredients. Marinate 8 to 24 hours. Grill over high flame for 16 to 18 minutes or until 165° (you want the pork to be a little pink in the middle). Let the pork rest at least 10 minutes for the juices to settle. Slice and serve.

Catherine McCord, Louisville, is a fashion model and actress. She has modeled for Victoria's Secret, L'eggs pantyhose, Calvin Klein and starred in television and movies such as Gridiron Glory, Two and a Half Men, Dick Clark's Rockin New Year's Eve.

Pheasant Pot Pie

John Michael Montgomery

2 c. cooked pheasant meat
1 can Veg-All (do not drain)
2 cans cream of potato soup

½ c. milk
salt and pepper to taste
4 pie crusts

Preheat oven to 375°. Combine ingredients in mixing bowl, then pour equal amounts into regular size pie crusts. Top with a pie crust and pinch sides together. Cut slits in the top of each pie. Bake for 40 minutes or until crust is golden brown. Makes 2 pies.
*Note: I sometimes add extra corn or green beans.

John Michael Montgomery from Danville, earned 15 number one singles, sold over 16 million albums, received 3 CMA Awards, 5 ACM Awards and 1 American Music Award. This one was given to him by a long time friend Len Doolen.

Tincy's Souse

Penn's Store
(Souse was made in the fall and enjoyed in the winter.)

1 hogs head
water to cover
3 Tbsp. salt
4 tsp. black pepper
1 garlic clove

1 Tbsp. cloves
1 Tbsp. red pepper
2 ½ tsp. allspice
1 qt. broth in which meat
    was cooked

Scrub and clean uncooked hog's head. Cut off ears and snout. Remove eyes and brain and all skin and fat from head. Cut into four pieces. Soak in salted water (½ cup salt per gallon of water) for 4 to 5 hours. Drain and wash in fresh water. Place on stove and bring to a boil. Turn down heat to medium and cook until tender. Remove meat from kettle and reserve one quart of broth. Let cool. Remove all meat from bones and chop fine. Place chopped meat and

Meats & Main Dishes

other ingredients in large pan. Place on stove and simmer for 10 to 15 minutes, mixing well. Pour mixture into a stone crock and store in a cool, dry place. Allow to jell. When jelled, the souse may be sliced as desired. Slices may be covered in vinegar for 1 to 2 hours and later served.

Penn's Store in Gravel Switch is the oldest country store in America run by the same family since 1850. Known for "The Great Outhouse Blowout Race" which brings competitors from all over the U.S. and Canada and is carried live on ESPN. The race started as a dedication of their new outhouse in 1992 and included a show by country singer Chet Atkins.

Petrino Italian Spaghetti

Bobby Petrino

1 lb. hamburger	2 cloves garlic or garlic salt
1 pkg. spaghetti seasoning mix	1 tsp. salt
	pepper to taste
1 small onion, chopped	1 tsp. oregano leaves,
1 (6 oz.) can tomato paste	crushed
1 (8 oz.) can tomato sauce	2 tsp. sugar

Brown hamburger; drain excess fat. Add onions and seasoning. Add tomato paste and sauce; simmer. Add water to desired thickness. Bring to boil. Simmer on low for 1 hour, stirring occasionally.

Cook spaghetti noodles, or favorite noodles per package instructions. Pour spaghetti sauce over noodles, mix together, and enjoy.

Bobby Petrino is an American college football coach and current head coach of Arkansas Razorbacks. He previously served as head coach for 4 seasons at the University of Louisville and considered one of the most innovative offensive minds in the college game.

Chicken Polly

Stu Pollard

olive oil	salt and pepper to taste
¾ stick butter	½ c. white wine
4 full boneless breasts of chicken	½ tsp. basil
	½ tsp. parsley

Season skillet with olive oil; turn on high. Add butter; melt. Add breasts of chicken, each folded in half. Keep on high until brown on the outside (3 minutes a side). Reduce heat; add salt and pepper to taste. Cover and simmer for 10 minutes. Add white wine, basil and parsley. Simmer for another ten minutes (and drink any leftover wine). Serve each breast in a lipped edge plate; pour remaining wine/butter reduction on as a sauce.

Award-winning producer and writer Stu Pollard is from Louisville and graduated from Georgetown. He hit the movie scene as writer and producer of the hit movie "Nice Guys Sleep Alone", starring Sean O'Bryan. Also wrote and produced "Keep Your Distance", which he filmed in Louisville.

❧ *Kentucky Bison Tenderloin With Buttered Leeks* ❧

Chef Michael Paley
Proof on Main

(Serves two)

2 (12 oz.) "bone-in" bison filets	2 Tbsp. unsalted butter
kosher salt to taste	2 sprigs fresh rosemary
freshly ground black pepper to taste	2 Tbsp. good quality extra-virgin olive oil
1 bunch leeks, diced and rinsed well in cold water	½ tsp. smoked sea salt (see note following)

In a medium, heavy-bottomed saucepan over medium heat, melt the butter and add the leeks.

Season with salt and pepper. Reduce the heat to low and slowly simmer the leeks until soft and buttery. Set aside and keep warm.

Place a large, heavy ovenproof skillet (such as an iron skillet) in a 500° conventional oven. Drizzle the skillet with a small amount of olive oil. Season the bison filet well with salt and pepper and place on the hot skillet. Return to oven for 5 minutes. Turn steaks and return to oven until steak reaches desired doneness; 10 to 12 minutes roasting time will give you a good medium-rare (135° to 145° on an instant-read thermometer). After cooking, allow the meat to rest for 5 minutes.

While the meat rests, make the rosemary oil. Warm the oil and rosemary gently in a small sauté pan to infuse the flavor, about 5 minutes. Remove the rosemary sprigs and reserve for garnish.

To Finish: Divide the leeks evenly in the center of two warm dinner plates. Place the bison filet on top. Drizzle with a little of the rosemary oil. Garnish with the sprigs of rosemary and the smoked salt. Serve with roasted fingerling potatoes.

Housed in 5 historic buildings in downtown Louisville, Proof on Main is part of the new 21c Museum Hotel, which opened in 2006 and developed by Louisville art collectors and philanthropists, Laura Lee Brown and Steve Wilson.

Oven Baked BBQ and Olive Oil Marinated Chicken Breast

Lee Reherman
LG Entertainment

4 chicken breasts   olive oil
BBQ sauce

Fill a deep oven pan about a good generous layer of BBQ sauce. Mix in a substantial amount of olive oil, but not TOO much.

Cut up several chicken breasts into smaller "chicken nugget" sized pieces. Wash the smaller pieces of chicken thoroughly (obviously), but put the chicken into the pan while still wet, as this will dilute the BBQ/olive oil into just the right marination where the BBQ sauce won't harden while cooking.

Mix the chicken in the pan, making sure all the pieces of chicken are covered thoroughly (you can let this set for a while, but it doesn't make that much difference). Cook in the oven on 375° to 400° for 30 minutes.

After cooking, immediately put all the contents of the pan, both chicken and marinade, into any container that can hold it all; cover, and let this sit for a couple of hours.

In that time, the BBQ/oil will continue to soak and cook right into the chicken, making it unbelievably juicy, tender and tasty.

Lee Reherman of Louisville was a standout at Cornell University before playing pro football with the Miami Dolphins as part of their offensive line. While working on his Ph.D. at UCLA, he could be seen as "Hawk" on the television series American Gladiators.

Meat Loaf Wellington

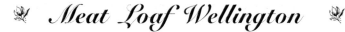

Tom Rickman

1 c. finely chopped onions	1 chopped tomato
1 celery stalk, chopped thinly	1 tube braunschweiger (or
1 Tbsp. minced garlic	liverwurst)
1 carrot, chopped fine	1 can mushrooms
2 Tbsp. unsalted butter	3 bay leaves
1 ½ lb. ground beef	1 onion
2 egg yolks, slightly beaten	puff pastry
1 c. bread crumbs	

Make the meat loaf the way Mama made it (mine, anway): a couple of pounds of hamburger, some diced onions and celery, maybe a carrot, and a chopped tomatoes. Cook until almost done, then remove.

To make the duxelle, pan-fry a can of mushrooms, a diced onion and a few bay leaves in butter, salting to taste. Mix this with the braunschweiger (or liverwurst) to make a loose paste.

Spread the paste on some store-bought puff pastry and wrap the meat loaf, the paste-side next to the meat. Poke a few holes in it to let the steam escape and brush the pastry with the egg yolks. Pop it back in the oven and cook until the pastry is the color of a Kentucky sunset in August. Remove, serve, and cross your fingers.

Tom Rickman from Sharpe, Kentucky, whose screenwriting/directing feature movie credits include Oscar-nominated "Coal Miner's Daughter" and "Truman" for which he received an Emmy nomination, "Breakfast with Morrie", "Berry Gordy's Motown", a miniseries.

Pastilla D'agneau Puree De Coco Et Pistou

Jeri Ryan and Christophe Eme

(Serves 2)

Duxelle:

Tbsp. olive oil	fresh squeezed juice of 1
8 shallots, chopped	lemon
2 kg white mushrooms,	salt and pepper to taste
chopped	bouquet garnit (thyme,
	parsley, leek)

Heat olive oil in pan and add chopped shallots. Sauté shallots until become clear (colorless). Add the chopped mushrooms with the lemon juice, bouquet garnit and the salt and pepper. Cook until the liquids have just evaporated; set aside.

Citron Confit:

1 lemon

For Syrup:

300 g sugar	1 basil stem (no leaf)
1 L water	10 whole peppercorns

Mince whole lemon finely, removing all seeds. Combine syrup ingredients in saucepan and bring to boil. Add minced lemon and bring to boil again. Set aside.

Tomato Confit:

1 kg tomatoes

For Marinade:

3 cloves garlic, minced	4 cl olive oil
5 sprigs thyme	salt and pepper to taste

Peel tomatoes, removing seeds and core. Cut tomatoes into 4 pieces and flatten so they look like tulip petals. Marinate tomato pieces in olive oil with the garlic, thyme, salt and pepper. Roast tomatoes in marinade for 4 hours at 90°C.

Pastilla:

1 rack of lamb (5 people, 1 slice each; 3 people, 2 slices each)	clarified butter (enough to coat 2 sheets of phyllo dough)
salt and pepper	Duxelle
3 basil leaves	Citron Confit
3 sheets phyllo dough	Tomato Confit

Debone and remove the fat from the rack of lamb. Season it with salt and pepper. Lightly sear lamb on both sides. Coat one side of phyllo dough with clarified butter. Place another sheet of phyllo on top, then coat that with clarified butter. Place the third sheet of phyllo dough on top. Place seared lamb in center of phyllo dough. Layer Duxelle on top of lamb. Place 3 basil leaves on top of Duxelle. Layer the Citron Confit on top of basil. Layer Tomato Confit on top of Citron Confit. Wrap lamb and layers with phyllo dough. Cook in oven for 20 minutes at 300°. Cut into 4 pieces. Place on top of Puree De Haricots Blancs, 2 pieces pastilla per plate.

Purée de Haricots Blancs:

200g small white beans	1 carrot
chicken stock (2 times volume of soaked beans)	bouquet garnit (thyme, parsley, leek)
1 onion	pinch of "piment d'espelette"
1 clove	5 cl olive oil

(Prep begins 1 day ahead.) Soak beans in water for 24 hours. After soaking, strain excess water. In a large pot, put the beans with chicken stock (two times volume of beans). Insert clove into onion and add to pot. Add whole carrot, bouquet garnit and pimento. Cook slowly on low heat 45 minutes to 1 hour. Remove all items from the beans. Blend beans with a bit of chicken stock, 5 cl of olive oil. Garnish bean purée with rosemary.

Garnishes:

4 grape tomatoes (whole)	10 nicoise olives, chopped
4 spring onions, blanched, halved and then grilled on both sides	

Mint Salad:

mesclin lettuce	sherry vinegar
5 small mint leaves	salt and pepper
olive oil	

Pistou (Sauce):

10cl olive oil	30g grated Parmesan
1 Tbsp. pine nuts	2 bunches basil
1 garlic clove	salt to taste

Blend ingredients.

Presentation: Two plates with bean purée on each. Place two pieces of lamb pastilla on top and place salad on the side. Arrange garnish around pastilla. Drizzle with pistou and lamb jus (purchase separately).

Actress Jeri Ryan, Paducah, and husband French Chef Christophe Eme sent this incredible recipe. They own Ortolan in L.A. Jeri performed at Market House Theatre while in high school and starred in Star Trek, Boston Legal and Shark.

Beef Steak Pie

John Scope

1 beefsteak, cut into small
  pieces
1 small onion, chopped

2 to 3 stalks celery, chopped
small amount of salt and
  pepper

Cover steak and vegetables with water and cook until done. Remove from broth (save broth) to cook optional dumplings.

Place cup (years ago a ceramic bird with opening in mouth for steam to escape was used) in center of pie plate. Place beef and vegetables around cup. Cover with piecrust; slit crust to allow steam to escape. Bake at 400° for 15 to 20 minutes until crisp.

John T. Scope III, Paducah, is buried in Oak Grove Cemetery. The book and movie "Inherit the Wind", starring Spencer Tracy, is based on him and the famous attorneys Williams Jennings Bryan and Clarence Darrow. Special thanks to his niece Mrs. Louise Wahl.

Conway's Fish Fillets

Conway Stone

4 boneless fish fillets (choose
  any freshwater fish, cod,
  bass, etc.)
½ c. flour
1 Tbsp. paprika

½ tsp. red pepper
½ tsp. salt
½ tsp. garlic powder
½ tsp. black pepper
2 Tbsp. vegetable oil

Mix flour, paprika, red pepper, salt, garlic powder and black pepper. Dip fillets in the mix and cover the entire fillet. Heat frying pan with vegetable oil. Brown fillets in frying pan for one minute on each side. Bake fish in oven for 10 minutes at 350°.

Conway Stone is a professional speaker and author based in Louisville, Kentucky. He is the author of two books, "Follow Your Dreams" and "Dream High." You can find Conway speaking to groups all over the world and you can find him anywhere there is great food. www.dreamhigh.com

Hush-Cat Nuggets

Stonefence Bistro

1 (8 oz.) pkg. hush puppy mix	1 Tbsp. hot pepper sauce
½ c. water	½ tsp. cayenne pepper
½ c. milk	vegetable oil (for frying)
1 large egg, beaten	1 ¼ lb. catfish fillets
1 Tbsp. finely minced jalapeno pepper	1 c. all-purpose flour
	Spicy Tartar Sauce (recipe follows)

In a medium-sized bowl, stir together hush puppy mix, water, milk, egg, jalapenos, hot pepper sauce and cayenne. Let stand five minutes.

Pour oil to a depth of ½-inch in a large deep skillet; heat oil to at least 350°.

Pat catfish fillets dry with paper towels, and cut into bite size pieces. Dredge catfish pieces in flour, then dip in hush puppy batter mixture. Drop catfish pieces into hot oil and fry, in batches, 3 to 4 minutes on each side, or until golden brown. Serve with Spicy Tartar Sauce.

Spicy Tartar Sauce:

1 c. mayonnaise	2 cloves garlic, finely minced
1 ½ Tbsp. finely minced jalapeno pepper	2 Tbsp. hot pepper sauce
1 Tbsp. finely minced red onion	½ tsp. lemon juice
	½ tsp. chili powder
	1 pinch of salt

Stir together all ingredients in a medium bowl. Cover and chill until ready to use.

The Stonefence Bistro is located at 730 Main Street in Paris, Kentucky. Mara Whalen sent this great recipe that is a variation/combination of the traditional hush puppy/fried catfish recipe.

Lisa's Favorite Roasted Pork Loin

"Thunder Over Louisville"

1 boneless pork loin	¼ c. Kentucky bourbon
1 apple, thinly sliced	2 Tbsp. Dijon mustard
32 oz. apple jelly	juice from 1 lemon

Bring to boil the jelly, mustard, lemon juice and bourbon, stirring until marinade is well mixed. Separate into 2 portions.

Pierce the roast with a fork. Layer bottom, center (if roast is split) and top of pork loin with sliced apples and baste well with marinade.

Place in 325° to 350° oven for two hours, basting every 15 to 20 minutes. When middle of roast reaches at least 145°, take out of oven and slice and put in pan. Using the separated portion, coat the sliced roast with marinade. Place in warm oven for at least 30 minutes or until ready to serve.

Kentucky Derby Festival and "Thunder Over Louisville" is sponsored by several businesses, including Ford Motor Company Louisville Truck Plant. "Thunder Over Louisville" is the nation's largest annual fireworks event. This recipe is from their company cookbook.

❧ *Chilled Shrimp With Basil* ❧ *Ponzu Sauce*

Toad Hollow Vineyards

2 Tbsp. thin or low-sodium
  soy sauce
2 Tbsp. freshly squeezed lime
  juice
2 Tbsp. freshly squeezed
  orange juice

2 Tbsp. light brown sugar
2 Tbsp. flavorless cooking oil
½ tsp. Asian chile sauce
1 Tbsp. finely minced ginger
1 clove garlic, finely minced
¼ c. chopped fresh basil

Shell and devein the shrimp (leaving the tail attached). Bring 4 quarts of water to a rapid boil. Add 1 pound of medium to large shrimp. Cook the shrimp until done, about 1 minute. Drain and transfer immediately to a large bowl of ice water. When chilled, drain and refrigerate until ready to use. In a small, nonreactive bowl, combine the sauce ingredients and mix well. If not using right away, refrigerate. The recipe can be completed to this point up to 10 hours before. To serve, toss the shrimp with the sauce, 10 minutes before serving.

Todd Williams, whose brother is actor and comedian Robin Williams, grew up in Versailles, Kentucky. He is owner and general manager to Toadhollow Vineyards located in Healdsburg, California in the Napa Valley.

Old Fashioned Chicken and Dumplings

Kipp Tribble

Broth:

2 c. water
4 c. chicken broth
½ Tbsp. salt

1 c. milk
½ tsp. pepper

Dumplings:

2 c. all-purpose flour
½ tsp. baking soda

½ Tbsp. salt
¾ c. buttermilk

Combine the water, broth and salt. Bring to a boil; cover and lower heat.

Dumplings: Combine the flour, baking soda and ½ teaspoon of salt. Add the buttermilk; knead in until the dough is a sticky ball. Unroll dough onto a floured surface. Use a rolling pin or glass to roll the dough down to under ⅕ of an inch in thickness. Cut squares (about an inch or two in size).

Raise broth heat again and stir in the milk and add the pepper. Some people add carrots, celery, chicken and other foods. This is a personal preference.

Drop the dumplings one at a time into the broth. Stir often so things won't stick together. Cook dumplings for 10 to 12 minutes. Makes 6 to 8 servings, although we often tripled the recipe!

Actor, writer and producer Kipp Tribble is from Lexington. He is CEO for Ship of Fools Productions. In addition to starring in "Sugar Cain" and "Up Michigan", he has produced various docudramas for the Discovery Network.

Grilled Salmon, Cream Cheese Grits and Caramelized Orange Sauce

Varanese

(Serves 8 people.)

8 (8 oz.) salmon filets

Lightly oil and season salmon. Grill to medium and serve over 4 to 5 ounces of Cream Cheese Grits and ladle 2 ounces of Orange Sauce over top. Complement the dish with your favorite seasonal vegetables and garnish with paprika around the rim.

Caramelized Orange Sauce:

1 orange (zest and squeeze)	½ c. Triple Sec
1 c. sugar	1 c. mandarin oranges
1 c. Karo	

Place sugar and Karo in saucepan and stir. Bring to simmer, brushing down the sides with water to keep crystals from forming. When an amber color is reached, turn off flame and cool for 5 minutes. Heat the Triple Sec with zest and juice in microwave for 1 minute. Whisk in the caramel. If it locks up, just heat up and continue to stir. When cools completely, fold in the oranges.

Cream Cheese Grits:

1 c. heavy cream	3 pt. water
¼ lb. cream cheese	12 oz. grits

Heat the cream and water in a pot; stir in grits and simmer until thick. Add softened cream cheese and season with salt and pepper

Varanese is located on Frankfort Avenue in Louisville. Owner and Executive Chef John Varanese graduated from the Culinary Arts program at Johnson and Wales University. The restaurant was selected as 1 of the top 5 best in the city by the Courier Journal.

Veal Gabrille

Vincenzo's

1 ½ lb. scallopine of veal	1 Tbsp. lemon juice
(each slice weighing 2 oz.)	4 oz. veal broth
1 oz. clarified butter	salt and pepper
1 tsp. shallots	3 crescents each honeydew
½ c. sliced mushrooms	and cantaloupe melon
½ tsp. drained capers	chopped parsley
1 oz. white wine	

Lightly dust veal in seasoned flour (flour, salt, white pepper). Saute veal in pan until just rare; remove from pan. Saute mushrooms and capers; cook until mushrooms are tender. Deglaze pan with wine, then add lemon juice and veal stock. Simmer until consistency is correct. Season with salt and pepper; pour over veal. Garnish with melon and parsley. Serves four.

Vincenzo's Italian Restaurant, Louisville, is owned by brothers Agostino and Vincenzo Gabriele who are from Palermo, Italy. The restaurant represents their personal dreams for a place of hospitality where friends, old and new, can come to enjoy a truly special evening.

—• *Extra Recipes* •—

Asparagus Baked in Foil

1 lb. asparagus, washed & trimmed
Salt & freshly ground pepper to taste
2 tsp. lemon juice
1/4 c. strong chicken broth
parsley and lemon rind (for garnish)

Vegetables

Preheat the oven to 350°. Place the asparagus
in the center of a large sheet of aluminum
foil. Keep the tips pointing the same way. Season
with salt and pepper. Add the lemon
juice and pour the chicken broth over all. Seal
tightly and place the foil packet over a cookie
sheet over a preheated oven. Bake until the
asparagus is cooked, about 30 minutes. Place
on a serving dish. Pour on the juices. Garnish
with parsley and lemon rind.

Recipe Favorites

Recipe Title:_____ _____

_____ _____

_____ _____

_____ _____

_____ _____

_____ _____

_____ _____

_____ _____

_____ _____

_____ _____

Family Favorites

Page No.

Recipe Title:_____ _____

_____ _____

_____ _____

_____ _____

_____ _____

Notes:_____

_____

_____

_____

Vegetables

Lady Anne's Hashbrown Heaven

Aire Castle Inn B&B

1 lb. sausage, bacon and/or ham
2 lb. pkg. pre-cooked cubed potatoes
1 ½ c. mushrooms

1 c. chopped red and green peppers
2 c. mixed shredded cheese
10 eggs
1 can Milnot or evaporated milk

Preheat oven to 375°. Spray 2 pie plate dishes with Pam.

Line dish with a thin layer of pre-cooked cubed potatoes. (You may use frozen or refrigerated potatoes.) (Layer toppings; may add more or less.) Sprinkle choice of meat topping(s), mushrooms, peppers and mixed shredded cheese.

Beat 10 eggs well and blend in a can of Milnot or evaporated milk. Salt and pepper to taste. Pour egg mixture over other ingredients and gently combine so eggs are throughout dish.

Bake 30 to 40 minutes or until center is firm. Slice into pie wedges and serve with warm salsa. (Recommend served with baked fruit and hot biscuits.)

This recipe was given to us by Mike and Ann Driver, owners of Aire Castle Inn B&B, 413 Salem Chapel Road North, Benton, Kentucky, near beautiful Kentucky Lake. This is their signature breakfast dish.

Putanaesca

Banana Tree Studio

(Serves 6 to 8)

25 to 30 Greek olives in brine, pitted and chopped
3 to 4 Tbsp. good capers
½ c. extra-virgin olive oil
¼ c. Italian parsley, chopped fine

6 to 8 fillets anchovies, chopped fine
¼ c. (4 to 5 Tbsp.) toasted bread crumbs
1 clove garlic
1 ¼ c. plum tomatoes, skinned (medium dice)

Preparation: 30 minutes. Cooking: 15 minutes.

Heat oil and fry garlic. Brown, flavor oil, discard. Water for vermicelli should be ready; add vermicelli; cook 6 minutes.

Whip chopped anchovies, olives and capers into oil. Stir. Add tomatoes. Bring to light boil and simmer until vermicelli is done.

Toss sauce into pasta. Sprinkle with toasted bread crumbs. NO CHEESE. Garnish with parsley.

Banana Tree Studios is located at 121 Electric Avenue in Flemingsburg, located in a mid-1800's warehouse that was originally a distillery and flour mill. Owners/artists Ken Macht specializes in silver and goldsmith pieces and his wife Kathy is a pastel artist.

Oven Roasted Potato Wedges

Bauer Haus Bed and Breakfast

4 baking potatoes (may be peeled or left with skins)
2 Tbsp. olive oil (or vegetable oil)

pinch of garlic
salt and cracked pepper to taste

Preheat oven to 350°. Scrub potatoes and cut in wedges. Place potatoes in a pan of water on top of the stove. Remove the pan from the stove when the water starts to boil. Remove the potatoes from the water and put potatoes in a bowl or a Ziploc bag. Sprinkle with the oil, salt, pepper and garlic. Shake the bag or lightly toss the potatoes in the bowl. Place potatoes on a baking sheet and put in oven until brown and tender. Approximate baking time is 30 minutes. Serves 4 to 6.

This 1880 Victorian home has lovely craftmanship and unique spaciousness from main hall to guest rooms. This fine home is in Kentucky's first permanent settlement, Harrodburg (1774). Bauer

Vegetables

Haus is listed as a Kentucky Landmark and on the National Register of Historic Places.

Beaumont Inn Corn Pudding

2 c. white whole kernel corn	4 tsp. sugar
4 eggs	2 oz. butter, melted
4 oz. flour	1 tsp. salt
1 qt. milk	

In a casserole dish, mix corn, salt, sugar and butter. Beat eggs and add to milk. Stir into the corn mixture. Preheat oven to 450°.

Place in oven for 10 minutes. Remove and stir with long prong fork, disturbing the top as little as possible. Return to the oven for 10 more minutes. Repeat stirring procedure. Return to oven for 10 more minutes. Repeat stirring procedure. Return to oven for 10 to 15 minutes. Top should be lightly brown and pudding should be firm.

Beaumont Inn, listed on the National Register of Historic Places, is located in the heart of the Bluegrass Region in Harrodsburg. Operating since 1919 by the Dedman family, it is Kentucky's oldest family-operated B&B inn (5 generations).

Polenta "Faux A La Mode"

Berea College

Polenta:

2 c. freshly stone-ground yellow cornmeal	2 Tbsp. unsalted butter
8 c. water	4 c. fresh sweet corn, cut from the cob
2 tsp. salt	

Put the 8 cups of water on high heat in a heavy saucepan. When the water boils, add the salt and reduce heat to a gentle boil. Whisk the cornmeal in slowly. Continue whisking until the polenta is back to a boil and has begun to thicken, and then turn the heat down to a low simmer. Cover the pot and cook slowly, stirring with a wooden spoon every ten minutes for 30 minutes. Stir in the butter and fresh corn; cover and continue simmering for another 10 minutes. Pour the polenta into two buttered round cake pans. Allow the polenta to cool and set up for a few minutes, then cover and refrigerate until you are ready to use them.

Sauce:

4 cloves garlic, chopped
1 medium yellow onion, finely chopped
2 to 3 stalks celery, sliced
½ sweet red peppers and ½ green peppers, coarsely chopped
3 carrots, finely chopped (or matchsticks)
3 (28 oz.) cans chopped tomatoes
1 (28 oz.) can crushed tomatoes
1 (5 oz.) can tomato paste
2 to 3 cubes Knorr vegetable bouillon
¼ c. chopped parsley
½ c. dry white wine
1 to 2 Tbsp. fresh rosemary, ground with mortar and pestle in olive oil or finely chopped
1 Tbsp. fresh marjoram, chopped finely
1 Tbsp. fresh sage, chopped finely
basil to taste
salt and pepper to taste

Saute garlic and onions in olive oil until the onions are translucent. Add remaining ingredients. Simmer for 3 to 4 hours. The flavors will blend better if the sauce is cooled overnight and reheated before using it.

Filling:

1 roasted large sweet red pepper (skin removed)
1 c. fresh basil leaves

Heat oven to 375°. Place the halved sweet red peppers (skin side up) on a baking sheet toward the bottom of the oven and cook until the pepper is a little charred and limp. You can cool it in a covered glass bowl for a few minutes to make it easier to peel. Remove the skin from the cooled pepper and coarsely chop it. Coarsely chop the basil and mix it with the pepper in a small bowl.

For the Cheese:

16 oz. good quality mascarpone cheese (cool but not cold)
6 tsp. freshly ground high-quality black pepper

Combine the pepper with the cheese thoroughly with a fork until fluffy.

To Fry the Polenta:

fat for frying (pancetta, butter, oil, or a combination)

Heat two heavy skillets that the round polenta cakes will fit in; add your choice of fat and allow it to get good and hot but not smoking. Lay the polenta cakes in the hot pans and cook on medium-high heat, trying not to disturb until they have become golden and crispy on the bottom. CAREFULLY turn the polenta over to cook the other side. This maneuver may be best accomplished with a buddy, gently supporting the entire polenta cake. Add more fat if needed.

To Assemble the Dish: Have the sauce warm on the stove and the pepper paste at room temperature. Place the first polenta cake on a serving dish. Spread the pepper and basil paste over the entire surface. Place the second layer of polenta. Slice individual pieces of "layer cake" onto plates. Pour a ladleful of hot sauce over each slice and top with a dollop (about a tablespoon and a half) of the peppered cheese. Serve.

Berea College, founded in 1855 as the 1st interracial and coeducational college in the South, charges no tuition and admits only academically promising students who have limited economic resources. It is known for preservation of Appalachian crafts.

Corn Pudding

Gov. Steve Beshear

(Serves 8)

3 c. fresh or frozen corn	1 tsp. salt
6 eggs	1 tsp. flour
3 c. heavy cream	½ tsp. baking powder
½ c. sugar	2 tsp. butter

Stir eggs and cream together. Add sugar, salt, flour, baking powder and butter. Pour into greased 9 x 13 casserole. Bake at 350° for one hour.

Governor Steven L. Beshear said this is a recipe that the chefs prepare at the Governor's Mansion for official and family functions. Democratic Governor Beshear and his wife Judy are from Dawson Springs. He has also served as Kentucky State Representative and Lt. Governor.

Fried Corn

Bluegrass Balloon Festival

12 ears fresh corn	2 to 3 Tbsp. sugar
8 slices bacon (uncooked)	2 tsp. salt
½ c. butter	½ tsp. pepper

Cut off tips of corn kernels into a large bowl; scrape milk and remaining pulp from cob with a paring knife. Set aside.

Cook bacon in a large skillet until crisp; remove bacon, reserving ¼ cup drippings in the skillet. Crumble bacon and set aside. Add corn, butter and remaining ingredients to drippings in skillet. Cook over medium heat 20 minutes, stirring frequently. Spoon corn mixture into a serving dish and sprinkle with crumbled bacon. Yields 12 servings.

The Bluegrass Balloon Festival is held in Louisville, at historic Bowman Field, which is the country's oldest continually operating airport. The 90+ balloon festival, which takes place every September, is free and includes the Wings and Wheels (air and car) Show.

❧ *Tomato Pie* ❧

Edgar Cayce

1 can crescent rolls	2 tomatoes
1 green pepper	2 c. Mozzarella cheese
1 onion	1 plus c. mayonnaise

Grease pan lightly. Press crescent rolls into pie pan. Sauté onion and pepper in butter. Add to pie pan. Thinly slice tomatoes over onion and pepper. Salt and pepper. Mix cheese and mayo together and spread over tomatoes. Bake at 350° for 45 minutes to 1 hour.

Edgar Cayce, Hopkinsville, was a 20th Century Psychic and Medical Clairvoyant for 43 years, demonstrated the uncanny ability to put himself into self-induced sleep-meditation. 300 books and papers have been written discussing his life and work. Christian County Tourism.

❧ *Breakfast Casserole* ❧

Christopher's Bed and Breakfast

12 eggs	2 c. shredded hash brown
1 c. plain yogurt	potatoes, thawed
1 tsp. Lawry's seasoned salt	¼ c. (or less) chopped onion
(or to taste)	1 c. grated sharp Cheddar
¾ stick butter or margarine	cheese

Preheat oven to 350°. Spray or grease a two-quart casserole dish with cooking oil.

Beat eggs, yogurt and salt together. Melt butter and lightly sauté onion. Add thawed potatoes. Stir to mix. Pour in egg mixture and lightly stir to blend ingredients. Pour into casserole dish. Sprinkle grated cheese over casserole. Bake at 350° for approximately 25 minutes or until knife comes out clean when inserted. If preparing the dish the night before, bake for approximately 45 to 50 minutes. Cut into 8 squares.

Christopher's Bed and Breakfast, located in Newpoet in the former late 1800's Christian Church, is named after the Patron Saint of Travelers. It has been voted by inngoers for three consecutive years as one of the Top 15 B&Bs/Inns for Best Design and Decor.

❦ *Broccoli Casserole* ❦

Bob C. Cooke

1 pkg. frozen broccoli (or cooked fresh)
8 oz. cooked rice (your choice of rice)
1 small can milk
1 can cream of mushroom soup
1 c. shredded cheese
1 medium onion, chopped
2 Tbsp. butter

Brown and saute onion with the butter. Remove from heat. Add remaining ingredients. Stir until cheese is melted and soup and rice are incorporated. Fold into a buttered baking dish. Bake at 350° for 35 minutes or until top is bubbly and brown.

Bob C. Cooke is from Lexington. He is both an actor and director with such movies as "Into the Woods" to his credit. His agency works to promote casting calls for movies, television and commercials filmed in and around Kentucky.

❦ *Baked Bean Medley* ❦

Davidson's Studio

1 ½ lb. ground beef
1 medium onion, chopped
salt to taste
1 (15.5 oz.) can dark red kidney beans
1 (15.5 oz.) can light red kidney beans
1 (15.5 oz.) can lima beans
1 (31 oz.) can pork and beans
½ c. tomato ketchup
¼ c. brown sugar
2 Tbsp. vinegar
1 can chopped mushrooms

Cook ground beef, onions and salt until brown. Drain grease. Then mix with all other ingredients. Pour into baking dish and bake at 350° for 35 minutes.

Mabel Davidson of Mt. Vernon is a descendant of 1 of the men who blazed the Wilderness Road with Daniel Boone. She was born in a renovated log structure once used as a stagecoach inn. As an artist, her work depicts a bit of Kentucky's Appalachian Mt. culture and her ancestral history.

Fresh Fries

Everly Brothers

6 to 8 potatoes   **sunflower oil**

Peel fresh potatoes. Then cut them over the length of the long potatoes in 6 to 8 slices. Fresh fries need to be fried twice. First, they are fried in sunflower oil at 158° for about 7 minutes. Then, they're taken out of the oil to rest 5 minutes or more. Then they get heated to 194° for 2 to 3 minutes until they get that light brown, golden tan.

The Everly Brothers, born in Central City, are one of the top acts in rock and roll history with such hit songs as "Bye Bye Love" and "Wake Up Little Susie". Each year, they return to Central City to perform for a local fundraiser, "Everly Brothers Homecoming."

Skillet Zucchini

Crystal Gayle

6 medium zucchini, sliced   **1 Tbsp. olive oil**
1 medium to large onion,   **1 Tbsp. sugar**
** coarsely chopped**   **salt and pepper to taste**

Pour olive oil in skillet. Add zucchini, onion, sugar, salt and pepper. Cover and cook over medium heat until squash is done and you have the consistency you like.

With more than 3 dozen hit records to her credit, Crystal Gayle has come a long way from her roots in the Appalachian coal mining town of Paintsville. The youngest of 8, Crystal started her career singing with her sister Loretta Lynn for a few weeks each summer, while still in school.

Vegetables

Fried Apples

Grapevine Inn Bed and Breakfast

Granny Smith apples (1 large per person)
cinnamon (personal desire)
allspice (personal desire)

sugar (amount determined by how sour they are)
½ to 1 stick butter (depending on how many apples used)

Melt butter in iron skillet. Cook covered on medium heat until tender; remove cover and continue to cook until apples are just beginning to caramelize. Remove and serve.

Grapevine Inn Bed and Breakfast is located in one of the elegant old homes of Middlesborough. Built in 1903, it belonged to one of the city's first merchants. The name comes from the beautiful grapevine stencil found under several layers of wallpaper in the dining room.

Bourbon-Baked Beans

Heaven Hill Distillery

2 (28 oz.) cans B&M brand baked beans
½ c. chili sauce
½ c. strong coffee (best if left over from the morning's brew, not fresh)

¼ c. Evan Williams straight bourbon
3 tsp. dry mustard

Combine all ingredients. Pour into 2-quart casserole dish. Bake at 350° for 1 hour.

Heaven Hill, Bardstown, is the largest family-owned producer of distilled spirits in the U.S. They asked Parker Beam, their 7th generation Master Distiller to submit his favorite recipe. He said, "There just aren't many things that bourbon and coffee won't improve."

Fried Pumpkin Blossoms

Erin Hill

12 pumpkin blossoms
1 c. cracker meal
1 c. bread crumbs
1 c. corn flake crumbs

cooking oil
1 egg
1 c. milk

Pick the pumpkin blossoms early in the morning before they close up. Break off and discard the end of each blossom, then rinse the remaining flower under cool running water. Lay the blossoms flat on a paper towel on a plate and cover with plastic wrap. Store in the refrigerator until ready to fry.

Make your breading mixture by mixing equal parts cracker meal, bread crumbs and corn flake crumbs. Pour ½ inch of cooking oil into an electric skillet and heat to 340°. Dip each blossom in a mixture of one beaten egg and one cup milk. Then coat the blossom with the breading mixture and fry until crisp and lightly browned on both sides. Serve with sliced, homegrown tomatoes.

Note: Squash blossoms may be substituted for the pumpkin blossoms, but they are smaller and not as tasty.

Actress, composer and musician Erin Hill is from Louisville. She has performed both on Broadway and television, including "Annie Blake" in "Another World". She is the harpist for performer "Kayne West". This is a 4th generation family recipe.

❧ *Fried Green Tomatoes* ❧

J.D. Legends

qt. buttermilk	¼ c. white pepper
8 c. flour	¼ c. garlic salt
¼ c. black pepper	¼ c. salt

Mix all ingredients, except flour, together first, then add to flour. Slice green tomatoes ¼-inch to ½-inch thick. Dip green tomatoes in flour first, then buttermilk, then back in the flour. Fry tomatoes in vegetable oil; heat oil to 350° and fry for 2 ½ minutes.

Serve with spicy Ranch. Take Ranch dressing and add salsa and blend to a light pink color.

JD Legends, Nicholasville, is a full-service restaurant, sports bar, and family entertainment center including a bowling alley, which has received national and international recognition in the bowling industry. They are legendary for their Fried Green Tomatoes.

Varina Davis' Stuffed Eggplant

Jefferson Davis

2 large eggplants	1 c. nuts, chopped
2 Tbsp. onion, minced	½ c. butter, melted
1 c. celery, chopped	2 c. tomatoes, stewed
½ tsp. pepper	½ c. cream
1 tsp. salt	3 Tbsp. cream
½ tsp. nutmeg	1 Tbsp. flour
1 tsp. parsley	1 tsp. parsley

Put the eggplants in a cast-iron kettle and cover with cold water. Parboil them for 10 minutes. Take the eggplants from the kettle and slit each down the side. Take out the seeds and lay the eggplants in a bowl of cold, salted water while preparing the stuffing as follows: Grease a cast-iron skillet with butter and fry the onion and celery until nicely browned. Blend these with the rest of the ingredients in a wooden mixing bowl. Fill the cavity of each eggplant with this stuffing. Wind thread around them to keep the slit shut. Place the eggplants on the rack of a roasting pan. Put a little water in the bottom of the pan and bake in a moderate oven (350°) for 25 minutes. Baste with melted butter and water as they bake. Now make the gravy: Add the cream to the drippings in the bottom of the roasting pan. Thicken this with the flour and then stir in the parsley. Bring to a quick boil and pour over the eggplant on a large platter. Serve immediately.

Jefferson Davis State Historic Site, Fairview, is a 371-foot memorial to the famous Kentuckian born here. He distinguished himself as a West Point graduate, Mexican War hero, U.S. Congressmen, U.S. Senator, Secretary of War, President of the Confederacy.

Grilled Summer Vegetable Terrine

Jewish Hospital

(Serves 10)

10 Portabello mushrooms	3 zucchini
3 eggplants	1 ½ c. virgin olive oil
3 red bell peppers	fresh squeezed lemon juice
3 yellow bell peppers	(4 lemons)
6 fresh garlic heads	½ c. fresh basil leaves
3 yellow squash	salt and pepper to taste

Turn oven to 375°. Place garlic head on baking pan and drizzle with ¼ cup of olive oil. Broil garlic until it becomes soft. Squeeze garlic out of the skin. Place in a mixing bowl and reserve until cool.

Clean all vegetables and cut eggplant and squash lengthwise in ½-inch thick slices. Cut all 4 sides of bell pepper; steam the tops of the mushrooms and remove the thin outer layer.

Place the lemon juice, basil and salt and pepper in a mixing bowl and slowly add the remaining olive oil until the mixture thickens. Pour dressing over vegetables and marinate for one hour in the refrigerator. Turn the oven to grill. Drain vegetables but keep marinade. Grill all vegetables (al dente - firm but cooked)

Line a terrine mold with plastic film and place the vegetables one by one in the terrine. Drizzle a soup spoon of dressing over each layer and "build" the vegetables in the terrine.

Now the most critical part: Keep a heavy weight on top of the terrine by wrapping a piece of cardboard with foil and placing it directly on the top of vegetables. Put some weight on top of the cardboard and refrigerate for two or three days.

Unmold the terrine on a platter and slice with a very sharp knife. Serve over mixed greens and use the marinade as a vinaigrette.

Greg Guiot is chef of Jewish Hospital's Trager Pavilion, an upscale floor that combines the finest medical care with hotel-type amenities to deliver five-star health care and accomodations. This recipe is low fat and works well for individuals on special diets.

❧ *Squash Souffle* ❧

Ken Jones

2 lb. yellow squash
2 eggs, lightly beaten
¼ c. bell pepper, chopped fine
¼ c. onion, chopped fine
1 c. mayonnaise
½ c. mild Cheddar cheese, grated
½ c. Mozzarella cheese, grated
½ tsp. salt
1 tsp. pepper
½ c. bread crumbs

Wash and cut squash into quarters. Cook in salted water until tender. Drain well. Mash lightly. Mix together in bowl all other ingredients except bread crumbs. Mix in squash and pour into buttered casserole dish. Bake 30 minutes at 350°. Sprinkle bread crumbs on the top and brown for additional 3 to 5 minutes.

Ken Jones is an Emmy nominated playwright and screenwriter. He has written and directed for television series airing on ABC,

HBO, Disney Channel and PBS. Jones is currently the Chairman for the Department of Theatre and Dance at Northern Kentucky University.

🌿 *Breaded Dandelions* 🌿

Ron Lewis

¼ c. milk	1 egg
2 Tbsp. powdered milk	½ c. flour
1 Tbsp. baking powder	14 large dandelion blossoms

Mix all ingredients except blossoms. Wash blossoms and lightly drain. Do not let them wilt. Dip into batter and fry in deep hot fat until golden. Yields 4 servings.

U.S. Representative Ron Lewis from Cecilia has served the 2nd District of Kentucky since 1994. Lewis is a member of the prestigious Ways and Means Committee. This recipe from him and his wife Kayi, is an old Eastern Kentucky recipe that her family enjoyed.

🌿 *Cheese Pudding* 🌿

Lincoln Museum

1 c. soda cracker crumbs	2 c. medium white sauce
½ lb. grated American cheese	1 (7 oz.) can pimento, grated
4 hard-cooked eggs, grated	buttered crumbs

Grease the casserole. Place a layer of crumbs, well moistened with sauce; stir with fork to see that all crumbs are moistened. Make a layer of grated cheese, a layer of eggs, a layer of grated pimento. Repeat layers; again stir with fork until all crumbs are moistened (the pudding will be dry unless crumbs are moistened). You may have to add milk to be sure crumbs are moistened. Top with buttered crumbs. Bake at 350° for about 30 minutes.

Hodgenville and LaRue County are the birthplace and boyhood home of Abraham Lincoln. Visit the Abraham Lincoln Birthplace National Historic Site, Knob Creek Farm, Lincoln Heritage House, Lincoln Homestead State Park and Lincoln Museum while there.

Kathy's Mashed Sweet Potatoes

3 c. mashed sweet potatoes
  (can be canned)
½ tsp. salt
2 eggs

⅓ stick butter
1 tsp. vanilla
4 tsp. cinnamon
½ c. milk

Topping:
⅓ c. dark brown sugar
⅓ c. flour

½ c. pecans

In large bowl, mix together potatoes, sugar, salt, eggs, softened butter, milk, vanilla and cinnamon. Stir until well blended, then pour into greased casserole dish. Spread topping over potatoes. Bake at 350° for 35 minutes. (Check at 25 minutes.)

The Louisville Chorus was established in 1939 and soon will be celebrating it's 60th season. This recipe comes from Kathy Curley Buskill. Her mother, Dot Curley, is the music librarian and has been involved in the chorus most years since 1942.

Asparagus-Ham Ring

May's Lick Asparagus Festival

½ c. chopped ham
¼ lb. fresh asparagus,
  chopped
¼ c. chopped onion
½ c. fresh parsley, snipped

1 ½ c. (6 oz.) grated Swiss
  cheese
2 Tbsp. Dijon mustard
1 tsp. lemon juice
2 pkg. refrigerated crescent
  rolls

Coarsely chop ham, asparagus and onion. Snip parsley and combine all ingredients except crescent rolls. Set this mixture aside. Arrange crescent triangles in a circle on a 13-inch baking (pizza) stone with base points overlapping and long points of rolls to the center of the stone and outside the perimeter of the stone. There should be at least a 3-inch diameter circle in the center when rolls are in place. Spread the vegetable mixture over the middle of the rolls, making a circle and attempting to distribute evenly. Fold points of rolls over the filling and tuck ends under base at the center. Filling will not be completely covered. Bake 25 to 30 minutes or until golden brown. Serving portions: approximately 8.

May's Lick was founded in 1788 by a group of families who purchased 1400 acres of land from William May near the salt lick.

Come on the 3rd Saturday in May and join one of the most earnestly quirky, homey, hilarious and genuinely unique festivals in the state!

❧ Cabbage Casserole ❧

McCreary County Museum

1 medium head cabbage,
  shredded
2 Tbsp. lemon juice
1 tsp. salt
1 Tbsp. sugar
¾ c. water
1 c. (10 oz.) cream of
  mushroom soup

⅓ c. milk
2 c. Cheddar cheese,
  shredded (set aside 1 c.)
1 small onion, chopped fine
½ c. sour cream or
  mayonnaise
3 c. seasoned croutons (crush
  1 c. and set aside)

In a large saucepan, combine the cabbage, lemon juice, salt, sugar and water. Stir. Cover the saucepan; boil 6 to 8 minutes. Drain. Set aside.

In a bowl, combine soup, milk, 2 cups cheese, onion, sour cream and 2 cups croutons. Stir until mixture is blended. Pour cabbage mixture into a 9 x 13-inch baking dish. Pour soup mixture over the cabbage. Sprinkle 1 cup Cheddar cheese and 1 cup crushed croutons over top. Bake at 350° for 20 to 30 minutes.

Located in the heart of historic downtown Stearns, the McCreary County Museum is housed in the old Stearns Coal and Lumber Co. Corp. headquarters built in 1907. The museum overlooks the town's craft and antique shops and Big South Fork Scenic Railway.

❧ Fried Potatoes ❧

Bill Monroe

1 to 2 lb. potatoes, sliced or
  cubed
1 medium onion, sliced
2 Tbsp. bacon drippings

1 tsp. salt
½ tsp. pepper
¼ tsp. garlic powder

Saute onions in bacon drippings until tender. Add potatoes and seasoning. Cook covered 20 minutes, turning occasionally until crispy.

Grammy winner and Country Music Hall of Fame member Bill Monroe was known as "the father of bluegrass." The music style took its name from his band "The Bluegrass Boys." His home and farm in Rosine is a museum and site of the Jerusalem Ridge Bluegrass Festival. The director of the Bill Monroe Foundation that sponsors the festival said "Bill Loved Fried Potatoes!"

❦ Blt's Made With Fried ❦ Green Tomatoes

Ro Morse

(Makes 2 sandwiches.)

1 green tomato, cut into 4 or 5 slices	2 whole leaves leaf lettuce
2 egg whites, lightly beaten	2 slices Swiss cheese
dash Tabasco sauce (optional)	4 slices bacon, crisply cooked, drained and cut in half
1 ½ Tbsp. cornmeal mix	4 slices wheat bread, toasted
vegetable cooking spray	Hellmann's mayonnaise

Dip sliced tomatoes in a mixture of egg whites and hot sauce. Lightly coat with the dry corn meal mix. Place slices in a single layer on a baking sheet coated with cooking spray. Lightly coat tomato slices with the vegetable spray, too. Broil about 3 inches from heat for about 3 minutes on each side. Tomatoes will be golden brown and tender. Layer the cheese, bacon and tomato slices on the toast. Top with another slice of toast. Cut in half and serve immediately.

Author Ro Morse, Paducah, has written 3 cookbooks. She owned and operated the local restaurant, Whaler's Catch, for 15 years. She was the former director of tourism for Paducah and is presently the Downtown Events Coordinator and for the past 12 years has shared recipes daily on 2 local radio stations.

❦ Hash Brown Potato ❦ Casserole

National Softball Association's Sports Hall of Fame

1 lb. frozen hash brown potatoes, thawed	1 ½ c. shredded Cheddar cheese
½ stick margarine (room temperature)	½ tsp. pepper
½ c. chopped onions	1 c. sour cream
1 tsp. salt	2 c. corn flakes, crushed
1 can cream of chicken soup	½ c. margarine, melted

Mix the ingredients in a large bowl. Pour into large baking dish. Top with the corn flakes and the melted margarine. Bake at 400° for one hour. Leave covered until the last 15 minutes. This can be refrigerated overnight before cooking.

The National Softball Association and Baseball Players Association was established in 1982 by Hugh Cantrell in Lexington, Kentucky. It is a full service organization that offers a division of play and a level of competition that youth through adults can enjoy.

Mushroom Rice

Cheryl Norman

(Serves 4)

1 c. raw long-grain brown rice
1 (14 oz.) can low-fat chicken broth
1 (8 oz.) can mushrooms (do not drain)
½ c. water
1 clove garlic, pressed
1 bay leaf

Place all ingredients into a 4-quart pressure cooker. Bring to pressure, then lower heat just enough to maintain pressure for 15 minutes. Remove from heat and allow pressure to drop on its own for 5 minutes. Then quick-release according to your pressure cooker's guidelines. After pressure is released, carefully remove lid. Fluff rice with a fork, remove bay leaf, and serve.

Cheryl Norman, Louisville, loves to experiment in her kitchen when she can break away from writing her romance and mystery novels. She's a member of the Kentucky Romance Writers, the First Coast Romance Writers, Romance Writers of America, and Sisters in Crime.

Bourbon Sweet Potatoes

Old Talbott Tavern

3 (1 lb. 2 oz.) cans sweet potatoes
1 c. sugar
½ c. butter
½ c. bourbon
½ tsp. vanilla
2 c. miniature marshmallows

Heat potatoes thoroughly over medium heat in large saucepan, stirring often. Remove from heat; drain and mash. Add other ingredients except marshmallows. Mix well and turn into large casserole. Sprinkle marshmallows over top and bake uncovered in a

Vegetables

350° preheated oven for 30 minutes or until marshmallows are golden brown.

Since the late 1700s, the Old Talbott Tavern in Bardstown has provided shelter, food and drink. It is the oldest western stagecoach stop in America as the westward expansion brought explorers from the east into Kentucky.

❧ *Otto Eitel's Holiday Onion* ❧ *Quiche*

Fess Parker

½ lb. Farmer's country-style cottage cheese
½ lb. sweet butter, softened
½ lb. white flour
caraway seed
8 slices smoked bacon, finely chopped

3 ½ lb. white onions, chopped
4 whole eggs
2 egg yolks
2 c. sour cream
black pepper, freshly ground
Lawry's Seasoning Salt

The Crust: Mix flour and butter until very finely crumbled. Add cottage cheese a little at a time. Shape into a ball, cover with plastic wrap and refrigerate overnight. Roll out dough on lightly floured board and transfer to Pyrex casserole dish with about 1 ½-inch edge to a 9-inch pie pan. Sprinkle bottom of pastry with about 2 tablespoons caraway seed and the bacon.

The Custard: Hand-cut onions as food processing makes them too mushy. In a covered earthenware (not stainless steel) container, put on an asbestos pad; sauté onion over very low heat. Stir from time to time (takes about 45 minutes). Cool completely. Beat the eggs and the egg yolks lightly and blend with sour cream. Add to onions and season with salt and pepper to taste, then pour on crust. Top with a sprinkling of caraway and the rest of the bacon. Bake in a preheated 375° oven for one hour until bubbly and brown. Serves four to six people as an entrée.

Actor Fess Parker is not from Kentucky, but has Kentucky ties as he starred in the television series "Daniel Boone." Boone was an explorer and one of the 1st settlers in Kentucky. He is buried in Frankfort. Parker now owns a vineyard in Santa Barbara, California.

Poke Sallet

Poke Sallet Festival

Pick a mess of new, young poke leaves. Rinse leaves. Boil for one hour and drain off water. (Rids toxins from the leaves.) Add fatback grease and salt to taste. Boil poke for additional hour.

Alternative method is to fry the first-boiled poke in a skillet with fatback grease and onions.

Poke Sallet Festival is almost 50 years old and is celebrated each year in Harlan. Poke, an indigenous mountain green, has a long history dating back to Native Americans. The wild green fed many pioneer families and was used for its medicinal purposes. This recipe is served at the festival with fatback bacon, boiled eggs, green onions, hoe cake and buttermilk.

Spinach Quiche

Mollie Sims

1 Tbsp. butter
1 onion, chopped
1 (10 oz.) pkg. frozen chopped spinach, thawed and drained well
1 (9-inch) refrigerated ready piecrust (½ box)
1 tsp. all-purpose flour
½ c. (about 2 oz.) grated Monterey Jack
½ c. (about 2 oz.) grated Parmesan
4 eggs
½ c. low-fat cottage cheese
½ tsp. salt
¼ tsp. pepper
⅛ tsp. ground nutmeg

Melt butter in heavy medium skillet over medium-high heat. Add onion and sauté until translucent, about 8 minutes. Add spinach and stir until spinach is dry, about 3 minutes. Cool slightly.

Preheat oven to 375°. Dust 1 side of crust with flour. Transfer to 9-inch diameter quiche dish or pie pan, floured side down. Press into pan, sealing any cracks. Trim edges. Sprinkle both cheeses over bottom of crust. Top with spinach mixture. Beat eggs, cottage cheese, salt, pepper and nutmeg in large bowl to blend. Pour over spinach. Bake until filling is set, about 50 minutes. Cool slightly. Cut into wedges and serve.

Actress and fashion model Mollie Sims, Boaz, Kentucky, has modeled for Vanity Fair and Cover Girl, but she is most famous as Delinda Deline in NBC's Las Vegas. She and her mom were at an auction in Mayfield, Kentucky, and she said she loved her Mom's Spinach Quiche.

Risotto With Butternut Squash

Art Wehrmann

1 ½ lb. cooked butternut
  squash
1 ¼ c. chicken stock
½ c. diced onion
1 Tbsp. chopped garlic

1 ¼ tsp. chopped fresh
  ginger
3 Tbsp. butter
½ c. arborio
¼ c. white wine
1 sliced green onion

Mix chicken broth and water together. Cook butter, onion, ginger and garlic in a saucepan for about two minutes or until the onion starts turning opaque. Add arborio. Stir for one minute. Add wine, continually stirring until it is absorbed. Turn temperature down to a simmer. Add ¼ cup of stock (continually stirring) until the liquid is absorbed. Add another ¼ cup of stock (continually stirring) until the liquid is absorbed. Add the squash. Add ¼ cup of stock (continually stirring) until the liquid is absorbed. Add the remaining liquid and continue stirring until all the liquid is absorbed. Stir in the green onions and salt and pepper to taste.

Art Wehrmann is the Executive Chef at Bristol Cafe located at The Inn at Jewish Hospital in Louisville. He likes risotto because it is something different. It's a rice, but it has a different shape and ends up with a different texture and taste than regular rice.

Squash Casserole

Whistle Stop

12 to 15 medium-sized
  yellow squash, sliced (or 2
  large bags)
1 lb. margarine
1 c. chopped onion

4 c. shredded Colby cheese
1 ½ c. real mayonnaise
  (Hellmann's is best)
⅓ c. sugar
salt and pepper

Cook squash until it is just starting to get tender; do not overcook. Drain well. Saute onions in 1 stick of the butter. Mix all ingredients together gently and pour into 2 pans, 9 x 13. Melt rest of margarine. Crush 4 packs Ritz crackers and stir in melted margarine. Mix well and sprinkle evenly over squash casserole. Bake in oven at 325° until set and done, about 45 minutes.

The Whistle Stop Restaurant, Glendale, offers the most unique atmosphere, nestled by the main line railroad track between Louisville and Nashville. Owner Lynn Cummins developed this recipe to use the fresh garden squash her neighbor grew for the restaurant.

Cheddar Cheese Souffle

Ed Whitfield

2 Tbsp. dry bread crumbs	dash of pepper
2 ½ Tbsp. butter	6 eggs
3 Tbsp. flour	¼ tsp. cream of tartar
¾ c. scalded milk	1 c. grated cheese
¾ tsp. salt	½ c. Parmesan cheese

Preheat oven to 350°. Set pan of water in oven. Prepare an 8-cup soufflé dish (4 to 5-inches high). Butter dish and sprinkle with bread crumbs. Cook butter and flour together slowly to make roux (foamy and frothy). Pour milk into roux, stirring with wire whisk; cook until thick. Add ½ teaspoon salt, pepper and 3 egg yolks to sauce. Beat 6 egg whites; add ¼ teaspoon salt and cream of tartar. Continue beating until soft peaks form. Put dollop of egg white in sauce. Add cheese. Fold remaining egg whites into sauce. Fill mold to ²/₃. Set in pan of water in oven. Bake 1 hour to 1 hour and 15 minutes. Can leave in warm oven for ½ hour if necessary. Serves 6 to 8.

Rep. Ed Whitfield, a native of Hopkinsville, was elected to Congress in 1994 to represent Kentucky's First Congressional District, which is home to Fort Campbell, home of the 101st Airborne. This is his favorite recipe prepared by his wife, Connie.

Lye Hominy

Wickliffe Mounds Research Center

8 c. sweet white corn	1 gal. boiling water
2 oz. concentrated lye	

Dissolve lye in the boiling water in an iron kettle. Drop corn into this solution and boil rapidly for 25 to 30 minutes. Drain and put into a pot of cold water. If possible, allow water to run over it for 3 to 4 hours to remove all traces of the lye. If this is not possible, wash through about six changes of fresh water. After this, place in a barrel churn and turn the churn for 5 to 10 minutes to remove the hulls and black eyes. After removing the hulls, place corn in an enamel kettle; cover with clear boiling water and cook until tender.

Wash again and remove any hulls or eyes that failed to come off in the churn. The hominy may now be seasoned for serving.

Designated Kentucky's 1st Archaeological Landmark Wickliffe Mounds Research Center is the site of a prehistoric Native American village of the Mississippian culture (1100-1350). The Wickliffe, Kentucky site owned by Murray State University is on the National Register of Historic Places.

—• *Extra Recipes* •—

Breads,
Rolls,
and Pastries

Recipe Favorites

Page No.

Recipe Title:_____

_____

_____

_____

_____

_____

_____

_____

_____

_____

Family Favorites

Page No.

Recipe Title:_____

_____

_____

_____

_____

_____

Notes:_____

_____

_____

_____

Breads, Rolls & Pastries

Knob Creek Kentucky Corn Cakes

Abraham Lincoln Library and Museum

2 c. cornmeal	1 egg, lightly beaten
1 tsp. salt	3 c. buttermilk
1 tsp. soda	

Sift together cornmeal, salt and soda. Add the egg and buttermilk. Mix well to blend, but do not overbeat. (The batter should be thin enough to form a lacy edge when baking.) Drop by small spoonfuls on a hot griddle; cook until golden, turn, and finish cooking. Stack cakes on a cookie sheet and place in a 250° oven to keep warm. (Makes 32 to 36 two-inch cakes.)

The Abraham Lincoln Library/Museum is located in Tennessee 1 mile from the Kentucky border near Cumberland Gap. The Gap was heavily fortified during the Civil War and changed hands 4 times during the war. The Museum houses over 25,000 Lincoln/Civil War artifacts.

Berea Spoonbread

Berea Spoonbread Festival

3 c. milk	3 large eggs
1 c. cornmeal	4 Tbsp. butter
1 tsp. baking powder	1 tsp. salt

Scald milk; stir in cornmeal and bring just to boil. Add butter and allow to cool. Beat eggs with salt and baking powder. Add to cornmeal mixture. Pour in preheated baker. Bake at 350° for 30 to 35 minutes. Best when served immediately with butter, honey or sorghum.

The Berea Spoonbread Festival is held in Berea, the Folk Arts and Crafts Capital of Kentucky. Centered on this local dish, the

3-day family event has gospel music concerts and family fun activities for all ages.

Jan's Best Yeast Rolls Ever

Gary Bertram

½ c. canola oil	1 egg
¼ c. sugar	½ c. warm water
1 tsp. salt	1 pkg. fast-acting yeast
½ c. boiling water	2 ½ c. bread flour

Mix together oil, sugar, salt and boiling water. Let cool. Then add 1 egg and mix. Mix together ½ cup warm water and yeast in separate bowl until dissolved and add to mixture. Then fold in flour until moistened. Roll out dough on floured board (will need about ½ cup flour to roll out) and cut into rolls. Let rise about 2 hours or until they reach the top of the pan. Cook at 350° for 25 to 30 minutes. Makes about 15 rolls.

Award-winning nature, wildlife, portrait and abstract artist Gary Bertram has exhibited in shows nationwide. He has also produced equine art of such high quality that it is registered with the Saddlebred Museum at the prestigious Kentucky Horse Park, Lexington.

Southern Spoon Bread

Boone's Tavern

3 c. milk	2 Tbsp. butter
1 ¼ c. corn meal	1 ¾ tsp. baking powder
3 eggs	1 tsp. salt

Stir meal into rapidly boiling milk. Cook until very thick, stirring constantly to prevent scorching. Remove from fire and allow to cool. The mixture will be cold and very stiff. Add well beaten egg, salt, baking powder and melted butter. Beat with electric beater for 15 minutes. If hand beating is used, break the hardened cooked meal into the beaten eggs in small amounts until all is well mixed. Then beat thoroughly for ten minutes using a wooden spoon. Pour into 2 well-greased casseroles. Bake for 30 minutes at 375°. Serve from casserole by spoonfuls.

Boone Tavern Hotel and Restaurant was built in 1909. Owned by the Berea College and operated with students, the facility is now in its 85th year. It features 58 elegantly designed guest rooms

Breads, Rolls & Pastries

furnished with fine crafted hand weavings and other items made in the College's craft programs.

 Kentucky Bourbon French Toast

Canaanland Farms

6 slices salt-risen bread*
2 c. eggnog (regular or low-fat)
¼ c. oil

1 to 2 Tbsp. Kentucky bourbon (this can be omitted or rum extract can be used)

Mix eggnog, oil and bourbon (or rum extract). Mix well. Dip slices of bread into mixture and place on cookie sheet (sprayed with nonstick). Bake in preheated 450° oven for 10 minutes. Serve on a platter with sprigs of mint. Can also be garnished with fresh fruit. Serve with warm maple syrup or hard sauce.

Hard Sauce:

½ c. unsalted butter
1 c. sugar, brown sugar or confectioners sugar

1 tsp. vanilla or dash of Kentucky bourbon

*It is important to use salt-risen bread, available at grocery stores or bakery, as regular bread gets soggy. Salt-risen has a wonderful taste and texture.

Canaan Land Farms in Harrodsburg is a Historic Bed and Breakfast. Guest may stay in Benjamin Daniel House, c. 1795, which is one of the earliest brick houses in Kentucky and on the National Register or the Philemon Waters Log House c. 1815. Canaan Land Farm was designated a Kentucky Historic Farm.

Apple Bread

Evans Orchard and Cider Mill
(My Favorite)

2 c. sugar
1 c. oil
3 eggs, beaten
3 c. flour
1 tsp. salt
1 tsp. cinnamon

1 tsp. soda
2 tsp. vanilla
3 c. peeled and chopped apples (sweet and tart)
1 c. nuts, chopped

Beat together sugar, oil and eggs. Sift together flour, salt, cinnamon and soda. Add to liquid mixture. Add vanilla, apples and nuts to mixture. Put into two greased loaf pans. Sprinkle tops with sugar. Bake at 325° for one hour until done.

Evans Orchard and Cider Mill in Georgetown, Kentucky is a 45-acre orchard, gift shop and restaurant serving lunch, apple pies and fudge. They have fresh produce, u-pick area, children's play area, and provide activities such as farm tours, hayrides, bonfires, live music and birthday parties.

Chocolate Waffles
Gallery House Bed and Breakfast and Art Gallery

1 ¾ c. flour	2 beaten egg yolks
¼ c. cocoa	1 ¾ c. milk
1 Tbsp. baking powder	¼ c. vegetable oil
½ tsp. salt	2 stiffly beaten egg whites

Sift together dry ingredients. Combine wet ingredients and stir into dry ingredients. Fold in egg whites. Bake in waffle maker according to manufacturer's directions.

Chocolate Ganache:

4 oz. heavy cream	4 to 6 oz. bittersweet chocolate

Bring cream to barely simmering. Take off heat. Stir in chocolate. Stir until melted.

Strawberry Coulis:

½ to 1 c. strawberries (frozen strawberries work fine)	¼ c. clear corn syrup

Process (in food processor or blender) strawberries and corn syrup until mixture is smooth. Warm gently.

Sliced Strawberries:

Hull and slice 1 pint of strawberries. Macerate strawberries with ¼ cup sugar.

Assemble: Place 3 waffles on plate. Drizzle chocolate ganache over waffles and edge of plate. Drizzle strawberry coulis over waffles and edge of plate. Spoon sliced strawberries into center of waffle. Top with whipped cream. Dust with confectioners sugar. Serves 2.

Gallery House B&B, 1386 S. 6th St., Louisville, sets amidst America's largest collection of Victorian homes. If you enjoy original art, great food and warm Kentucky-style hospitality, come join Leah Stewart, a graduate of Sullivan University with a degree in Baking and Pastry Arts.

Pancakes With 7-Up
Gateway Bed and Breakfast

1 ¼ c. sifted flour
3 tsp. baking powder
1 Tbsp. sugar
½ tsp. salt
1 beaten egg

¼ c. milk
¾ c. 7-Up (room
  temperature)
2 Tbsp. salad oil or bacon fat

Sift together flour, baking powder, sugar and salt. Combine 7-Up, egg, milk and salad oil; add to dry ingredients, stirring just until flour is moistened (batter will be lumpy). Makes about eight 4-inch pancakes.

Gateway B&B is a beautifully restored 1878 Italianate Townhouse, built by Henry Schriver and restored by the present owners, Ken and Sandy Clift, located next door to the Water Tower Square in the East Row Historic District of Newport, just across the river from downtown Cincinnati.

Buttermilk Biscuits
Helm House

2 c. all-purpose flour
1 Tbsp. baking powder
¾ tsp. salt
½ tsp. baking soda

5 Tbsp. chilled Crisco
  shortening
1 c. buttermilk

15 minutes prep, 12 to 15 minutes baking. Makes 12 biscuits. Preheat oven to 425°. In large bowl, sift together flour, baking powder, salt and baking soda. Using a pastry blender, cut the shortening into the flour mixture until coarse crumbs form.
Add the buttermilk, tossing with a fork until a dough forms.

Turn dough out on a lightly floured surface. Gather into a disk. Knead lightly a few times just until smooth. (The dough can be made up to 2 hours ahead, wrapped in plastic wrap, and refrigerated until ready to use.)

Pat the dough to ¾-inch thick. Using a biscuit cutter, cut out biscuits. Place the biscuits 2 inches apart on an ungreased baking sheet. Bake until golden, 12 to 15 minutes. Serve hot.

The Helm House, Morgantown, is a spacious Victorian home built in 1898 by Hon. W.A. Helm. The Bed and Breakfast is conveniently located near Mammoth Cave, the Corvette Museum, new Bluegrass Museum and Riverfront Art Center in Owensboro.

Muffins

Liz Curtis Higgs

Muffins:

½ c. butter, softened	2 c. flour
½ c. sugar	1 tsp. baking soda
1 c. mashed ripe bananas	½ tsp. salt
2 eggs, beaten	¾ c. roasted and salted
½ c. honey	peanuts, chopped

Glaze:

2 Tbsp. butter, softened	2 Tbsp. honey

Preheat oven to 325°. Cream butter. Add sugar. Beat well. Stir in bananas, eggs and honey. Blend. Sift flour, soda and salt together in a separate bowl. Stir into banana mixture. Add peanuts and stir until just combined. Bake in greased muffin tins for 25 to 30 minutes or until muffins spring back when tested.

To make glaze, combine butter and honey in small bowl and stir until smooth. Brush warm muffins with glaze. Serve warm.

Liz Curtis Higgs of Louisville is the author of twenty-six books, with more than three million copies in print, including best selling series "Bad Girls of the Bible." She is a gifted international speaker and has been a featured speaker on both television and radio. She was awarded the Gold Medallion for Excellence and Christy Award for Best Historical Fiction for her religious novels.

Breads, Rolls & Pastries

Peach French Toast

Jailer's Inn

1 c. brown sugar
½ c. margarine
2 Tbsp. water
1 (29 oz.) can sliced peaches

5 eggs
1 ¼ c. milk
1 Tbsp. vanilla
6 slices white bread

Drain peaches and reserve syrup. Heat margarine in micro-wave for one minute. Add 1 cup brown sugar and microwave one minute more, then add 2 tablespoons water. Continue microwaving until thick and foamy, about 1 to 2 minutes. Pour into 13 x 9 baking dish and cool for 10 minutes. Place peaches on cooled caramel sauce and cover with slices of bread placed close together. Beat eggs, milk and vanilla until mixed. Pour over bread; cover and refrigerate overnight. Bake at 350° for 40 minutes. Loosely cover with foil the last 10 minutes if browning too fast. Serve with warmed peach syrup. Makes 10 to 12 servings.

Iron bars on windows, 30-inch thick stone walls, may not sound like the typical tourist accommodation. However, the historic Jailer's Inn, Bardstown, circa 1819, offers a unique and luxurious way to "do time." The Bed and Breakfast is beautifully decorated with antiques and heirlooms.

Caramel Apple French Toast

Kavanaugh House Bed & Breakfast

1 c. firmly packed brown
  sugar
1 tsp. vanilla
2 Tbsp. light corn syrup
½ c. butter
1 c. chopped pecans
3 to 4 peeled, thinly sliced
  apples

¼ tsp. ground nutmeg
12 to 18 slices Italian bread
1 ½ tsp. cinnamon
6 eggs
½ tsp. salt
1 ½ c. milk
Caramel Sauce

Combine the brown sugar, butter and corn syrup in a small saucepan and cook over medium heat until thickened, stirring con-stantly. Pour into a 13 x 9-inch baking dish and sprinkle half the pecans over the syrup. Place apples on caramel sauce and pecans. Place 6 to 9 slices of bread on top of the syrup mixture and sprinkle

9010 *Breads, Rolls & Pastries* 111

the remaining pecans on top of the bread. Top with the remaining 6 to 9 slices of bread.

Combine the eggs, milk, vanilla, nutmeg, cinnamon and salt in a blender. Pour evenly over the bread slices; cover the baking dish and chill 8 hours. Bake uncovered in a preheated oven, 350°, for 40 to 45 minutes or until lightly browned. Drizzle the sauce over the toast right before serving.

Caramel Sauce:

½ c. firmly packed brown sugar

¼ c. butter
1 Tbsp. corn syrup

In a small saucepan, combine the brown sugar, butter and corn syrup and cook until thickened, stirring constantly.

Kavanaugh House (Lawrenceburg) was built in the 1880s by Dr. Charles Kavanaugh. It later became a military prep school educating 150 Annapolis midshipmen and 15 West Point appointees. This beautiful historic home now serves as a B&B and Tea Room.

Miniature Corny Jalapeno Muffins

Kentucky Corn Growers Association

¾ c. yellow cornmeal
¼ c. all-purpose flour
1 Tbsp. plus 1 tsp. finely chopped sweet red pepper
1 Tbsp. minced jalapeno pepper
1 ½ tsp. baking powder

¼ tsp. garlic salt
⅓ c. skim milk
1 egg, beaten
½ c. corn
1 Tbsp. corn oil
corn oil spray

Combine first six ingredients in a medium bowl, stirring well. Combine milk, egg, corn oil and corn. Stir well. Add to dry ingredients, stirring just until dry ingredients are moistened. Spoon batter into miniature muffin pans coated with corn oil spray, filling ⅔ full. Bake at 425° for 10 to 15 minutes or until lightly browned. Yield: 18 muffins.

This corn recipe was featured at the Kentucky State Fair cooking school. The goal of the Kentucky Corn Growers Association is to help producers provide the best possible product to all customers, whether we are feeding livestock or nations around the world. The Kentucky Corn Growers Association is a state affiliate organization of the National Corn Growers Association. We increase knowledge about corn and awareness of Kentucky's corn

Breads, Rolls & Pastries

industry through educational programs, promotional activities and media.

Very Best Blackstrap Molasses-Raisin Muffins

Leah Lail

2 ½ c. flour
1 ¼ c. sugar
1 ½ tsp. baking powder
½ c. chopped walnuts
¼ c. honey
½ c. molasses

3 eggs
⅓ c. plus 1 Tbsp. butter, melted
⅓ c. raisins
¼ c. milk

Mix first four ingredients in large bowl. In a separate bowl, mix remaining ingredients. Add dry ingredients to the wet, being careful to break up big lumps. Spoon into greased muffin tins. Bake for 15 to 20 minutes until fork comes out clean. Serve immediately. Yields 2 ½ dozen.

Leah Lail was raised on a horse farm near Lexington. She played Hank Kingsley's wife on HBO's "The Larry Sanders Show" and starred on V.I.P. as Kay Simmons, system communications director. Movies to her credit: Little Nicke, Late Last Night and Denial.

The Derby Benedict

Last Call Film Festival

2 Tbsp. butter
2 Tbsp. all-purpose flour
1 tsp. Dijon mustard
1 tsp. Worcestershire sauce
½ tsp. black pepper

½ c. BBC Jefferson Reserve Bourbon Barrel Stout
¾ c. heavy cream
6 oz. sharp Cheddar cheese
toasted whole-wheat bread
eggs

Put a saucepan on low heat and add the butter. Once the butter has melted, add the flour, mustard, Worcestershire, pepper and beer. After adding the beer, combine the ingredients by stirring with a whisk. Add the cream to the mixture in the saucepan and combine again with the whisk. Begin to add the cheese in small amounts, only adding more as it melts while stirring.

Once the sauce has been brought together, it's time to make toast and eggs. I use two pieces of toast and one egg for each plate I'm making. Toast bread to desired setting and fry an egg sunny side up in a nonstick skillet. Arrange toast in the center of the plate. Add the egg on top of the toast. Then drizzle your amazing homemade bourbon cheese sauce over the egg and toast.

The famed Last Call Film Festival is a 3-day event created by Andy Schanie and held annually in June at the historic Rudyard Kipling multi-performance space in Louisville. It has both performances and film with directors on hand to do a Q&A after the screenings.

Locust Grove's Hearth-Baked Irish Soda Bread

Locust Grove

2 c. all-purpose flour
1 tsp. salt
1 tsp. sugar
1 tsp. baking powder
½ tsp. baking soda
3 Tbsp. butter, margarine or shortening
¾ c. buttermilk

Preheat oven to 375°. Butter a baking sheet. Combine dry ingredients in a large bowl. Cut in butter, margarine or shortening, using a fork. Knead a few times on a lightly floured surface; dough will resemble biscuit dough. Form into a mound about 5 inches in diameter and about 2 inches high.

Place dough on the cookie sheet and slash a cross in the top and down the sides, about 1 inch into the dough.

Bake for 35 to 40 minutes or until loaf sounds hollow when rapped with the fingers.

Cut into slices no more than ½-inch thick. Serves 6.

Locust Grove, a National Historic Landmark, was a 694 acre farm where George Rogers Clark, founder of Louisville and Revolutionary War hero, lived until his death in 1818. It hosted 3 U.S. Presidents and was a stopping point for famed explorers Lewis & Clark.

Cardamon Braid (Pula)

Sean Moth

2 ¼ c. flour
½ tsp. salt
1 pkg. active dry yeast
2 Tbsp. sugar

2 Tbsp. butter
1 tsp. cardamon
⅔ c. warm milk
1 egg, well beaten

Combine flour, salt and cardamon; set aside. Sprinkle yeast over milk; stir until dissolved. Add sugar, egg and flour mixture. Mix well. Add 2 tablespoons melted butter. Knead until smooth and satiny. Turn into greased bowl; let rise until doubled. Punch down. Cut dough into three equal pieces. Roll each into a 24-inch rope. Braid into a circle or straight loaf on greased cookie sheet. Brush with melted butter; let rise under damp cloth until doubled. Bake 12 minutes at 425°. Cool. Drizzle with frosting. Decorate with nuts/cherries.

Frosting:

1 c. powdered sugar
2 Tbsp. milk

¼ c. blanched, sliced
   almonds
½ tsp. vanilla

Sean Moth of Louisville is the public address announcer and Assistant Sports Information Director (SID) for the University of Louisville's Athletic Department. Before coming to Louisville, he was the announcer for the Colorado Avalanche and the Denver Nuggets.

Banana Nut Bread

National Corvette Homecoming

1 c. sugar
½ c. melted margarine or
   butter
2 eggs

2 Tbsp. milk
1 c. self-rising flour
2 bananas (overripe)
1 c. chopped nuts

Cream together the first 2 ingredients and add the next 3. Mix well and fold in bananas. Add 1 cup chopped nuts. Grease and flour a loaf pan. Pour into pan. Bake about 45 minutes to 1 hour at 325°. The longer this ages, the more moist it gets.

National Corvette Homecoming is held each year in Bowling Green. This is the location of the only General Motors Corvette

Assembly Plant in the world. In its 28th year, the celebration is a "Homecoming" for all Corvettes and their owners.

❦ Fried Sweet Bread ❦

Old Bardstown Village

2 c. all-purpose flour	1 c. raw sugar
1 c. milk or water	

Mix all together. Dip out tablespoons of dough and place in a hot skillet of 2 cups of vegetable oil. Fry on both sides until golden brown. When done, sprinkle raw sugar over top of hot bread.

Old Bardstown is an authentic village of ten log cabins dating from between 1776 and 1820. Along with frontier homes, Wheel Wright's Shop, Forge and Stillhouse, there is an Indian Museum and Civil War Museum also on site. Located in Bardstown, Kentucky.

❦ School's Whole Wheat ❦ Bread

Pine Mountain Settlement

1 cake yeast	½ c. dried milk
2 c. warm water	¼ c. hot water
2 Tbsp. sugar	¼ c. brown sugar
3 c. white flour	3 Tbsp. shortening
2 tsp. salt	3 c. whole-wheat flour

Soften yeast in lukewarm water. Add sugar, salt, white flour and dried milk. Beat smooth. Set in warm place (82°) until light and bubbly.

Combine hot water with brown sugar and shortening. Cool to lukewarm and add to the sponge. Add whole-wheat flour and mix smooth. Let rise. Place in greased loaf pans and let rise until double.

Bake in moderate oven (350°) for 40 minutes. Makes 3 one-pound loaves.

National Historic Landmark, Pine Mountain Settlement School was founded in 1913 as a school for children in Kentucky's remote southeastern mountains. Today, the 625-acre site provides student and adult instruction in Environmental Ed, Appalachian Culture and Crafts.

Breads, Rolls & Pastries

Banana Bread

Pinecrest Park Resort

1 stick butter (room temperature)	1 ½ tsp. baking powder
2 eggs	½ tsp. baking soda
1 c. sugar	¼ tsp. salt
1 tsp. lemon juice (or orange juice)	2 c. flour
	4 very ripe bananas, mashed
2 Tbsp. milk	1 c. walnuts or pecans (optional)

Preheat oven to 350°. Grease a 9 x 5-inch loaf pan. Cream butter, eggs, sugar, lemon juice and milk in a bowl with an electric mixer. Add remaining ingredients and mix on low until blended. Pour into pan and bake about 1 hour and toothpick inserted in center of bread comes out clean. Cool 15 minutes. Remove from pan and cool completely on a wire rack.

Pinecrest Park Resort near Russell Springs is perched high on a peninsula above beautiful Lake Cumberland. In addition to one and two bedroom cabins, they have an RV park, fishing pond, swimming pool, playground and boat storage area.

French Toast Casserole

Red Dog and Company

1 loaf French bread, cut into 1 ½-inch slices	1 ½ c. pecans
2 Tbsp. light corn syrup	5 eggs
5 Tbsp. butter	1 ½ c. milk
1 c. light brown sugar	1 ½ tsp. vanilla

Mix the corn syrup, butter and brown sugar until it boils and pour into 9 x 13 baking pan. Sprinkle pecans on top of syrup mixture. Place French bread slices on top.

Mix eggs, milk and vanilla. Beat all together. Pour over bread; set in refrigerator overnight. Bake at 350° for 45 minutes. Flip over on large platter. Serve with fresh sliced strawberries, whipped cream and maple syrup.

Michael Angel, owner of Red Dog Chairs, Londo, created his own line of traditional "mule-ear" chairs, so-called because the back posts of the chairs stick up, like ears on a mule. The hickory-bottom chairs are made from scratch, including weaving and carving.

9010 *Breads, Rolls & Pastries* 117

Banana Stuffed French Toast

Rose Hill Inn

1 loaf bread (unsliced)	1 c. milk or cream
2 bananas (not overripe)	1 tsp. vanilla
2 c. brown sugar	1 Tbsp. sugar
3 c. pecans	3 c. unsalted butter
3 to 4 large eggs	

Slice the bread into pockets (don't use the ends), with each slice being about 2-inches with a sliced pocket in center. Peel and slice your bananas. Lay the bananas in the pocket and stuff in about 5 pecans. Put about 1 tablespoon brown sugar on top. Mix together eggs, milk, vanilla and sugar. Dip each French toast into egg mixture and place into skillet with melted butter. Cook and turn. Keep heat on medium to prevent the butter from burning.

Enjoy these wonderful banana toasts with powdered sugar, maple syrup or even whipped cream.

Rose Hill Inn is an elegant 1823 Victorian Mansion in the Historic District of Rose Hill in Versailles. This home was a hospital during the Civil War. This Kentucky landmark is on the National Historic Register and has provided shelter and security for almost 200 years.

Mom's Pancakes

Tillie Sowders

1 c. plain flour	1 egg, beaten
1 ¼ tsp. baking powder	1 Tbsp. vegetable oil
½ tsp. baking soda	1 c. buttermilk (do not
1 Tbsp. sugar	substitute)

Mix the dry ingredients together. Add the other ingredients and mix well. Heat a griddle (electric skillet works best) to medium-hot and butter it generously. Pour on 3 to 4-inch blobs of batter. Cook about 1 minute, then turn and cook until golden brown.

Artist Tillie Sowders has lived all of her life in her turn-of-the-century Danville home. Many of her paintings support local, charitable fundraisers. In addition to a great talent in painting, she is also active in the deaf community, serving as an interpreter.

Breads, Rolls & Pastries

Fr. Stan's Favorite Dressing

St. Joseph Catholic Church

4 ½ c. cornbread crumbs
1 (16 oz.) pkg. herb stuffing mix
2 (10 ¾ oz.) cans cream of chicken soup
2 (14 oz.) cans low-sodium chicken broth
1 medium onion
½ c. chopped celery
4 large eggs
1 Tbsp. rubbed sage
½ tsp. salt
½ tsp. pepper
2 Tbsp. butter, cut up

Stir together cornbread crumbs, stuffing mix, and next 8 ingredients in a large bowl. Pour cornbread mixture into a lightly greased 5 ½ or 6-quart slow cooker. Dot with butter. Cook, covered, on low 4 hours or until cooked through and set.

On the National Register of Historic Places, Saint Joseph Catholic Church, Bowling Green was established in 1856. It rose in stages from this small 1860 brick building to the final addition, which was consecrated May 4, 1889.

A Storybook Inn Blueberry Muffins

Storybook Inn

1 ½ c. unbleached all-purpose flour
¾ c. sugar (Domino)
2 tsp. baking powder (use the kind without aluminum)
1 egg
¼ tsp. sea salt
⅓ c. vegetable oil
⅔ c. buttermilk
1 c. wild blueberries*

*(Folded in gently after the batter is complete so that the batter remains a lovely ivory color. If you beat too briskly, the batter will turn blue, which may be fine if you are a Kentucky Wildcat's fan, or you could just call them "Blueblood Muffins." They still taste great.)

First, mix all the dry ingredients thoroughly with whisk. Please don't leave out this step. Then add wet ingredients and stir until mixed well with large spoon, but not mixer. Fold in wild blueberries, enough for 12 medium size muffins. May sprinkle cinnamon and sugar on top with crushed walnuts or put on a streusel topping by mixing together:

½ c. white sugar
⅓ c. all-purpose flour
¼ c. butter, cubed
1 ½ tsp. ground cinnamon

Put on top of unbaked muffins or just use the more simple cinnamon-sugar sprinkled on top with crushed walnuts, or bake the muffins with no topping at all. Delicious!

Built in 1843, Storybook Inn Bed and Breakfast is located in the historic Rose Hill section of Versailles, Kentucky, as seen in the movie Elizabethtown (filmed in downtown Versailles and on Rose Hill Avenue). Chosen in 2007 as 1 of top 10 B&B's in the nation.

Curried Muffins

Robert Penn Warren

¼ c. chopped green onions	1 Tbsp. baking powder
3 Tbsp. vegetable oil	2 Tbsp. sugar
1 ¾ c. cornmeal	1 Tbsp. curry
¾ c. all-purpose flour	1 egg
¾ tsp. salt	1 c. milk

Heat oven to 425°. Cook the onions in oil until tender. Sift together cornmeal, flour, salt, baking powder, sugar and curry powder into a bowl. Add egg, milk and the cooked onions. Stir until just combined. Fill greased muffin cups ⅔ full. Bake 14 to 18 minutes.

Guthrie native Robert Penn Warren was an American poet, novelist, and literary critic. He won the Pulitzer in 1947 "All the King's Men" and won his subsequent Pulitzers for poetry in 1957 and 1979. Recipe provided by Pennyroyal Area Museum, has an exhibit on Warren.

Corn Bread Supreme

Weisenberger Mills

1 c. self-rising cornmeal	8 oz. sour cream
½ c. cooking oil	2 eggs
8 oz. can cream-style corn	

Mix well. Pour in greased pan. Bake 35 to 40 minutes at 400°.

Weisenberger Mills is located on the South Elkhorn Creek near Midway. The creek has provided the water to power the mill's twin turbines since the early 1800's. Six generations of Weisenbergers have operated the mill, which sells over 70 items for baking purposes.

Breads, Rolls & Pastries

White Hall Biscuits

White Hall State Historic Site

2 c. self-rising flour   **¼ c. shortening**
1 c. buttermilk

Get a good fire going, and once enough coals are formed from the fire, put them on the lid and underneath a cast-iron Dutch oven (this will warm the oven up just like preheating a modern stove). Or preheat modern oven to 400°.

Cut shortening into flour until grainy. Pour in milk. Knead on board. Roll out to desired thickness and cut with biscuit cutter.

Place in Dutch oven. Once biscuits are in the oven, remove burned out coals and replace with fresh on top and bottom of Dutch oven. Bake for 25 minutes or until brown on top and bottom. (The Dutch oven can vary in temperature from time to time, depending on what kind of wood one uses, how hot the oven is and how many coals one places around it, thus each baking time may be different.) If Dutch oven is not preheated, it will take about 40 to 45 minutes to bake the biscuits, and fresh coals will need to be added at least once in the baking process. Or place biscuits on baking sheet and bake for 12 to 15 minutes.

White Hall, Richmond, not only preserves 1860's architectural history and furnishings, but also commemorates its owner, one of Kentucky's most colorful and historical figures, Cassius Marcellus Clay, noted emancipationist, politician, publisher, Minister to Russia, and friend to Abe Lincoln.

Biscuits Monte Cristo

Dwight Yoakam

(Makes 4 servings.)

4 Bakersfield biscuits, sliced   **8 slices ham**
**   in half**   **8 slices Provolone cheese**
2 eggs   **2 oz. orange marmalade**
1 oz. milk   **1 Tbsp. butter**

Time: 10 minutes.

Preheat oven to 400°. Mix the eggs and the milk together. Warm up in a pan with butter. Dip the biscuit halves into the mix and pan-fry it on both sides (like French toast). Place a slice of ham and slice of cheese on each and bake for 5 minutes. Close the biscuits as a sandwich and serve with marmalade.

Dwight Yoakam of Pikeville has won Grammies for "Aint That Lonely Yet" and "Same Old Train." His film credits are "Red Rock

West", "Sling Blade," and "Panic Room." He is now serving the world with his Dwight Yoakam's Bakersfield Biscuits.

—•*Extra Recipes*•—

Cakes,

Cookies,

and Desserts

Recipe Favorites

Page No.

Recipe Title:_____ _____

_____ _____

_____ _____

_____ _____

_____ _____

_____ _____

_____ _____

_____ _____

_____ _____

_____ _____

Family Favorites

Page No.

Recipe Title:_____ _____

_____ _____

_____ _____

_____ _____

_____ _____

Notes:_____

_____

_____

_____

Cakes, Cookies & Desserts

Old Fashioned Banana Pudding

Ace Folkfest Rendevous

9 egg yolks (yellows)
3 c. sugar
6 c. milk (whole)
¾ lb. butter

1 ½ c. flour
7 bananas
1 Tbsp. vanilla
1 box vanilla wafers

Cook milk and butter on medium-high heat until butter is melted. Do not scald milk. Add flour, sugar and beaten egg yolks; after mixed well, add vanilla. Cook until pudding begins to thicken; remember to thicken but not all the way. Let cool, then beat again until smooth texture. Get a Pyrex bowl or square big enough to hold alternating layers of wafers, pudding and bananas plus topping. Alternate layers of vanilla wafers, pudding and sliced bananas. Top with vanilla wafers, then Cool Whip if you do not want to make the egg old-fashioned meringue for pies. Mom always made egg white and sugar meringue; beat about 6 egg whites only and add about 3 tablespoons sugar in the mixer to taste. Fluff with spoon on top of banana pudding. Toast the top in the oven on about 350° for golden color. Use Pyrex so not to break in oven.

Ace Folkfest takes place annually in June and October in Harford, Kentucky, and promotes artists, barbeque and chili cookers, craftspeople, musicians, muzzle loaders, performers, re-enactors, old-time demonstrations and dancers as an American Cultural Experience!

Kahlua Brownies

Actors Theatre of Louisville

1st Layer:
any brownie mix (to make 9 x 13 pan of brownies)

¼ c. Kahlua

Brush Kahlua over brownies when you take out of oven. Let set one hour.

2nd Layer:

2 c. powdered sugar   3 Tbsp. Kahlua
1 stick melted butter

Mix together and make 2nd layer on brownie. Let set one hour.

3rd Layer:

6 oz. chocolate chips $1/3$ c. milk
1 c. miniature marshmallows

Melt over low heat and make top layer of brownie. Refrigerate for one hour.

This delicious recipe is by one of Actors Theatre of Louisville's longtime dedicated volunteers Doris Elder. The Tony award winning theatre is in its 45th season located at 316 W. Main St., Louisville, Kentucky.

❧ *Pears In White Zinfandel* ❧

Aleksander House

8 pears   zest of 1 lemon
2 c. white zinfandel   1 tsp. vanilla
2 Tbsp. lemon juice   creme fraiche
1 c. sugar   mint leaves
2 tsp. cinnamon

Peel and core pears. Set aside. In a deep saucepan, combine wine, lemon juice, sugar, cinnamon, lemon zest and vanilla. Bring to a boil. Add pears, stems up, and scoop spoonfuls of liquid over them. Simmer until pears are tender (10 to 20 minutes). Remove pears and place in individual serving dishes. Strain liquid and boil until reduced by half. Pour wine sauce over pears. Let cool. Serve with creme fraiche on the side. Garnish with mint leaves.

The Aleksander House B&B is an elegant home built in 1882, complete with antiques and decor. On the National Register of Historic Places, the home has 12-foot ceilings, original hardwood floors, moldings and 5 fireplaces. It is located in historic Old Louisville, near Churchill Downs.

Burnt Sugar Cake

Barlow House Museum

1 ½ c. sugar
¾ c. cold water
¾ c. shortening
2 eggs, separated
1 tsp. vanilla

1 c. milk
2 ½ c. plain flour
1 tsp. baking powder
1 scant tsp. soda

Brown ½ cup sugar in heavy skillet (preferably iron) over medium heat to a deep brown. Add the water and while over the heat, stir well until all sugar dissolves; cool. Cream shortening and remaining sugar together; add beaten egg yolks, milk and dry ingredients; mix. Add burnt sugar/water mixture and mix well. Fold in beaten egg whites and vanilla. Pour into three 9-inch prepared pans (sprayed with flour/oil mixture). Bake in 350° oven 30 minutes. Frost with the following:

Frosting:

2 c. sugar
¾ c. shortening
1 c. milk

pinch of salt
1 tsp. vanilla

Cream shortening and sugar. Place on stove in a heavy 3-quart pan and brown until light brown/cream color. Take off stove and add milk. Mix well (careful, this mixture will boil up severely). Put back on stove and cook until a soft ball forms in cold water. Cool slightly; add vanilla and salt and with a strong spoon beat well until the glossy shine is dimmed. While still warm, spread between layers and over top and sides of cake. Store in a tight container. This cake keeps well and will continue to be moist for several days.

Vivian Barlow was a music teacher at the private Choate's School. His students included John and Robert Kennedy. Upon retirement, he returned to his beloved home built in the 1800's in Barlow, Kentucky. Now a museum, the home has his private collection and memorabilia.

Green Apple Pies (1862)

Battle of Perryville

6 good raw green apples
1 c. sugar
3 Tbsp. melted butter
4 eggs

lemon juice
2 Tbsp. brandy
dried currants
spice

Grate raw apples; add sugar, melted butter, eggs, a little lemon juice, brandy, a few dried currants and a little spice. Line plates with a paste (pie crust). Fill and bake without an upper crust. Bake at 350° for about 45 minutes or until apples are soft and bubbly.

Civil War Battle of Perryville with 40,000 soldiers was fought October 8, 1862. This recipe was shared by Debbie Rogers, who was described by John Downs of Kentucky State Parks as "the Battlefield Cooking Guru."

Snow Ice Cream

John Belski

1 c. milk	**1 tsp. vanilla**
½ c. sugar	

Mix ingredients together and add clean, fresh snow to desired consistency.

Emmy award winning meteorologist John Belski has been the meteorologist at WAVE-TV in Louisville for 20 years. He likes this recipe because it is directly related to the weather and can make it feel a little like summer in the middle of winter.

Pink Meringue Cookies

Pete Biagi

2 egg yolks	**¾ c. sugar**
2 ½ c. flour	**⅔ c. shortening**
1 tsp. salt	**¼ c. milk**
½ tsp. baking powder	**1 tsp. vanilla**

Blend ingredients. Form into balls. Flatten with glass dipped in sugar, then prepare the meringue.

2 egg whites	**½ tsp. vinegar**
¼ tsp. salt	**1 c. chocolate chips**
½ c. sugar	**1 c. coarsely crushed candy**
½ tsp. vanilla	**canes**

Beat whites with salt until soft mounds form, then add sugar and beat until stiff peaks form. Fold remaining ingredients in. Put a spoonful onto flattened base.

Cakes, Cookies & Desserts

Bake at 325° for 20 to 25 minutes.

Award winning cinematographer Pete Biagi is from Louisville. He is a graduate of Columbia with a BA in Film/Video. His work includes over thirty short and twelve feature length films, as well as numerous local and national television commercials.

❧ *Edna's Blackberry Cake* ❧

Roger Bingham

2 c. unsweetened
   blackberries (fresh berries,
   no jam)
2 c. sugar
2 eggs
1 stick margarine (soft)
enough water to cover
   berries in saucepan

1 ½ tsp. baking soda
¼ tsp. salt
1 tsp. cinnamon
1 tsp. nutmeg
¼ tsp. allspice
2 c. flour

Cook berries in water for 10 minutes; let cool. Do not drain. Cream sugar, eggs and margarine until light and fluffy. Add blackberries. In separate bowl, mix remaining ingredients except flour. Now, gradually add to cream mixture with flour. Pour into greased and floured 9-inch cake pan. Bake at 350° for 35 to 40 minutes. Cake will be very moist.

Caramel Icing:

3 c. brown sugar
⅔ c. evaporated milk
½ stick butter

1 tsp. vanilla
3 Tbsp. Karo syrup
confectioners sugar

Mix all ingredients except confectioners sugar in pan and boil until ball forms when testing in cold water (approximately 10 minutes after starts to boil). Pour into bowl; let cool. Beat in enough confectioners sugar until stiff. If hard to spread, add milk to thin. Spread on cake.

Roger Bingham of Crittenden was on the 2001 Survivor Australian Outback and survived 12 of the 14 episodes. Roger teaches industrial arts at Grant County High School. This blue ribbon recipe was handed down for years in his 82-year-old mother-in-law's family.

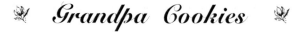

Grandpa Cookies

Toni Blake

2 sticks butter or margarine	1 ½ tsp. vanilla
1 ½ c. confectioners sugar	2 ½ c. flour
1 egg	1 tsp. baking soda
1 tsp. cream of tartar	¼ tsp. salt

Cream together first 5 ingredients. Combine salt, soda and flour in separate bowl, then mix gradually into creamed mixture. When well blended, cover and chill for 8 hours or overnight.

Preheat oven to 375°. Roll dough to approximately ¼-inch or less, if possible, using sprinkled flour to achieve desired rolling consistency. Cut into desired shapes and place on cookie sheet.

Bake on lower oven shelf until cookies are slightly puffed, then move onto upper shelf and bake until edges are lightly golden. Entire baking time is approximately four to six minutes, depending upon cookie thickness. Do not overbake. Cool on rack.

Eat cookies plain or cover with glaze:

2 c. confectioners sugar	milk (add to desired
a dash of salt	consistency)
1 tsp. vanilla	

Stir ingredients together, then add food color if desired. Apply to cooled cookies with pastry brush.

Author Toni Blake writes for Harlequin Romances with 14 novels to her credit. She and her husband Blair live in Northern Kentucky. When not writing, she enjoys traveling, scrapbooking, genealogy, and snow skiing. This recipe was given to her by her grandmother.

Candy Bar Cookies

David Bottrell

¾ c. butter	¼ tsp. salt
¾ c. powdered sugar	2 c. all-purpose flour
1 tsp. vanilla extract	

Mix butter. Gradually add powdered sugar. Add vanilla extract, salt and 2 cups of all-purpose flour. Roll out ½ of dough at a time on floured surface to a rectangle (about 12 x 18-inches). Trim sides. Cut into 1 x 1 ½-inch pieces and place on ungreased cookie sheet. Bake at 325° for 10 to 14 minutes until lightly

Cakes, Cookies & Desserts

browned. Cool on racks and top with caramel-pecan topping (see following). Allow to cool, then top with chocolate icing (see following).

Caramel Topping:

28 Kraft caramels	1 c. powdered sugar
¼ c. evaporated milk	1 c. finely chopped pecans
¼ c. butter	

Combine in top of double boiler (or just a regular pan over low heat) caramels and evaporated milk. Heat until caramels melt (try not to boil), stirring occasionally. Remove from heat; add butter. Stir in powdered sugar and pecans.

Chocolate Icing:

1 c. semi-sweet chocolate chips	2 Tbsp. butter
	1 tsp. vanilla extract
¼ c. evaporated milk	½ c. powdered sugar

Melt 1 cup chocolate chips with evaporated milk over low heat. Remove from heat and stir in butter, vanilla extract and powdered sugar. Top candy bar cookies that already have pecan topping. You can also top it off with a single pecan per cookie.

Actor and screenwriter David Dean Bottrell is from Louisa. He is recognized as attorney Lincoln Meyer on Boston Legal and written several scripts including "Kingdom Come" starring Whoopi Goldberg. This is his favorite recipe made by his mother Ruth Day Bottrell.

❧ Apple Bread Pudding With ❧ Bourbon Cider Sauce

Bramble Ridge Orchard

4 large eggs, beaten	6 c. cubed raisin bread or
2 ½ c. heavy cream	cinnamon bread (if other
1 c. apple cider	bread is used, double the
1 c. brown sugar	amount of cinnamon)
2 Tbsp. melted butter	1 Granny Smith or Pink Lady
½ tsp. salt	apple, cored and diced
1 tap cinnamon	1 c. dried apples, diced

Preheat oven to 350° and grease a 9 x 13 dish. Into a large bowl, put eggs (beaten) and add next 6 ingredients. Stir until mixed and add bread, apple and dried apples. Stir again until mixed and pour into greased dish. Cover with plastic wrap and chill for at least an hour. Remove the plastic wrap and bake at 350° for 1 hour. Cut into squares and serve with:

Bourbon Cider Sauce:

¼ c. butter	2 c. powdered sugar
¼ c. brown sugar	2 Tbsp. bourbon
¼ c. half and half	⅛ tsp. salt
¼ c. apple cider	

In a small heavy pan, heat and stir until sugar dissolves the butter, brown sugar, half and half and apple cider. Add and bring to a boil and boil for 1 minute the powdered sugar, bourbon and salt. Cool and serve over warm bread pudding. Delicious!

Nestled between the foothills of the Appalachian Mountains and Kentucky Bluegrass region, Bramble Ridge Orchard with 2700 trees and 13 varieties of apples is located in Mt. Sterling. This recipe has been a favorite recipe at the orchard's Green Apple Tea Room.

Grasshopper Pie

Brass Lantern Restaurant

(For 4 Pies)

1 ½ bags mini marshmallows	¾ c. green creme de menthe
2 c. milk	2 qt. whipping cream
¾ c. white creme de cacao	4 Oreo pie crusts

Place marshmallows in a glass bowl and pour ½ cup milk over them. Microwave for one minute to completely melt marshmallows. Add white creme de cacao and green creme de menthe and let cool. Chill your mixing bowl and beaters. Beat whipping cream until stiff. Fold in the chilled marshmallow mixture. Put in your Oreo crusts and freeze. You can decorate by topping it with Hershey chocolate syrup in a zig-zag pattern over each, immediately prior to serving. Serve frozen.

At the Brass Lantern located in Aurora on Kentucky Lake, Victorian elegance can be seen throughout. There are special dining rooms, to the "cozy" balcony overlooking the huge fireplace, or the spacious Garden Room that wraps around two ancient oaks.

Cakes, Cookies & Desserts

Wynema Brown's Red Velvet Cake

W. Earl Brown

Cake:

2 c. Wesson oil
1 ½ c. sugar
2 eggs
¼ tsp. salt
1 tsp. vanilla

2 ½ c. plain flour (not self-rising)
1 c. buttermilk
2 Tbsp. cocoa
1 tsp. baking soda
1 oz. red food coloring

Cream oil and sugar. Add eggs. Beat well. Add flour and buttermilk alternately. Make paste of cocoa and red coloring. Add to mixture. Add salt, soda and vanilla. Mix well. Bake 25 minutes in 350° oven in buttered and floured long cake pan. (Single layer is best for this dense, moist cake!)

Icing:

1 box sifted powdered sugar
1 stick butter, softened
1 c. chopped pecans

8 oz. cream cheese, softened
1 tsp. vanilla

Beat everything well, except nuts. Stir in nuts and ice cooled cake.

Actor W. Earl Brown is from Murray. Best known as Dan Dority on TV's "Deadwood," he has also starred in numerous movies, including "There's Something About Mary." Said his mother's Red Velvet Cake was better than the one at Hollywood's Doughboys.

Bull Nelson Rum Cake

Camp Nelson Heritage Park

1 c. nuts (half walnuts and half pecans), chopped and toasted
1 (3 oz.) pkg. instant vanilla pudding

½ c. cold water
½ c. rum
1 pkg. yellow cake mix
½ c. oil
4 eggs

Sprinkle nuts on bottom of greased Bundt pan. Mix pudding, water, rum, cake mix and oil. Beat in eggs, one at a time. Pour batter into pan and bake one hour at 325°. Let cool briefly and then remove cake from pan. Poke holes all over with small fork.

Glaze:

¼ c. melted butter   ⅓ c. rum
½ c. sugar

Mix well and pour slowly over hot cake.

Camp Nelson is located near Nicholasville. It was the site of the 4,000 acre Union Armies Civil War Fortification and was named in honor of the late Major General William "Bull" Nelson. This cake is served at teas in the restored Civil War era "White House."

Pig-Poke Buttermilk Pie
Coffee Tree Cabin

4 eggs   1 stick melted margarine
2 c. sugar   1 tsp. vanilla
½ tsp. salt   1 c. buttermilk

Beat eggs. Add sugar and beat. Add the melted margarine and beat. Mix well. Add buttermilk and pour into unbaked pastry shell. Bake at 325° for 35 to 40 minutes until lightly brown. Note: This makes 2 pies. Serve with ice cream or Cool Whip. A wonderful and easy pie to make.

Coffee Tree Cabin Bed and Breakfast is a 4-room, elegant log home on 41 acres in Bardstown. It has large porches, cobblestone fireplace, gardens, private lake, hiking and fishing, evening desserts and full breakfasts, decorated with antiques. Just minutes from "My Old Kentucky Home."

Achy Breaky Cake
Billy Ray and Miley Cyrus

1 yellow cake mix   1 (16 oz.) Cool Whip
1 can Borden's condensed   2 large Butterfinger bars,
  milk   crushed
1 small squeeze bottle
  Smucker's or Hershey's
  caramel sauce

Bake cake according to package directions in 9 x 13-inch pan. When cooled, poke numerous holes in cake with straw. Combine

Cakes, Cookies & Desserts

milk and sauce until smooth and pour over cooled cake. Ice cake with Cool Whip. Sprinkle crushed Butterfingers over top just before serving. Keep refrigerated.

Billy Ray Cyrus, Flatwood, and his daughter Miley star in the television show Hannah Montana and he also is host of "Nashville Star." This is one of his family's favorite recipes. The Cyrus family has had a phenomenal career in film, television and the music world.

Mudbog Pie
Daniel Boone National Forest Trailblazers

16 Oreo cookies
½ c. crushed pecans
¼ c. melted butter

1 ½ pt. vanilla or coffee ice cream
fudge sauce (I use Hershey's)

Crush Oreo cookies. Mix with melted butter. Line pie pan. Freeze until firm. Soften ice cream. Place in shell; freeze until firm. Sprinkle with crushed pecans. Spread fudge sauce over all and freeze until firm. When serving, garnish with whipped cream.

Daniel Boone National Forest with its sandstone cliffs is located in eastern Kentucky and encompasses over 707,000 acres. Daniel Boone Trailblazers partner with the U.S. Forest Service in efforts of safeguarding safe, recreational riding in National Parks and Forest.

Floating Fruit Cobbler
Dippin' Dots Ice Cream

1 c. sugar
1 c. self-rising flour
1 c. whole milk

1 stick butter
1 egg

Mix all the ingredients together; add approximately 2 ½ cups of sweetened fruit (blackberries and peaches are my personal favorite), and bake at 350° until slightly brown. Cool and serve with high quality ice cream.

Dippin' Dots Ice Cream's International Headquarters is in Paducah. CEO Curt Jones shared this recipe given to him by Grace Jones, a dear friend and neighbor of his mother. This freeze-dried ice cream is sold in all 50 states and internationally.

Jim Driver's Fruit Cream Cheese Pie

Jim Driver

Use a 9-inch pre-baked pie crust.

1 pkg. cream cheese
1 can Eagle Brand milk

your choice fresh or frozen
well-drained fruit *

*Strawberries, blueberries, bananas, pineapple chunks, raspberries, mandarin oranges, to name a few; mix fruits if you like; base mix plus fruit can make two pies; note: bananas will darken within 24 hours.

Blend cream cheese and Eagle Brand milk to a creamy texture. Fold in gently the fruit. Fill pie shells to the top; refrigerate overnight, then top off with your choice of whipped cream topping.

Variations:

Lemon Cream Pie: Fold in 1 to 2 tablespoons of lemon juice plus garnish with shredded lemon zest.

Lemon-Lime Cream Pie: Fold in 1 tablespoon lemon juice plus 1 tablespoon lime juice plus garnish with lime zest.

Creme de Coco Pie: Fold in 2 tablespoons of creme de coconut and blend to creamy for a hint of coconut flavor, then sprinkle shredded coconut lightly over the top.

This recipe was submitted in loving memory of Paducah Restaurateur Jim Driver by his son Mike Driver. He owned Drive-R-In 1952-53 era, Hickory House, Cape Codder Seafood, and Granny's Country Cookin', all in Paducah, Kentucky.

Cappuccino Brownies

Explorium of Lexington

**2 lb. semi-sweet chocolate
   chips**
½ c. instant coffee granules
1 c. unsalted butter, softened
1 c. white sugar
1 c. brown sugar

8 eggs
3 Tbsp. vanilla extract
1 tsp. ground cinnamon
1 tsp. salt
2 c. all-purpose flour

Preheat the oven to 375°F (190°C). Grease and flour four 8 x 8-inch baking pans. Place the chocolate chips and the coffee

Cakes, Cookies & Desserts

granules in a double boiler over simmering water. Cook over medium heat, stirring occasionally, until melted and smooth. Set aside.

In a large bowl, cream the butter and sugar together until light and fluffy. Beat in the eggs two at a time, mixing well after each addition. Stir in vanilla and salt, and then mix in the melted chocolate. Mix in flour until just blended. Divide the batter equally into the prepared pans, and spread smooth. Bake for 35 minutes in preheated oven, or until the edges pull from the sides of the pans. Cool on a wire rack. Melt cream cheese frosting in the microwave for 1 minute. Pour over the cold brownies. Sprinkle with additional coffee granules and cinnamon.

Located in the heart of the Horse Capital of the World, Explorium of Lexington is one of the oldest children's museums in the United States. With 9 discovery zones filled with interactive exhibits, kids of all ages have experiences that can last a lifetime.

Coconut Bread

Fleming County

(Makes 1 loaf. Serve toasted or warm.)

½ c. butter, softened
1 c. white sugar
2 eggs
2 tsp. coconut extract
1 c. fancy shredded coconut

1 c. sour cream
2 c. all-purpose flour
1 tsp. baking soda
1 tsp. baking powder

Cream together butter and sugar. Beat in eggs and extract, then the sour cream. Add the coconut. Fold in the flour, baking powder and soda. Turn into lightly greased loaf pan and bake at 350° for about 45 minutes or until done. Makes 1 loaf, 10 slices.

Fleming County is located northeast of Lexington. Known as the Covered Bridge Capital of Kentucky, it was also the home of Franklin Sousley (born in Hilltop). He was 1 of 6 Marines in Joe Rosenthal's famous photograph of raising the flag on Iwo Jima in World War II.

Dutch Chocolate Cake

Ernie Fletcher

1 c. sifted cocoa
2 c. boiling water
2 c. sifted flour
¾ tsp. salt
1 c. butter, softened

4 eggs
2 tsp. baking soda
½ tsp. baking powder
2 ½ c. sugar
1 ½ tsp. vanilla

Mix first 2 ingredients well and cool completely.

Preheat oven to 350°. Sift together dry ingredients. Beat together butter, sugar, eggs and vanilla until light and fluffy (5 minutes at high speed). At low speed, beat in dry ingredients alternately with cocoa mixture. Divide evenly into three 9-inch pans. Bake 30 minutes or until toothpick comes out clean; cool completely, fill and frost.

Filling:

1 c. butter	1 c. powdered sugar
½ c. sifted cocoa	2 eggs

Beat all ingredients together until light and smooth; fill between cake layers when cooled.

Frosting:

2 c. heavy whipping cream	¾ c. sifted powdered sugar
1 tsp. vanilla	

Combine all ingredients; beat until stiff enough to spread. Frost sides and top of filled cake; refrigerate at least one hour before serving. Keep refrigerated. Flavor improved if allowed to sit for one day.

Ernie Fletcher has served as both Governor and 6th U.S. Congressional District Representative (3 terms). He received a B.S. degree from the University of Kentucky College of Engineering and an MD degree from the University of Kentucky College of Medicine.

❧ *Pavlova* ❧

Ford Motor Company

6 egg whites	1 ½ tsp. vanilla essence
2 c. (12 oz.) very fine sugar	1 pt. strawberries
1 ½ tsp. vinegar	½ pt. cream, whipped

Beat egg whites at full speed until they stand in peaks. Sift sugar and gradually add 1 tablespoon at a time, beating at high speed only until all sugar has been added. Lastly fold in vinegar and vanilla essence.

Draw a 7-inch circle on greased paper or aluminum foil and put on oven slide (baking sheet). Heap egg white mixture on the circle on paper. Mold up the sides with a spatula and make a slight depression on top to form a well-shaped meringue when cooked. Cook for 1 ½ hours in a 200° oven (which has been preheated to

375° prior to putting Pavlova in). After 1 ½ hours, turn off oven and leave Pavlova in until it has cooled.

When cool, spoon whipped cream high in the center. Decorate with fruit.

Ford Motor Company is celebrating its 100th Anniversary this year. John Crew is the Plant Manager of Ford Motor Co. Truck Plant in Louisville, Kentucky, where heavy duty trucks and F series trucks are produced. John and his wife Anne are from Australia.

White Chocolate Bread Pudding With Maker's Mark Bourbon Sauce

Good Ol' Days

(12 Servings)

day-old French bread	1 stick butter
4 c. heavy cream	6 oz. Snicker's butterscotch
4 beaten eggs	topping
1 c. sugar	6 oz. crushed pineapple
2 tsp. vanilla extract	6 oz. golden raisins
8 oz. white chocolate, melted	1 Tbsp. cinnamon

Cover pan with bite size pieces of bread. Mix ingredients well, allowing liquid to soak into bread. Bake at 325° with cover for 25 minutes, then uncover and continue to bake for 15 minutes or until having a light toasted finish. Cover with Maker's Mark Bourbon Sauce.

Maker's Mark Bourbon Sauce:

½ c. bourbon	½ c. heavy cream
½ c. melted butter	½ c. sugar

Heat until sugar comes to boil.

Good Ol Days in Midway is known for its fine food, bluegrass music and farm-fresh produce. This recipe was developed by the restaurant as a signature dessert for the Kentucky Cooperage hosting a private catering for VIP Bourbon Distillers at the annual Bourbon Festival.

Pumpkin Gooey Butter Cake

Grand Rivers Hunters Moon Festival

Cake:

1 box yellow cake mix
1 stick butter, softened

1 egg
dash pumpkin pie spice

Filling:

1 pkg. cream cheese,
  softened
1 (15 oz.) can pumpkin
3 eggs
2 tsp. vanilla

1 stick butter, melted
2 c. powdered sugar
1 Tbsp. pumpkin pie spice
Cool Whip or whipped
  cream (garnish)

Preheat oven to 350°. Combine cake mix, butter, spice and egg with mixer. Pat into a greased 9 x 13 pan. Set aside.

In a large bowl, beat cream cheese and pumpkin with mixer until smooth. Add eggs, vanilla, butter, sugar and spices gradually. Mix well. Pour mixture over cake batter and bake for 40 minutes being careful not to overbake. Should be slightly gooey in center. Allow to cool and serve with a dollop of whipped cream.

2008 marks the 30th anniversary of the famous Grand Rivers, Kentucky Hunters Moon Festival (15,000 attending). It includes children's activities, street parade, food vendors, artisan, craft and antique vendors. One of the favorite festival activities is an old fashion cakewalk.

Chewy Chocolate Peanut Butter Cookies

T.L. Gray

1 ¼ c. butter or margarine,
  softened
2 c. sugar
2 eggs
2 tsp. vanilla extract
¾ c. Hershey's Cocoa

1 tsp. baking soda
½ tsp. salt
1 c. (12 oz. pkg.) peanut
  butter chips and 1 c.
  semi-sweet chocolate chips

Preheat oven to 350°. In large mixer bowl, cream butter and sugar until light and fluffy. Add eggs and vanilla; beat well. Combine flour, cocoa, baking soda and salt and gradually blend into

Cakes, Cookies & Desserts

creamed mixture. Lastly, stir in peanut butter and chocolate chips. Drop by teaspoonfuls onto ungreased cookie sheet. Bake 8 to 9 minutes. (Do not overbake.) Cookies will be soft. They will puff up while baking, then flatten out while cooling. Cool slightly; remove to wire rack. Let cool completely. Makes approximately 4 ½ dozen chewy cookies.

Kentucky native and award-winning author T.L. Gray grew up reading Harlequin Romances, Nancy Drew and The Hardy Boys. Naturally, her favorite books are ones where romance and mystery are entwined. She's a member of Romance Writer's of America.

Grandmother's Lemon Meringue Pie

D.W. Griffith

Pie Crust:

3 c. premium flour	1 level tsp. salt
½ level tsp. baking powder	¾ c. lard

Sift together dry ingredients; add a pinch of sugar, and work in lard with knife, then moisten with water. Place dough on a board dusted with flour and roll flat, then put in pie pan. Trim edge and punch holes in bottom and sides to keep it from rising. Bake until done (about 15 minutes at 350°). Allow to cool.

Lemon Filling:

¾ c. sugar	3 Tbsp. lemon juice
¾ c. boiling water	1 tsp. butter
1 Tbsp. flour	grated rind of 1 lemon
2 egg yolks	

Mix flour and sugar, adding boiling water constantly. Cook for two minutes before adding butter, egg yolks, rind and juice. Pour into pie crust and add meringue. Return to oven and bake until meringue is tinged a soft brown.

Meringue:

2 egg whites	1 tsp. lemon juice or ¼ tsp.
1 tsp. water	vanilla extract
2 Tbsp. powdered sugar	

Beat egg whites and water until stiff. Gradually add powdered sugar. Continue whipping and add lemon juice or vanilla extract.

Shane Woodson, Louisville, has starred in over 20 movies and TV. Joseph Woodson Oglesby, Louisville, is a playwright, novelist and journalist and nominated for 2 Pulitzer prizes. Recipe from his book on their uncle, producer/director and Crestwood native D.W. Griffith.

Pudding Cake

Suzanne Gutierrez

Crust:

1 ½ c. flour
1 c. chopped pecans

1 ½ sticks butter or
  margarine

Mix together and press in bottom of greased 9 x 13 pan. Bake approximately 20 minutes at 375°. Watch closely not to burn. Let cool completely.

Filling #1:

1 (8 oz.) tub soft cream
  cheese
1 c. powdered sugar

1 c. Cool Whip (12 oz.
  container)

Mix/beat until fluffy. Spread on cooled crust. Let it sit in refrigerator while preparing the other filling.

Filling #2:

2 small pkg. instant pudding   3 c. milk

Follow directions of packages, but use a total of 3 cups of milk. Let sit until firm. Spread on top of first filling.

Filling #3:

Spread the rest of the Cool Whip on top. Refrigerate.

Actress and casting director Suzanne Gutierrez has starred in film, television, theatre and comedy improv. She was born in Milwaukee, Wisconsin. Her Kentucky connection: She was a scholarship gymnast for the University of Kentucky in Lexington.

Cakes, Cookies & Desserts

Fruit Cocktail Cake

Hillcrest Collectibles

1 ½ c. sugar	½ c. brown sugar, packed
¼ tsp. salt	2 c. flour
2 tsp. soda	2 eggs
1 can fruit cocktail	1 tsp. vanilla
½ c. pecans	½ c. coconut

Mix sugar, salt, soda, flour and egg. Add fruit and vanilla. Stir well; pour in a greased loaf pan. Sprinkle top with brown sugar, pecans and coconut. Bake at 350° for 40 to 50 minutes.

Topping:

1 stick butter	¾ c. condensed milk
1 c. sugar	1 tsp. vanilla

Bring to boil. Pour over cake while hot.

Karen O'Nan Martin has been weaving for 20 years. She owns Hillcrest Collectibles, a retail/wholesale basket studio. Located in rural Henderson, Kentucky, her custom-made baskets are sold in Kentucky state parks, craft shops and galleries throughout the United States.

Emma's Pumpkin Cheesecake

Historic Crescent-Hill 4th of July Celebration

Crust:

1 ½ c. gingersnap crumbs	4 to 6 Tbsp. melted butter
¾ c. chopped pecans or walnuts	

Combine and press into greased spring-form pan. Chill 30 minutes.

Filling:

1 ½ lb. cream cheese (room temperature)	½ tsp. cloves
½ c. white sugar	¼ tsp. nutmeg
½ c. brown sugar, lightly packed	1 (15 oz.) can pumpkin (not pie filling)
1 tsp. cinnamon	5 eggs
¾ tsp. ginger	½ c. heavy cream

Beat cheese until smooth. Beat in sugars and spices until light and fluffy (4 minutes). Beat in pumpkin, then eggs one by one, then cream. Scrape into pan. Cover bottom of spring-form pan with foil and place in roasting pan. Bake at 350° for 55 to 70 minutes until center does not jiggle when pan is touched. Do not underbake. Turn off oven but leave cake in with door propped open for 1 hour. Then remove and let cool. Best eaten the next day.

This celebration is held on July 4th at the historic Peterson-Dumesnil House, which was built in 1869. Historic Crescent-Hill, founded in the 1850's, is known for its unique restaurants, shops and historic homes. It is located 4 miles east of downtown Louisville.

Ice House Icebox Cookies

Ice House Gallery

2 c. brown sugar	1 tsp. cream of tartar
½ c. butter	3 c. unsifted flour
2 unbeaten eggs	1 tsp. vanilla
1 tsp. soda	½ c. chopped pecans

Cream butter and sugar, then add eggs, one at a time. Add remaining ingredients. Form into two rolls; wrap in wax paper and chill overnight. Slice and bake in a 350° oven for 10 minutes.

The Mayfield/Graves County Art Guild in Mayfield is located in the historic 3,200 square foot Ice House. The gallery, workshop and weaving area provide exhibit space and educational opportunities for local and regional artists and students. They also sponsor Gourd Patch Festival.

Woodford Pudding

Inn at Woodhaven

The Pudding:

1 c. butter (melt and cool)	2 c. sugar
6 eggs	2 c. all-purpose flour
1 c. buttermilk	2 tsp. baking soda
2 c. Kentucky Windstone Farm blackberry jam (we use seedless)	2 tsp. cinnamon

Cakes, Cookies & Desserts

The Sauce:

We double this cause it is so good!

1 c. light brown sugar	glug glug of Kentucky
1 c. heavy cream	bourbon (about ¼ c.)
1 stick butter	

Heat oven to 350°. Mix butter, eggs and buttermilk, then stir in jam. Combine dry ingredients and add to liquid. Mix until creamy. Spray a 9 x 13-inch pan or a large Bundt pan with vegetable oil. Bake for 45 minutes or until pudding is just set.

In saucepan, combine brown sugar and cream and bring to a boil, stirring constantly. Add butter and whisk until blended. Add bourbon. Pour over warm cake and set some aside for extra drizzling.

Serves 10 to 12.

The Inn at Woodhaven Bed and Breakfast located in Louisville is a historic gothic revival mansion built in 1853. The home and carriage house were built on a 500-acre plantation by Theodore Brown. Marsha Burton is the owner and innkeeper.

❦ *Picker's Pay-Off* ❦
International Bluegrass Music Museum

4 Tbsp. flour	½ stick butter
1 c. sugar	1 tsp. vanilla flavoring
2 c. milk	4 bananas
1 egg, beaten	½ box vanilla wafers

In large bowl, slice bananas into ½-inch slices. Add vanilla wafers. Combine flour, sugar, milk and beaten egg into saucepan and cook until it thickens. Add butter and vanilla and stir until melted. Pour over bananas and wafers and stir lightly. Top with nondairy whipped topping or whipped cream.

International Bluegrass Music Museum, Owensboro, is located in a 32,000 square foot facility. It is dedicated to preserving and promoting bluegrass history, music and artifacts. Famous for their Bill Monroe-style mandolin camps that draws national and international musicians.

S'mores Brownies

Terry Mike Jeffrey

10 whole graham crackers	2 c. miniature marshmallows
1 pkg. fudge brownie mix	1 c. chocolate chips

Arrange crackers in a single layer in a greased pan (long). Prepare brownie mix and spread over crackers. Bake at 350° for 30 minutes. Sprinkle with marshmallows and chocolate chips. Bake 5 minutes longer until marshmallows are golden.

Terry Mike Jeffrey is a singer and Emmy-nominated songwriter from Paducah. He was the musical director and star of the Broadway musical "Elvis: An American Musical," performed at the Elvis Presley 20th and 25th Anniversary with the Jordanaires and Elvis' TCB Band.

Mrs. Joy's Jelly Cookies

Annie Fellows Johnston

1 c. sugar	2 c. flour
1 c. butter	2 tsp. baking powder
3 egg whites	¾ c. milk

Mix ingredients; drop cookie batter by teaspoonful on greased baking sheet. Bake at 350°. When cookies are done and still warm, spread small amount of favorite jelly on one cookie and place other cookie on top to make a sandwich. Sprinkle with powdered sugar while warm.

Annie Fellows Johnston (Peewee Valley), a celebrated author of children's and juvenile fiction, wrote The Little Colonel Series and The Little Colonel movie (1935), starring Shirley Temple. Special thanks to Oldham Co. Historical Society for use of recipe.

Berry Delight Cake

Jubilee in the Breaks Concerts

1 box white cake mix	1 (16 oz.) jar blackberry
½ c. oil	preserves (with seeds are
½ c. water	the best)
	3 egg whites
	1 can fluffy white cake icing

Mix cake mix, egg whites, oil and water together. Separate into 3 (9-inch) round cake pans. Bake at 350° for 30 minutes or until a toothpick comes out clean. Let cool. Place first layer of cake on cake plate and spread with preserves. Do the same with the second layer. Put a good amount of preserves between the 2 layers. Spread cake icing on top and sides of cake. This cake is better if it sits for a day or 2 so that the preserves can soak into the cake. It's so delicious!

Jubilee in the Breaks is a 3-day gospel event held Memorial Day weekend at the Breaks Interstate Park on the Kentucky/Virginia border. It draws numerous Kentucky gospel groups and is sponsored by Hometown Gospel Promotion of Pikeville, Kentucky.

Museum Winner's Pie

Kentucky Derby Museum

1 stick butter	2 Tbsp. Kentucky bourbon
1 c. sugar	(or 1 tsp. vanilla)
2 eggs, beaten	1 c. chocolate chips
½ c. flour	1 c. chopped pecans
pinch of salt	1 (9-inch) pie shell, partially baked

Preheat oven to 350°. Cream butter and sugar. Add beaten eggs, flour, salt and Kentucky bourbon (or vanilla). Add chocolate chips and nuts. Stir well. Pour into partially baked pie shell and bake for 30 minutes or until center is set. Serve with whipped cream or vanilla ice cream. Serves 6 to 8.

At historic Churchill Downs, the Kentucky Derby Museum is one of Kentucky's premier cultural attractions that capture the pride, tradition and excitement of "the greatest 2 minutes in sports." It also expands awareness, appreciation and understanding of the Kentucky Derby and Thoroughbred racing.

Ashley's Four-Layered Dessert

Ashley Judd

First Layer:

1 stick or ½ c. butter	¾ c. pecans
1 c. all-purpose flour	

Preheat oven to 350°. Line an 8 x 8 x 2-inch pan with aluminum foil. Coat lightly with nonstick cooking spray. Bake 10 minutes and allow cooling.

Make first layer and press into pan.

Second Layer:

1/3 c. heavy cream or 1 c. nondairy whipped topping

1 (8 oz.) pkg. cream cheese (at room temperature)
1 c. confectioners sugar

Cream sugar and cream cheese. Fold in whipped topping. Place on top of first layer.

Third Layer:

1 c. sugar
1/3 c. unsweetened cocoa powder
3 Tbsp. all-purpose flour
2 Tbsp. cornstarch

pinch of salt
3 large egg yolks
2 c. milk
2 Tbsp. butter or margarine

Mix all ingredients. Bring to boil over low heat until thickens. Allow cooling. Place on top of second layer.

Top with 2 cups nondairy whipped topping and 1/3 cup nuts.

An 8th generation Eastern Kentuckian, Ashley Judd graduated from U.K.. She starred in The Divine Secrets of the Ya-Ya Sisterhood (directed by Paducah native Callie Khouri), De-lovely, and Catwoman. She is married to Indy 500 race winner Dario Franchitti.

The Perfect Bar

Judeen's Art Gallery

2 sticks softened butter
1 c. firmly packed brown sugar
2 tsp. vanilla
dash of salt

2 c. flour
6 oz. semi-sweet chocolate chips
1 c. chopped walnuts

(I prefer using about 1/4 cup chocolate chips and adding 1/2 cup of dried diced pineapple, 1/2 cup dried cranberries, 1 cup dried diced apricots and 1/2 cup coconut.)

Preheat oven to 350°. Beat butter, sugar, vanilla and salt until well blended. Add flour and mix well. Stir in chocolate and walnuts (and other goodies). Press mixture into ungreased 15 x 10 x

Cakes, Cookies & Desserts

1-inch baking pan. Bake 25 to 30 minutes until lightly browned or longer. Cut into 40 bars while warm.

Judeen's Art Studio and Gallery features contemporary original works by artist/owner Judeen Theis as well as changing exhibits of national artists, photographers and quilters. The studio is part of the nationally acclaimed Paducah Lowertown Art District.

🍃 *Keeneland Bread Pudding* 🍃
and Bourbon Sauce

Keeneland

1 Tbsp. butter, softened
2 c. sugar
¼ tsp. salt
1 Tbsp. cinnamon
6 c. whole milk
8 large eggs, beaten

1 Tbsp. vanilla
12 c. densely packed and
   cubed day-old French
   bread, crust removed
1 c. golden raisins

Bourbon Sauce:

1 lb. unsalted butter
2 lb. powdered
   (confectioners) sugar

1 c. bourbon

Preheat oven to 325°. Generously grease 3-quart ovenproof dish with softened butter. In large bowl, combine sugar, salt and cinnamon. Whisk milk into dry ingredients until sugar is dissolved. Add eggs and vanilla, stirring well to incorporate all ingredients. Soak bread in mixture for half hour. Pour into buttered ovenproof dish. Sprinkle raisins on top and press into bread. Bake at 325° for 1 hour and 15 minutes or until firm to touch and golden brown.

For sauce, soften butter to room temperature and add powdered sugar. Beat with electric mixer until combined. Whip bourbon into mix until it achieves frosting consistency. Ladle sauce over hot bread pudding. Sauce will "melt" on its own.

Keeneland (Lexington), founded in 1934, is a thoroughbred horse racing facility known for the Bluegrass Stakes. Their thoroughbred auction sales complex attracts buyers worldwide. The racing scenes of the 2003 movie Seabiscuit were shot at Keeneland.

Australian Christmas Pudding

Kentucky Down Under

½ lb. flour
½ lb. fresh breadcrumbs
1 lb. butter
1 lb. brown sugar
pinch of salt
½ lb. raisins
½ lb. sultanas (small raisins)
½ lb. citrus peel
½ lb. maraschino cherries
¼ lb. figs and dates
9 eggs
1 gill or more of brandy (gill equals ¼ pt.)
1 tsp. nutmeg
1 tsp. mixed spice
½ tsp. bicarbonate of soda (baking soda)
½ c. blanched almonds

Prepare fruit and combine in a large bowl. Cream butter, sugar, eggs and brandy. Stir in fruit; add bread crumbs and other dry ingredients and mix well. Grease a large basin and line with wax paper, leaving 1 ½ inches from the top. Pour pudding into basin and cover top with more wax paper and foil. Cook in moderate oven for 6 hours. Cool and store in cool dry place for 3 weeks. Once each week, pour ½ gill (¼ pint) of brandy over pudding. On day to be used, cook for another 3 hours in moderate oven.

Kentucky Down Under is an interactive Australian Animal Park in Horse Cave, Kentucky. Hop with our kangaroos in the outback, meet our lizards in the Discovery Area, hand-feed our birds in the aviary, learn about Australian culture in the Coroboree, and tour the cave. Owner, Judy Austin, is from Australia and this is her mother's recipe.

Transparent Pie A La Bush

Kentucky Gateway Museum Center

1 stick butter, softened
1 ½ c. sugar
½ pt. whipping cream
1 tsp. (plus a "dab") vanilla
4 egg yolks

Preheat oven to 350°.
Mix sugar and butter; beat until creamy. Add about 1 tablespoon of flour to sugar/butter mixture, then add vanilla and egg yolks. Beat until creamy. Add cream at lower blender speed. Pour into 9-inch piecrust and bake about 45 minutes; watch closely!

Cakes, Cookies & Desserts

When it begins to brown, turn down to 300°, about 20 minutes at 350° and 25 minutes at 300°.

Established in 1878, Kentucky Gateway Museum, Maysville, tells the story of explorers, movie stars, artists, pioneers, and slaves that passed through this part of Kentucky or called it home. It also has one of the highest quality private miniature collections in the country.

🌿 *Basic Pound Cake* 🌿
Kentucky High School Invitational Rodeo

1 lb. butter (room temperature)	10 large eggs
3 ⅓ c. granulated sugar	4 c. all-purpose flour
	2 tsp. vanilla

Cream together butter (room temperature) and sugar. Beat in eggs one at a time with mixer on high. Turn mixer speed on low and slowly add flour, then vanilla. Pour into 10-inch tube pan and bake in preheated oven at 325° for one hour. Enjoy this cake sprinkled with powdered sugar, with fresh fruit, slices toasted and spread with jelly or preserves, with ice cream or whipped cream, or just plain.

Established in 1991, the Rodeo Scholarships, Inc. hosts the Kentucky High School Invitational Rodeo in the covered arena of the Kentucky Horse Park each Memorial Day weekend. This rodeo is the state finals and main provider of scholarships for rodeo youth throughout the state. It attracts numerous leaders in the equestrian industry and celebrities, including former Kentucky Derby winning jockeys.

🌿 *Strawberry Shortcake Swirls* 🌿
Kentucky Poultry Producers

3 c. all-purpose flour, sifted	3 pt. strawberries
4 ¼ tsp. baking powder	1 c. sugar
1 ½ tsp. salt	8 oz. whipping cream
5 Tbsp. sugar	8 oz. Cool Whip
¾ c. shortening	½ stick butter
4 eggs, beaten	vegetable spray
½ c. milk	

Preheat oven to 450°. Sift together flour, baking powder, salt and 5 tablespoons sugar. Cut in shortening until mixture is consistency of coarse cornmeal. Combine eggs and milk and stir quickly into dry ingredients. Turn onto a floured board, and roll into an 8 x 21-inch rectangle. Brush well with melted butter and roll as for jelly roll. Cut into 1-inch slices. Lay cut side up on greased baking pan. Brush tops with whipping cream and bake in oven for 15 minutes. Meanwhile, wash, hull and cut strawberries in halves. Add remaining 1 cup sugar and chill. Spoon over hot pinwheels and serve with Cool Whip.

Poultry farming and related agribusiness (eggs) is a thriving industry in Kentucky, which ranks 10th in the nation in terms of broiler production. Kentucky's poultry business is a $680 million industry, which is about 28% of what livestock cash receipts bring to the state.

❧ *Creamy Wheat Cake* ❧

Lanette Freitag
LanMark Farm

1 c. butter	4 tsp. baking flour
1 c. sugar	¾ tsp. salt
¾ c. Splenda	1 ¼ c. milk
6 eggs	1 tsp. vanilla
3 c. whole-wheat flour (stone ground)	½ c. walnuts

Cream butter. Gradually add sugar. Beat until fluffy. Add eggs two at a time, beating after each. Add flour. Combine rest of the ingredients. Beat until smooth. Bake in 2 greased and lightly floured 9 x 1 ½-inch round pans in moderate oven (350°) for 30 to 35 minutes or until cake tests done. Fill and frost cooled layers with butter type frosting.

Lanmark Farms located in Sharpsburg is a working sheep farm that has been supporting families since 1824 and home to Kentucky Wool Society. They offer tours, workshops and make "Kentucky Proud" products using fibers that they shear from sheep and llamas.

❧ *Lavender Rum Cake* ❧

Lavender Hills Farm

1 pkg. yellow cake mix	½ c. water
1 pkg. vanilla pudding mix	4 medium eggs
½ c. vegetable oil	½ c. pecans, chopped
½ c. rum	1 tsp. dried culinary lavender

Glaze (enough for 2 cakes):

¼ c. butter or margarine   1 c. sugar
¼ c. water   ½ c. rum

Preheat oven to 325°. Grease and flour Bundt cake pan. In a small mixing bowl, toss chopped nuts with a few lavender buds. Sprinkle nut mixture over the bottom of the pan. In large bowl, beat together cake mix, pudding, vegetable oil, rum and water. Add eggs and the remaining lavender until smooth. Do not overbeat. Pour batter over nuts. Bake for 60 minutes. The cake is done when a toothpick comes out clean. Cool down for a minute or two and then turn out onto wire rack to cool completely.

To Make the Glaze: Bring the butter, water and sugar to a boil, stirring constantly. Remove from heat and let stand for one minute. Add rum and stir. Poke holes into the cake with a skewer. Brush and spoon half the glaze over the cake.

Lavender Hills of Kentucky is a 109-acre family-owned and operated lavender farm beginning its fourth year of operation. Located in Northern Kentucky near Brooksville, it provides workshops, farm tours, gift shop and you pick opportunities.

❧ *Chocolate Cream Pie* ❧

Homer Ledford

(For 9-inch Pie)

1 ½ c. sugar   ½ tsp. salt
½ c. cocoa (or you can use 3   3 c. milk
  sq. unsweetened chocolate,   3 egg yolks
  etc.)   1 Tbsp. butter
3 Tbsp. cornstarch (that is 3   1 ½ tsp. vanilla
  Tbsp.)

Mix sugar, cornstarch and salt in saucepan. Add milk slowly. Cook over medium heat, stirring constantly until mixture thickens and boils.

Boil one minute. Stir half of hot mixture into egg yolks slowly. Then blend in rest. Boil one minute more, stirring constantly. Remove from heat and add butter and vanilla.

Pour into baked pie shell. (I use Jiffy mix for my crust or the frozen crust.)

Cover top with meringue using the egg whites after beating and adding sugar, etc.

Follow directions for baking any meringue.

Homer Ledford lives in Winchester. He is an internationally known dulcimer maker, having made over 6000 dulcimers plus many guitars, mandolins, banjos and violins. He invented the dulcitar. His handcrafted instruments are in the Smithsonian Institute.

Chocolate Chestnut Bourbon Torte With Kentucky Bourbon Cream

Lilly's Bistro

6 eggs, separated, plus 2 egg yolks
1 ½ c. sugar plus ⅓ c.
4 Tbsp. bourbon plus 2 tsp.
2 ½ c. pureed unsweetened chestnuts
¾ c. ground pecans plus pecan pieces for garnish

2 tsp. instant coffee
6 Tbsp. chilled butter, cut into pieces
1 ½ oz. bitter chocolate, chopped
¾ lb. bittersweet chocolate
3 ½ c. whipping cream
½ c. confectioners sugar

Make the Cake: Heat oven to 350°. Grease and flour two nine-inch cake pans. Beat 6 egg yolks well. Stir in 1 ½ cups sugar and 1 ½ teaspoons bourbon, then blend in 2 cups chestnut puree. Stir in ground pecans. Whip egg whites with a pinch of salt until stiff. Fold whites into batter. Divide mixture between the two cake pans and bake for 25 minutes. Cool on a cake rack, then remove from the pans.

Make the Filling: Beat the 2 egg yolks with ½ cup of sugar. Add instant coffee and 1 tablespoon hot water. Beat chilled butter into mixture, then add ½ teaspoon bourbon and stir in remaining ½ cup chestnut puree. Stir in chopped bitter chocolate. Cover bowl with plastic wrap and refrigerate.

Melt bittersweet chocolate with heavy cream over low heat. Stir in 2 tablespoons bourbon. Transfer to a bowl. Cover with plastic wrap and refrigerate.

To Assemble Cake: Spread the chilled chestnut filling atop one cake layer and cover with the other. Cover the torte with the chocolate icing and sprinkle with chopped pecan pieces. Chill before serving. Meanwhile, prepare a bourbon chantilly to pass at the table: Whip the 2 cups of cream to soft peaks; gradually beat in the confectioners sugar and then fold in 2 tablespoons of bourbon.

Cakes, Cookies & Desserts

Yield: 10 servings.

Lilly's Bistro is on Bardstown Rd. in Louisville. It is a favorite of the area because of its dedicated team of professionals. The owner, Cathy Cary, takes pride in using locally grown produce in her creations and even has "God bless our local farmers" on her menu.

🌿 *Joel Ray's Favorite Banana Pudding* 🌿

Lincoln Jamboree

6 eggs, separated	3 c. milk
1 ¼ c. sugar	3 Tbsp. cornstarch
dash of salt	2 tsp. vanilla
5 or 6 bananas, sliced	vanilla wafers
cream of tartar	¼ c. powdered sugar

Beat egg yolks; pour into milk. Stir in sugar and cornstarch and salt. Cook in double boiler. Stir constantly to keep from lumping. Cook until smooth and thick; remove from heat. Add vanilla. Make layer of vanilla wafers and bananas in dish, then pour in part of the custard; make another layer of wafers and bananas and custard. Beat egg whites until stiff. Add pinch of cream of tartar and powdered sugar. Spread over top. Bake in 400° oven for 5 to 7 minutes until lightly browned.

In its 54th year, the Lincoln Jamboree, Hodgenville, continues the family show tradition each Saturday night with special guests and the Lincoln Jamboree Band. Featured in the October 2005 Forbes Magazine, they refer to the Lincoln Jamboree as an immortal talent.

🌿 *Lemon Blossoms* 🌿

London Dragway

18 ½ oz. pkg. yellow cake mix	4 large eggs
3 (12 oz.) pkg. lemon instant pudding mix	¾ c. vegetable oil

Glaze:

4 c. confectioners sugar	3 Tbsp. vegetable oil
⅓ c. fresh lemon juice	3 Tbsp. water
1 lemon, zested	

Preheat oven to 350°. Spray mini muffin pans with cooking spray. Combine cake mix, pudding, eggs and oil. Blend well until smooth, about 2 minutes. Pour in muffin trays, filling them half full. Bake 12 minutes. Turn out onto tea towel.

When making glaze, sift sugar into bowl. Add lemon juice, zest, oil and 3 tablespoons water. Mix until smooth.

Dip the cupcakes while warm, covering as much as possible. Place on wire racks with wax paper underneath. Let set about 1 hour. Store in covered containers. Enjoy!

Opened in the summer of '99, London Dragway is one of the nicest drag racing facilities in the state of Kentucky. It is located in London, Kentucky on the outskirts of the Daniel Boone National Forest with a racing schedule that run March through November.

Mary Margaret's Vinegar Pie

Market House Theatre

1 c. sugar
3 heaping Tbsp. all-purpose flour
1 c. cold water
3 eggs (yolks and whites separated)

1 whole egg
2 Tbsp. butter
6 Tbsp. vinegar
1 tsp. cream of tartar
1 (9-inch) pie crust, baked

Mix sugar and flour in saucepan. Add water, egg yolks, whole egg, butter and vinegar. Cook until thick. Pour into baked 9-inch pie shell.

To Make the Meringue: Beat 3 egg whites until stiff. Add 4 tablespoons sugar and cream of tartar. Spread over pie. Brown meringue lightly in oven at a very low temperature (I use 225°).

Market House Theatre, in its 44th season, is located in Paducah. Mary Margaret Hoffman has volunteered and served as a mentor from its inception (performing there with actresses Jeri Ryan and Molly McClure). She remembers her grandmother making this pie.

Cakes, Cookies & Desserts

Sour Cream Chocolate Cake With Coconut-Pecan Frosting

William I. May, Jr.

2 c. flour	2 c. sugar
1 c. water	¾ c. dairy sour cream
¼ c. shortening	1 ¼ tsp. soda
1 tsp. salt	1 tsp. vanilla
½ tsp. baking powder	2 eggs
4 oz. melted unsweetened chocolate (cool)	

Heat oven to 350°. Grease and flour two 9-inch or three 8-inch round layer pans. Measure all ingredients into large mixer bowl. Mix ½ minute on low speed, scraping bowl constantly. Beat 3 minutes on high speed, scraping bowl occasionally. Pour into pans. Bake 30 to 35 minutes or until top springs back when touched lightly with finger. Cool. Frost.

Coconut-Pecan Frosting:

1 c. evaporated milk	1 tsp. vanilla
1 c. sugar	1 ⅓ c. flake coconut
3 slightly beaten egg yolks	1 c. chopped pecans
½ c. butter or margarine	

Combine first 5 ingredients. Cook and stir over medium heat until thickened, about 12 minutes. Add coconut and pecans. Cool until thick enough to spread; beat occasionally. Makes 2 ½ cups.

Mayor William I. May is a graduate of Frankfort High School and Kentucky State University. A Frankfort native, May took office as mayor of Kentucky's capital city on January 1, 1996. Mayor May was elected to a second term in 2000.

Fruit Nut Torte

Joan McCall

The Cake:

1 egg	1 c. flour
¾ c. granulated sugar	1 tsp. soda
1 c. fruit cocktail (juice and all)	¼ tsp. salt

Topping:

½ c. walnuts, chopped   ¼ c. brown sugar

Frosting:

¼ c. granulated sugar   ⅓ c. oleo margarine
½ c. evaporated milk   ½ tsp. vanilla extract

Beat well together egg, sugar and fruit cocktail. Stir in flour, soda and salt and mix thoroughly again. Pour into a greased 9-inch round pan.

Combine walnuts and brown sugar and sprinkle evenly over top of batter. Bake at 350° for 30 minutes. Eight minutes before cake is done, begin to prepare icing. Combine sugar, evaporated milk and oleo margarine. Bring to a boil and boil three minutes, stirring. Remove from heat. Add vanilla. Spoon hot icing over cake as it comes out of the oven. Serve with whipped cream or ice cream. Serves 8.

Joan McCall, a graduate of Berea College, is President and Director of Hollywood Writers Studio and a prolific screenwriter, actress on Broadway, in films and wrote "When I Knew Al" (the story of Al Pacino) with husband and film producer David Sheldon. She is also a religious science minister.

Cranberry Goodin Puddin

Merri Melde

1 ¾ c. fresh cranberries   ½ c. sugar
1 Tbsp. sugar   ½ c. flour
¼ c. chopped pecans   1 egg
¼ c. butter   ½ tsp. vanilla
2 Tbsp. shortening

Butter a 9-inch pie plate. Spread cranberries in plate. Sprinkle 1 tablespoon sugar and pecans over cranberries.

In medium mixing bowl, melt butter and shortening in microwave. Stir in ½ cup sugar, flour, egg and vanilla until blended. Pour batter over cranberries. Bake at 325° until lightly browned (40 to 45 minutes). Cut in wedges and serve hot or cold with dollop of whipping cream or ice cream. Serves 8. Freezes well.

Merri Melde is an award-winning equine photographer and writer featured in Texas Thoroughbred, Equus, Trail Blazer, the books Straight From the Heart, and Chicken Soup for the Horse

Lover's Soul II. Her work also includes the Keeneland Yearling Sales.

𝒫residential 𝒞hocolate 𝒯orte

Filling:

⅓ c. all-purpose flour
3 Tbsp. sugar
1 tsp. salt
1 ¾ c. milk

1 c. chocolate syrup
1 egg, lightly beaten
1 Tbsp. butter
1 tsp. vanilla extract

Batter:

½ c. butter, softened
1 ¼ c. sugar
4 eggs
1 tsp. vanilla extract
1 ¼ c. all-purpose flour

⅓ c. baking cocoa
¾ tsp. baking soda
¼ tsp. salt
1 ½ c. chocolate syrup
½ c. water

Frosting:

2 c. heavy whipping cream
¼ c. chocolate syrup

¼ tsp. vanilla extract

For filling, in a small saucepan, combine flour, sugar and salt. Stir in milk and syrup until smooth. Bring to a boil over medium heat, stirring constantly; cook and stir for 1 to 2 minutes or until thickened.

Remove from heat. Stir a small amount of hot mixture into egg; return all to the pan, stirring constantly. Bring to a gentle boil; cook and stir for 2 minutes. Remove from heat; stir in butter and vanilla. Cool to room temperature, stirring often.

In a large mixing bowl, cream butter and sugar until light and fluffy. Add eggs, one at a time, beating well after each. Stir in vanilla. Combine dry ingredients; add to creamed mixture alternately with syrup and water. Beat just until combined.

Pour into two greased and floured 9-inch round baking pans. Bake at 350° for 30 to 35 minutes or until a toothpick comes out clean. Cool for 10 minutes; remove from pans to wire racks to cool.

Cut each cake in half horizontally. Place one bottom layer on a serving plate; spread with a third of the filling. Repeat layers twice. Top with remaining cake. In a mixing bowl, beat frosting ingredients until stiff peaks form; spread or pipe over top and sides of cake. Yield: 16 servings.

Dr. Robert J. Imhoff is President of Mid-Continent University. Located in Mayfield, Mid-Continent has a four-year liberal arts program accredited by the Southern Association of Colleges and

Schools. Professional basketball player Winston Bennett is the coach there.

Fruit Cocktail Cake

Mountain Art Center

2 eggs
½ c. vegetable oil
1 ½ c. sugar
1 tsp. baking soda
¼ tsp. salt

2 c. plain flour (not
 self-rising)
1 can fruit cocktail
2 c. flaked coconut

Beat eggs. Add vegetable oil, sugar and salt and mix well. Add juice from the can of fruit cocktail (reserving the fruit for later) and stir. Add flour and baking soda, stirring again. Add the fruit cocktail and stir until well mixed. Pour into a greased and floured standard size rectangle cake pan. Sprinkle the flaked coconut on top. Bake at very low heat (275° to 300°) for about an hour.

Sauce:
1 stick (or ½ c.) butter
¾ c. sugar

½ c. evaporated milk
1 tsp. vanilla flavoring

Mix all ingredients in a saucepan, and bring to a boil over very low heat. Pour over top of cake as soon as cake is done baking (while cake is still very hot). Serve cake warm or cooled.

Pat Bradley, Director Mountain Art Center, Prestonburg, home to Kentucky Opry and U.S. 23 Talent Showcase where local performers have an opportunity to follow other U.S. 23 Kentucky folk: Billy Ray Cyrus, Judds, Ricky Skaggs, Loretta Lynn, Crystal Gayle, Tom T. Hall, Dwight Yoakam, Pattie Loveless.

Gloria Pruitt's Cake and Sauce

Murray Spring Classic and Custom Car Show

1 white cake mix (bake in sheet cake pan)

To Make Sauce:
4 Tbsp. cocoa
2 c. milk
2 Tbsp. butter
2 c. sugar

1 tsp. vanilla
⅛ tsp. salt
about 3 Tbsp. flour

Boil until somewhat thickened and let cool. Cut cake into squares and drench with chocolate sauce.

The Murray Spring Custom and Classic Car Show is held annually in Murray, Kentucky at the MSU's Regional Special Events Center. It is an open car show featuring cars, trucks and bikes. Show organizer Joe Pruitt said this was a "comfort food" made by his mother.

Yo Yo Brownies

National Quilt Museum

2 sticks butter
2 c. sugar
½ c. cocoa

1 c. self-rising flour
4 beaten eggs
1 c. nuts

Melt butter and add sugar. Add eggs and mix well. Add dry ingredients and nuts. Pour into 9 x 13-inch greased and floured pan and bake at 350° for 20 to 25 minutes. Cool, cut and sprinkle with powdered sugar. Enjoy!

National Quilt Museum and American Quilter's Magazine is a part of the American Quilter's Society headquartered in Paducah. Museum Director Jessica Byassee sent recipe from Yo Yo Quilter's Club who demonstrate quilting in the Museum's lobby.

Strawberries With Rebecca Sauce

National Society Sons of the American Revolution

2 qt. fresh strawberries
1 pt. sour cream
½ c. brown sugar
1 Tbsp. vanilla

1 Tbsp. dark rum, brandy or
bourbon (bourbon makes a
more Kentucky tasting
sauce)

Wash berries. Drain on paper towels. Place in a decorative bowl or basket. Combine sour cream, brown sugar, vanilla and rum or bourbon. Stir to mix well. Use as a dipping sauce for strawberries or spoon over any kind of fruit. Refrigerate until ready to use. Makes 3 cups.

The National Society Sons of the American Revolution Headquarters in Louisville is the leading male lineage society. A historical, educational and patriotic organization, it seeks to maintain and expand patriotism, respect for our national symbols, and the value of citizenship.

❧ *Mom's Date Nut Bars* ❧

New Coon Creek Girls

¼ c. melted butter
1 c. sugar
3 eggs, well beaten
1 c. flour

½ tsp. baking powder
dash of salt
1 c. pitted chopped dates
1 c. chopped nuts (pecans)

Mix in order given and pour into 11 x 13-inch baking dish that has been lined with wax paper. (Batter will be very thick.) Bake for 20 minutes at 350° or until delicately brown. Cut into finger-shaped pieces and roll in confectioners sugar while still warm.

New Coon Creek Girls (1979-present) and the original Coon Creek Girls (1937-1957) were formed by the late John Lair and now led by Vicki Simmons of Berea. Extraordinary in their musical talent, they were the first professional female stringband to break gender barriers in radio.

❧ *Cheesecake* ❧

Ann Northup

1 ½ lb. cream cheese
3 medium eggs
1 c. sugar

dash of salt
juice of ½ lemon

Crust:

1 ½ c. graham crackers, crushed

1 stick butter
½ c. sugar

Beat first 5 ingredients and pour into crust. Sprinkle top with nutmeg before baking. Bake 25 to 30 minutes at 375°.

Ann Northup, Louisville, represents the U.S. House of Representatives 3rd District. She said she was "honored to submit a family recipe that has been a favorite over the years with her 6 children and 10 siblings. Preparing dinner for my large family is a true joy."

Cakes, Cookies & Desserts

White Chocolate Cake

Old Kentucky Candies

4 oz. white chocolate	2 ½ c. sifted cake flour
½ c. boiling water	½ tsp. salt
1 c. butter or margarine	1 tsp. baking soda
2 c. sugar	1 c. buttermilk
4 egg yolks (unbeaten)	4 egg whites, stiffly beaten
1 tsp. vanilla	

Melt chocolate in boiling water. Cool. Cream butter and sugar until fluffy; add egg yolks, one at a time, beating well after each addition. Add melted chocolate and vanilla. Mix well. Sift flour, salt and soda together and add alternately with buttermilk to chocolate mixture. Beat well (until smooth), then fold in egg whites. Pour into three 8 or 9-inch pans lined on bottoms with paper. Bake in a 350° oven 30 to 40 minutes. Cool and ice tops of layers only.

Rich White Chocolate Frosting:

4 oz. white chocolate	2 Tbsp. hot water
2 Tbsp. butter	1 egg yolk
¾ c. confectioners sugar	½ tsp. vanilla

Melt chocolate and blend in sugar, salt and hot water. Add egg yolk and beat well. Add butter, 1 tablespoon at a time, beating thoroughly after each addition. Stir in vanilla. Makes about ¾ cup or enough to frost tops of layers.

Old Kentucky Candies, Lexington, is home of Old Kentucky Bourbon Chocolates, Old Kentucky Derby Mints, Chocolate Thoroughbreds, and The Colonel's favorite (Old Fashion Pulled Creams). They have been a Kentucky tradition for over 30 years.

Poppy Seed Cake

Bob Pilkington

Cake:

1 ½ c. sugar	2 tsp. baking powder
⅔ c. butter	1 c. milk
4 egg whites	1 c. poppy seeds
2 c. flour	

Filling:

1 c. milk	2 Tbsp. sugar
4 egg yolks	½ tsp. vanilla
1 tsp. cornstarch	

Icing:

2 ½ c. light brown sugar	1 Tbsp. butter
1 ¼ c. cream/evaporated milk	1 tsp. vanilla

Cake: Cream butter and sugar. Add lightly beaten egg whites. Mix flour and baking powder. Add milk mixed in alternately, dry/wet. Mix in poppy seeds.

Bake at 350° until done. Layers (if desired) for filling.

Filling: Mix all ingredients except vanilla in saucepan. Boil slowly until thick. Stir in vanilla. Spread evenly on cake layers.

Icing: Cook brown sugar with cream/evaporated milk until it forms a soft ball in cold water. Add butter and vanilla. Remove from heat and beat until RIGHT CONSISTENCY TO SPREAD!

Bob Pilkington of Louisville is a freelance producer and director of television, film and video projects and a researcher at Locust Grove. This is his all-time favorite recipe, as made by my late wife, whom he was married to for over 40 years.

❦ *Southern Pecan Bars* ❦

Jeff Rogers Photography, Inc.

Crust:

1 ⅓ c. sifted all-purpose flour	⅓ c. butter or margarine, softened
½ tsp. baking powder	½ c. firmly packed pecans

Sift together flour and baking powder; set aside. Cream butter and sugar together in a large mixing bowl. Add dry ingredients; mix with a pastry blender until particles are fine. Stir in pecans, mixing well. Pat dough into the bottom of a well-greased 13 x 9-inch baking pan. Bake at 350° for 10 minutes; let cool.

Pecan Topping:

2 eggs	½ tsp. salt
¼ c. firmly packed brown sugar	1 tsp. vanilla extract
3 Tbsp. all-purpose flour	¾ c. coarsely chopped pecans
¾ c. dark Karo syrup	30 pecan halves

Beat eggs until foamy in a small mixing bowl. Add corn syrup, flour, salt and vanilla; mix well. Add chopped pecans, stirring well. Pour topping over cooled crust. Bake at 350° for 8 minutes. Remove from oven; arrange pecan halves evenly over top. Bake 25 minutes or until done. Let cool in pan; cut in bars. Yield: 30 scrumptious bars.

Jeff Rogers has been a full time professional photographer since 1988. Working out of Lexington, Kentucky, his commercial and stock photography is regularly seen in publications that go around the globe. His work is often associated with the Thoroughbred Industry.

❧ *Mom's Blackberry Cobbler* ❧
Phil Roof

1 qt. fresh or canned blackberries	**sugar**
cornstarch	**prepared pie crust**

Sweeten blackberries to taste and cook on top of stove. Thicken with cornstarch.

For cobbler, sprinkle sugar on top of prepared pie crust and bake according to directions. Crumble baked piecrust in individual bowls and pour desired amount of cooked berries on top of crumbled crust. Top with vanilla ice cream. DELICIOUS.

Phil Roof, Paducah, played for the Oakland A's and Minnesota Twins and is one of several pro players from Paducah, including brother Gene Roof (St. Louis), Steve Finely (Arizona) and Terry Shumpert (Colorado). He is coach for Edmonton Trappers, Triple A affiliate of the Minnesota Twins.

❧ *Blue Monday Cream Pie* ❧
Ruth Hunt Candy

6 (1 oz.) Blue Monday candy bars	**16 oz. heavy cream, whipped Cool Whip**
24 large marshmallows	**1 chocolate graham cracker crust**
½ c. milk	

Coarsely chop 5 Blue Mondays; set aside.

In a 2-quart saucepan, over medium heat, stir marshmallows and milk until melted and smooth. Cool completely. Measure out 2 cups of whipped cream and fold into cooled marshmallow mixture. Fold in coarse Blue Mondays. Spoon into graham cracker crust pie shell; chill 4 hours or until firm.

To serve, garnish with Cool Whip and 1 crushed Blue Monday candy bar sprinkled on top (could also use Mint Blue Mondays).

In 1921, Ruth Hunt began to sell candy in her home in Mt. Sterling. In 1930, it was moved to its own permanent location where customers still tour the factory (an official Kentucky landmark). They are the "Official Candymaker of Churchill Downs and Kentucky Derby."

❧ High Bridge Coconut Cake ❧

Paul Sawyier

Cake:

2 c. sugar	2 c. flour
1 c. shortening	½ tsp. baking powder
5 eggs	1 tsp. salt
1 tsp. coconut extract	1 (13 to 14 oz.) can grated
1 c. buttermilk	coconut (or fresh coconut)

Cream sugar and shortening. Add eggs one at a time, beating 2 minutes after each addition. Add extract, buttermilk and flour that has been sifted with baking powder and salt. Add coconut. Stir until well mixed, then beat 2 ½ minutes with electric mixer. Bake in a greased and floured tube pan for 1 hour at 350°.

Glaze:

1 c. sugar	1 tsp. coconut extract
½ c. water	

Boil sugar and water for 1 minute. Stir in extract; pour over cake while it is still warm in the pan. Let cool completely before removing from pan.

This cake was developed as part of the outdoor drama, "The Paul Sawyier Story", held at the High Bridge Pavilion. He is considered Kentucky's most famous artist and lived on a shanty boat on the Kentucky River, beneath High Bridge in Jessamine County.

❧ Old Fashion Rice Pudding ❧

Terry Shumpert

2 c. cooked white rice	4 eggs
4 c. evaporated milk	2 c. sugar
½ c. butter	1 tsp. nutmeg
3 Tbsp. vanilla	

Cakes, Cookies & Desserts

Thoroughly combine rice with remaining ingredients. Pour into lightly greased (glass) baking dish. Bake at 375° for 45 minutes or until lightly browned.

Paducah native Terry Shumpert played professional baseball for the Kansas City Royals, Boston Red Sox and Colorado Rockies. This was his favorite recipe made by his mother for her 5 children. It was given to her by his grandmother.

❦ *Making A Cobbler Pie* ❦
South Central Kentucky Cultural Center

Pour the fruit such as peaches, apples, grapes, cherries, strawberries or blackberries from the jar into saucepan and let it come to a boil. Sweeten the fruit when you put it on to heat if it was not sweetened before it was canned. Roll regular biscuit dough until it is thin and put it in a pan. The dough should be bigger than the pan so it will droop over the sides. Pour the hot fruit into the dough in the pan. Now pull the dough that has drooped over the outside of the pan so it will cover the hot fruit. Be careful that you do not put dough on top of dough since that will keep the dough from browning and cooking as it should. Put it in the stove and let it bake until the dough starts to brown. Then add sugar and butter over the top and put it back into the oven to complete browning and to allow the butter to melt.

South Central Kentucky Cultural Center, Glasgow, has 30,000 square feet of quality exhibits, including displays of central Kentucky around 12,000 B.C., Native American exhibits, life in the 1800's, military collection, model of early town square, and research center.

❦ *Cozy's Peanut Butter* ❦ *Cookies*
Speed Art Museum

1 c. lard shortening	3 c. flour
1 c. white sugar	2 tsp. baking soda
1 c. brown sugar	1 tsp. vanilla
2 eggs	pinch of salt
1 c. peanut butter	

Mix in order given. Shape into balls the size of walnuts. Place on cookie sheet and press down with fork to resemble waffles. Bake in moderate oven 10 minutes (350° to 375°).

Established in 1927, the Speed Art Museum, Louisville, has over 12,000 pieces in its permanent collection, which spans 6,000 years, ranging from ancient Egyptian to contemporary art. It has distinguished collections of 17th and 18th century Dutch, Flemish and French paintings.

Sweet Potato, Sorghum and Bourbon Pie

Spindletop Hall and Farm

3 c. cooked sweet potatoes, mashed
2 oz. butter
1 tsp. vanilla extract
3 eggs
1 egg yolk
¾ c. cream

⅓ c. sorghum
½ c. brown sugar
¼ c. Kentucky bourbon
¼ tsp. nutmeg
1 tsp. cinnamon
⅛ tsp. ground cloves
1 (9-inch) pie shell

Cream butter and brown sugar together. Add eggs one at a time until all are incorporated. Add remaining ingredients together and mix completely. Scrape the bowl. Place in a 9-inch deep dish pie shell and bake at 350° for 35 to 45 minutes. Cool and serve with fresh whipped cream, slightly sweetened.

Spindletop Hall and Farm, Lexington, was established in the 1930's by Miles and Pansy Younts after they struck oil at Spindletop in Texas. The 1,066 acre farm and 50 room mansion and stables were a showplace for Kentucky and American Saddlebred horses.

Butter Pecan Pound Cake

Redd Stewart

1 box Betty Crocker butter pecan cake mix
1 can Betty Crocker coconut pecan frosting
4 eggs
⅔ c. oil

1 c. milk
1 tsp. vanilla
1 c. pecans, chopped (optional, but really makes the cake)

Mix eggs, oil, milk and vanilla together. Beat until well mixed. Add cake mix and beat until well mixed, 1 to 2 minutes. Add nuts. Stir in can of frosting. Spray Bundt pan or tube pan well. Pour batter into pan and bake at 350° for 50 to 60 minutes. Dust with powdered sugar.

Country music writer and singer Redd Stewart grew up in Louisville. He started writing at age 14. A charter member of the Nashville Songwriters Hall of Fame and numerous No. 1 hits, he is most famous for his song "Tennessee Waltz."

🌿 *Apricot Cream Cheese Thumbprints* 🌿

Sharon Stewart

(Makes 7 Dozen)

1 ½ c. butter, softened	1 ½ tsp. lemon zest
1 ½ c. sugar	4 ½ c. all-purpose flour
1 (8 oz.) pkg. cream cheese, softgened	1 ½ tsp. baking powder
	1 c. apricot preserves
2 eggs	⅓ c. confectioners sugar
2 Tbsp. lemon juice	

In a large bowl, cream together the butter, sugar and cream cheese until smooth. Beat in the eggs, one at a time, then stir in the lemon juice and lemon zest. Combine the flour and baking powder; stir into the cream cheese mixture until just combined. Cover and chill until firm, about 1 hour.

Preheat oven to 350°. Roll tablespoonfuls of dough into balls. Place dough balls 2-inches apart on ungreased cookie sheets.

Using your finger, make an indentation in the center of each ball and fill with ½ teaspoon of apricot preserves. Bake for 15 minutes or until cookie edges are golden. Allow cookies to cool on the baking sheets for 2 minutes before removing to wire racks to cool completely. Sprinkle with confectioners sugar.

Sharon Stewart and her musician husband Billy Stewart own and operate Ambridge Music, Inc., Hats Off to Her Unique Gifts, and manage the Redd Stewart Tribute Website (www.reddstewart.com) to preserve the memory of their father, Country Music Hall of Fame member Redd Stewart.

Frozen Lemon Ice Box Pie

Lily Tomlin

3 eggs, separated
½ c. sugar
5 Tbsp. lemon juice

1 c. stiffly beaten whipping cream
1 c. crushed vanilla wafers

Beat 3 egg whites stiff. Add sugar. Add yolks; beat well. Stir in lemon juice. Fold in whipping cream. Generously butter a Pyrex dish. Sprinkle crushed vanilla wafers to coat dish. Pour off excess wafer. Pour batter into dish. Sprinkle remaining crumbs on top and freeze.

Lily Tomlin is best known for "Laugh-In" characters Edith Ann and Ernestine. Her role in "Nashville" earned her an Oscar nomination and she stars in the hit series West Wing. Her grandmother lived in Ballard County in Western Kentucky and she stayed summers there.

Petersburg Christmas Pudding

Varden's Café

3 oz. flour
5 oz. French bread crumbs
5 oz. suet (chill and flake apart)
1 ¼ lb. mixed dried fruit
1 small orange
1 small lemon
1 small apple
2 eggs

½ tsp. mixed spice
½ tsp. cinnamon
½ tsp. nutmeg
1 small carrot
6 oz. dark brown sugar
1 oz. bourbon (no short cuts, only the best)
pinch of salt

Mix flour, bread crumbs, suet and mixed dried fruit into a large bowl. Add grated orange and lemon rind and juice. Add grated cooking apple. Mix well. Add eggs, spices and grated carrot. Add sugar, salt and bourbon. Mix well. Allow mixture to stand overnight in a covered bowl. Place mixture into well-greased pudding bowl (or any large bowl). Cover with grease-proof paper and secure with large rubber band. Pressure-cook according to pressure cooker instructions. Allow to mature for approximately a week before finally serving.

Cakes, Cookies & Desserts

On the serving day: Warm through using a saucepan of water on a low heat with pudding bowl on top for two hours, being careful not to let any water enter the pudding or the saucepan to boil dry.

The pudding may then be flamed at the table. Pour two tablespoons of high proof brandy over pudding and set aflame. (Be very careful.)

Varden's Cafe, Speciality Foods and Emporium is housed in a historic 1891 drugstore in the heart of beautiful downtown Paris, Kentucky. Paris, located in Bourbon County, has long been known for its horses, history and hospitality.

Mom's Blackberry Jam Cake

Brewier Welch

1 c. raisins
1 (8 oz.) can crushed
  pineapple
1 c. butter
1 c. white sugar
5 eggs
1 c. blackberry jam

2 ½ c. self-rising flour
1 tsp. baking powder
1 Tbsp. cinnamon
1 Tbsp. nutmeg
1 Tbsp. cloves
⅔ c. milk
1 c. walnuts

Grease and flour four 8-inch cake pans. Soak the raisins several hours or overnight in pineapple juice. Mix the butter and sugar together until creamy. Stir in eggs one at a time. Stir in jam. Sift dry ingredients together and add to the creamed butter and sugar. Stir in milk. Stir in pineapple, raisins and walnuts. Bake at 350° until done. This makes a four-layer cake.

Icing:

1 stick butter
1 ½ c. brown sugar
½ c. evaporated milk

1 tsp. vanilla
powdered sugar

Melt the butter, then add the brown sugar. Cook until it bubbles. Add the vanilla, then stir in powdered sugar a little at a time until the icing reaches the correct consistency.

Actor Brewier Welch grew up in Kentucky just outside the little town of Carrollton. He has starred in film, television and commercials, most recently in "Recount" with Kevin Spacey. This is his favorite recipe made by his mother, who still lives in Carroll County.

Pineapple Walnut Cake

Weller Haus Bed and Breakfast

2 c. flour	2 tsp. baking soda
2 c. sugar	1 c. chopped walnuts
2 eggs	1 (20 oz.) can crushed
1 tsp. vanilla	pineapple (not drained)

Mix dry ingredients. Add remaining ingredients by hand. Put into greased 13 x 9-inch pan. Bake at 350° for 45 minutes. Do not cool. Frost immediately.

Frosting:

8 oz. softened cream cheese	1 ⅓ c. powdered sugar
½ c. margarine	1 tsp. vanilla

In mixer, blend cream cheese and margarine. Add powdered sugar and vanilla. Frost as soon as cake is removed from oven. Cover with chopped nuts. Refrigerate.

The Weller Haus, Newport, was built in the 1880's and listed on the National Register of Historic Places, with original millwork and 18th century period pieces. This Victorian Gothic home in Taylor Daughter's Historic District is a mile from Cincinnati.

Sweet Potato Pie

Tom Wood

2 medium sweet potatoes	¼ tsp. allspice
(about 1 c.)	½ tsp. vanilla
1 c. brown sugar	2 eggs
¼ tsp. salt	1 small can evaporated milk
1 tsp. cinnamon	

Bake potatoes in microwave 10 to 12 minutes (pierce with fork to allow steam to escape). Mix all ingredients with peeled sweet potatoes. Beat well with electric mixer. Pour in an unbaked pie shell and bake at 350° for 30 to 40 minutes.

Tom Woods became close to the hearts of many West Kentuckians when he was here for the filming of "U.S. Marshalls", with Tommy Lee Jones and Wesley Snipes. Tom Wood has also starred in such movies as "Apollo 13", "Bushwhacked" and "Tinseltown."

Cakes, Cookies & Desserts

Edna's Yummy Apple Pie

John Yarmuth

Crust:

2 ½ c. all-purpose flour	1 ½ c. shortening
1 tsp. salt	smidge of ice water

Roll it out. Spread bottom crust in pan. Save layer for top.

Filling:

6 to 8 Granny Smith apples	couple shakes nutmeg
½ c. sugar (or until sweet)	Tbsp. butter
½ tsp. cinnamon	

Put filling into crust; lay top crust on top. Cut 2 or 3 slits in top crust. Spread a sliver of butter on top. Sprinkle cinnamon and sugar. Crimp edges to seal. Cover edges with foil to prevent burning. Bake for ½ hour or until brown and crisp at 400°.

U.S. Representative John Yarmuth, Louisville, represents Kentucky's 3rd Congressional District. Prior to his election, he was known for debating local and national politics as co-host and commentator on WAVE 3's "Yarmuth and Ziegler."

—•Extra Recipes•—

The Classic Smoothie
1 cup orange juice
2 medium bananas,
    frozen and sliced
1 cup hulled and quartered
    strawberries, frozen

Pour orange juice into a
blender. Add bananas and
strawberries. Blend until
smooth. Yield: 2 servings

Beverages, Microwave, and Misc.

Recipe Favorites

Page No.
_____

Recipe Title:_____

_____   _____

_____   _____

_____   _____

_____   _____

_____   _____

_____   _____

_____   _____

_____   _____

_____   _____

Family Favorites

Page No.
_____

Recipe Title:_____

_____   _____

_____   _____

_____   _____

_____   _____

_____   _____

Notes:_____

_____

_____

_____

Beverages, Microwave & Miscellaneous

Uncle John's Rub

A Taste of Kentucky

(For Chicken, Pork and Beef)

¾ c. paprika
¼ c. fresh ground black pepper
¼ c. salt
¼ c. sugar

2 Tbsp. chili powder
2 Tbsp. garlic powder
2 Tbsp. onion powder
2 tsp. cayenne

Just mix together and store in cool dark place.

A Taste of Kentucky, based in Louisville, brings together Kentucky's distinctive style, heritage, history and special flavors that bring you home to Kentucky no matter where you are. They have unique Kentucky-made gifts, foods, crafts and delightful gift baskets.

Mrs. Alben Barkley's Salad Dressing

Vice President Alben Barkley

1 pt. olive oil
⅔ c. powdered sugar
juice of 1 lemon
juice of 1 orange
3 Tbsp. vinegar

1 tsp. Worcestershire sauce
2 tsp. paprika
1 tsp. salt
1 tsp. onion juice
½ tsp. red pepper

Mix oil and sugar until well blended. Add remaining ingredients and shake well. Refrigerate.

Born in Lowes, Kentucky, Alben Barkley was a U.S. Representative and a U.S. Senator. He was elected Vice President of the United States with President Harry Truman. He is buried in Paducah, Kentucky. His granddaughter Dottie Barkley Holloway shared this recipe.

Party Mix From The Beaton Family

Ron Beaton

10 c. Crispix
6 c. Cheerios
1 can mixed nuts
2 c. pretzel sticks

2 sticks butter or margarine
2 ½ tsp. seasoned salt
4 Tbsp. Worcestershire sauce

Preheat oven to 250°. Heat butter in baking pan in oven until melted. Stir in seasoned salt and Worcestershire sauce. Add cereal, nuts and pretzels. Mix until well coated. Heat one hour, but stir every 15 minutes. Spread on absorbent paper to cool.

Ron Beaton was a news anchor for NBC affiliate WPSD-TV in Paducah for over 30 years. Mr. Beaton now uses all of his energy for his Money Matters Certified Financial Planning business that grew out of his "Money Matters" segments on WPSD and WKYX radio.

Puppy Chow

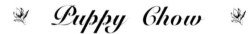

Steve Curtis Chapman

1 tsp. vanilla
1 ½ c. powdered sugar
½ c. peanut butter

1 (6 oz.) pkg. semi-sweet
  chocolate chips (1 c.)
¼ c. margarine or butter*
9 c. Rice Chex cereal

Measure cereal into large bowl; set aside. Microwave chocolate chips, peanut butter and margarine in 1-quart microwavable bowl, uncovered on High 1 minute; stir. Microwave 30 seconds longer or until mixture can be stirred smooth. Stir in vanilla. Pour chocolate mixture over cereal in bowl, stirring until evenly coated. Pour into large plastic food storage bag; add powdered sugar. Seal bag; shake until well coated. Spread on waxed paper to cool. Store in airtight container in refrigerator. 9 cups snack.

*Do not use spread or tub products.

Steve Curtis Chapman from Paducah is the winner of 5 Grammy Awards and 50 Dove Awards. He has a signature sound that has resulted in 41 No. 1 hits and sales of more than 10 million albums. Chapman's father has a music store in Lone Oak (pop. 1200), where he still teaches guitar lessons.

Hot Whiskey Toddy

Irvin S. Cobb

1 lump sugar
1 piece cinnamon
1 piece lemon peel

4 whole cloves
1 jigger of bourbon whiskey

Dissolve sugar in a little hot water; add other ingredients and fill glass with hot water.

Writer, actor and humorist Irvin S. Cobb, Paducah, authored more than 60 books, 300 short stories and was a reporter for Joseph Pulitzer's New York World and Saturday Evening Post. Of this recipe, he said, "I took my 1st of these to cure a cold, but why wait for a cold?"

Peach and Honey

Diamond Caverns

4 parts peach-flavored brandy (70 proof)

1 part fresh honey

Serve chilled, only adding ice after the brandy and honey are mixed well.

Gary Berdeaux, Managing Partner of Diamond Caverns, submitted this pre-Civil War recipe served to guests of Bell's Tavern (stagecoach and hotel) located at Three Forks (now Park City). It was the departure point for the 8-mile stagecoach trip to Mammoth Cave.

Chocolate Gravy

Larry Elmore

16 oz. milk
1 ½ tsp. cocoa powder
1 c. sugar

2 Tbsp. flour
¼ stick butter or margarine
1 tsp. vanilla

Over medium heat, warm milk. In medium bowl, mix cocoa powder, sugar and flour. Slowly add the dry mixture to the milk, stirring constantly. Continue to stir until you get a smooth mixture. Keeping over medium heat, bring to a boil, stirring constantly. Once it comes to a boil, cook, stirring constantly, for 4 to 5 minutes.

Take off of the heat and add butter or margarine and vanilla. Stir and serve warm. This is very good with hot country biscuits!

Larry Elmore Productions in Owensboro has been creating fantasy and science fiction art for over 25 years. His work includes covers of Dragonlance book series, Dungeons and Dragons, comics, computer games, magazines, fantasy and science fiction books.

Dried Apples

Sidney Farr

One method of preserving foods in Appalachia was by air and sun-drying. After coring and peeling, apples were cut in half, then cut into quarters. Each quarter was cut into two or three thin slices. When the apples were ready, they were spread on a large white cloth and placed on top of a shed or other flat area to dry in the sun. A fine wire screen put over them kept out flies and bugs. This method was chancy because of cloudy skies and often rain. However, apple slices can be dried near a wood-burning stove, in a sunny window, or in the oven at a low temperature. They can also be dried by stringing the slices with a needle and stout thread and hung up to dry. The apple slices shrivel and turn brown. When completely dry, they are stored in cloth bags, glass canning jars and the freezer.

Sidney Farr of Berea is past editor of Appalachian Heritage, having retired in December 1999. He is the compiler of three cookbooks: More Than Moonshine, Table Talk, the Spoon Bread Cookbook and has four other published books.

Four Roses Eggnog

Four Roses Distillery

6 eggs
¾ c. sugar
1 pt. cream

1 pt. milk
1 pt. Four Roses
1 oz. Jamaica rum

Beat separately yolks and whites of eggs. Add ½ cup of sugar to yolks while beating. Add ¼ cup of sugar to whites after they have been beaten very stiff. Mix egg whites with yolks. Stir in cream and milk. Add Four Roses and rum. Stir thoroughly.

Makes 5 pints of the grandest eggnog ever ladled into a cup. Serve very cold with grated nutmeg.

The Four Roses Distillery is located in Lawrenceburg on the banks of the Salt River. It began in the 1860's with founder Paul Jones, Jr. and on the National Register of Historic Places. Four Roses has earned a reputation as 1 of the finest names in the bourbon world.

Orange Slush

Hillbilly Days Gospel Jubilee
Gary Chaney

1 c. milk
½ c. sugar
1 c. water
1 tsp. vanilla

½ large can orange juice
  (about 6 oz.)
12 to 16 ice cubes

Blend all together in a blender until ice is chopped. Serve immediately. Kids will especially love this frozen drink.

Hillbilly Days Gospel Jubilee is held annually in April at Pikeville College Booth Auditorium in Pikeville, Kentucky. It draws numerous Kentucky gospel groups such as Carolyn Johnson, Twin Hearts, Sounds of Salvation, Still Waters and Wings of Faith.

Wake Up Smoothie

Homestead Bed and Breakfast

1 large ripe banana
1 c. hulled strawberries
  (frozen is okay)
½ c. raspberries (frozen is
  okay) or 2 kiwi

1 c. plain yogurt
¼ c. orange juice
2 Tbsp. honey

Place all in a blender and process on high speed until smooth (30 to 45 seconds). Makes 2 to 4 servings. Serve with a straw. Very pretty drink.

The Homestead Bed and Breakfast built of massive hand-hewn tulip poplar logs in the late 1700's is located on Highway #62 E four miles from Bardstown, an area that cherishes its history. It is furnished with period antiques and has a gift shop with unique Kentucky Crafts and Antiques.

Martha's Super Suet Bird Feeder

Land Between the Lakes

1 c. crunchy peanut butter
1 c. lard (not shortening)
2 c. quick-cook oats

2 c. cornmeal
1 c. white flour
$\frac{1}{3}$ c. sugar

Melt the lard and peanut butter in the microwave or over low heat. Stir in the remaining ingredients and pour into square freezer containers about 1 ½-inches thick. If these are too thick for your suet basket, pour the next batch a little thinner. Store in freezer or refrigerator. Makes about 6 to 8 cakes.

When the Cumberland and Tennessee Rivers were impounded to create Kentucky Lake and Lake Barkley, an inland peninsula was formed. The 170,000 acres called Land Between The Lakes is the cornerstone of the region's $600 million tourism industry in Western Kentucky.

Colista's Jam

Colista Ledford

3 to 4 c. sugar (granulated)

6 c. fresh berries (in a pot, strawberries, raspberries or blackberries)

Put over a low heat until sugar and berries are well mixed, stirring occasionally. Continue boiling over high heat. Jam is ready when you can dip a spoon into the pot and have 2 or 3 big drops clinging on the spoon side by side.

I gave this recipe to Michael Johnathon and he used it in his book Woodsongs, and he entitled a song, Colista's Jam, which is heard on Woodsong Old Time Radio Show broadcast every Monday at the Kentucky Theater in Lexington.

Colista Ledford, wife of world-renowned bluegrass performer and craftsman Homer Ledford, stars on Woodsongs Old-Time Radio Hour, Lexington. It now broadcasts on over 190 radio stations in the

USA, Canada and Europe and has a weekly audience approaching a half million listeners.

❧ *Kentucky Lemonade* ❧
Maker's Mark Distillery

1 ½ shots Maker's Mark bourbon
½ shot Triple Sec

2 oz. sour mix or 4 oz. lemonade
2 oz. 7-Up

Shake and pour over crushed ice!

Maker's Mark Distillery is located in Loretto and was founded in the 1840's by T.W. Samuels (stepfather of Frank and Jesse James). It is the only operating distillery in America to be designated a National Historic Landmark.

❧ *Grandmother's Boiled Custard* ❧
Bobbie Ann Mason

4 c. milk
2 or 3 eggs, beaten thoroughly
⅓ c. sugar

2 tsp. vanilla
pinch of salt
nutmeg

Put milk and salt in double boiler on high heat. Stir in sugar until it dissolves. Stir in beaten eggs gradually as milk heats. Begin adding them while milk is warm, not too hot. It's best to pour the eggs in from a measuring cup, slowly, in a thin stream, while stirring the milk with the other hand. Cook the mixture, stirring until it coats the spoon. Remove from double boiler and stir in vanilla. Cool. Serve cold, with a sprinkling of grated nutmeg

A major literary voice chronicling the changing landscape of the contemporary South, Bobbie Ann Mason is an American novelist and short story writer born in Mayfield. Her first volume of short stories, "Shiloh and Other Stories" won the 1983 Ernest Hemingway Foundation Award and "In Country" was made into a film starring Bruce Willis.

❧ *Dr. McDowell's Cherry Bounce* ❧
McDowell House Museum, Inc.

6 lb. ripe Morella cherries
6 lb. large black cherries

3 lb. sugar
2 gal. whiskey

Put cherries into wooden bowl or tub; mash so as to crack stones. Mix in the sugar and put into a large stone jar. Pour on the whiskey. Cover closely. Let stand two or three months. Shake every day during the first month. Strain and bottle. Improves with age.

In 1809, Dr. Ephraim McDowell, Danville, performed the 1st successful removal of an ovarian tumor (weighed 22 pounds). The surgery, which was unknown to the medical profession at the time, was performed without anesthetic. Mrs. Crawford lived another 32 years.

The World's Best Bourbon Balls

Robert McAtee

⅓ c. soft butter	½ tsp. salt
6 Tbsp. Kentucky bourbon	1 lb. box sifted confectioners
white corn syrup	sugar

Measure bourbon into a ⅓ cup and finish filling with white corn syrup. Blend butter, Kentucky bourbon, corn syrup and salt. Add sugar all at once, mixing first with a spoon and then with hands. Knead until mixture is well blended. Make into small balls and refrigerate overnight before dipping.

The next day, make the Dipping Chocolate:

½ (8 oz.) bar semi-sweet chocolate	4 Tbsp. melted paraffin
½ (4 oz.) bar German sweet chocolate	½ lb. whole pecans

Melt chocolate in top of double boiler; add melted paraffin and mix well. Keep warm while dipping. Using a dipping fork or long-handled fork; roll candy until coated. Press a pecan on top and then place on waxed paper to harden. Store in the refrigerator for a little while before you serve them. Enjoy!

Robert McAtee, Louisville, is an actor, writer, director, producer, composer. He shot most of the film Trail of Crumbs in Kentucky and can be seen acting in several films, including playing a young Hugh Hefner in an upcoming film about the life of Roman Polanski.

Molasses Taffy

butter
2 c. sugar
2 tsp. vinegar
1 c. light molasses

2 Tbsp. butter
½ tsp. baking soda
⅓ c. water

Butter sides of heavy 3-quart saucepan. In it, mix sugar, molasses and water. Heat slowly, stirring constantly until boiling. Stir in vinegar and cook to soft-crack stage. Remove from heat and add butter. Sift in baking soda and mix. Pour into a buttered 15 x 10 x 1-inch pan. Cool until easy to handle. Butter hands and gather taffy into a ball and pull. When golden and hard to pull, pull into strands ½-inch thick and cut in short lengths. Wrap in wax paper.

Mountain Home Place is located on Paintsville Lake, Paintsville, Kentucky. It is a working farm depicting the times of 1850 to 1875, how people lived in that time, and where history comes alive. In addition to the farm, there is a blacksmith shop and gristmill.

Little Silver Charms Horse Treats

Old Friends Equine

3 c. old-fashion (not instant) rolled oats
2 c. all-purpose flour
1 c. wheat bran
⅓ c. flax seed
1 tsp. salt

1 tsp. cinnamon (optional)
1 c. molasses
½ c. applesauce
1 egg
1 Tbsp. vegetable oil
warm water (as needed)

Combine dry ingredients. Whisk together wet ingredients and add to dry ingredients. Mix into stiff dough, adding small amount of warm water if mixture is too difficult to work. Place dough (well covered) in refrigerator.

When ready to bake, preheat oven to 300°. Line 2 cookie sheets with parchment paper or use nonstick cookie sheets. Pat dough out to ½-inch thickness and cut with cookie cutter. Bake 45 minutes. Turn oven off. Leave horse treats in oven 15 minutes or longer until they are crunchy.

Old Friends Equine brings "at risk" racehorses, those whose racing and breeding careers have come to an end, to Georgetown, provide them with the dignified retirement they deserve, and open the space to educate the public. They have over 30 thoroughbreds, including the horse from Seabiscuit.

Homemade Honey Granola

Raegan Payne

1 c. old-fashioned oats
½ c. sliced almonds
½ c. chopped walnuts
2 Tbsp. flax seed oil (can substitute other cooking oils)

3 Tbsp. local honey
1 tsp. vanilla extract
dried fruit

Preheat oven to 350°. Mix oats, almonds and walnuts together. Add oil, honey and vanilla extract (adding oil first will help the honey slide off the measuring spoon easier). Mix well. Pour into lightly oiled baking sheet. Cook for 10 minutes. Pull out granola and turn it over. Cook for another 10 minutes. Allow to cool and add favorite dried fruit.

Writer and actress Reagan Payne was born and raised in Murray. Having graduated cum laude from Sewanee, she has performed in theatre, film and television, including co-starring in "Charmed" and "The Closer". As a vegetarian, this is her favorite recipe.

Bourbon Ball Hot Chocolate

Rebecca-Ruth

1 (16 oz.) bag Rebecca-Ruth Bourbon Ball Boo-Boo's

1 qt. milk

Put bourbon balls in a bowl. Add milk. Microwave at full heat for 5 to 10 minutes, or until milk is hot to the touch. (Do not let the milk boil over.) Mix well with a wire whisk and serve.

Rebecca Ruth Candies of Frankfort was founded in 1919 by two substitute school teachers in their mid-twenties, Ruth Hanly (Booe) and Rebecca Gooch. In operation for nearly a century, the company is famous for bourbon balls, first created by Ruth. This recipe was submitted by Charles Booe, her grandson and president of the company.

The Kentucky!

Alex Simon

1 ½ oz. 86-proof bourbon
½ oz. lemon juice
½ oz. pineapple juice
1 tsp. maraschino liqueur

Shake well with ice. Strain into pre-chilled, sugar-frosted cocktail glasses. It kicks like a Kentucky thoroughbred racehorse!

Alex Simon, Lexington, is Editor-in-Chief of Venice Magazine, Los Angeles' premiere arts and entertainment publication and a motion picture screenwriter. His most recent film, "My Brother's War", won the "Best Feature" at the annual Hollywood Film Festival.

Swann's Nest Granola

Swann's Nest at Cygnet Farm

18 oz. regular oats
6 oz. pecans
11 oz. jar honey-crunch
   wheat germ
11.8 box Hodgson Mills oat
   bran
8 oz. vegetable oil
½ tsp. ground cinnamon
1 c. each golden raisins,
   dried cranberries and
   chopped dates
1 c. honey
grated rind of 1 orange

Preheat oven to 300°.

Mix the oats, wheat germ, oat bran, pecans and vegetable oil in a large roasting pan and stir well to distribute oil evenly over the ingredients. Toast until golden brown, stirring every 10 minutes or so for a total time of one hour. Add the remaining ingredients while mixture is warm. Stir and let cool completely before storing in an airtight container. For an average family, this recipe can be reduced by half.

This recipe was developed for Swann's Nest by John Groah, chef at The Thoroughbred Club of America in Lexington.

Swann's Nest, the main home on Lexington's Cygnet Farm, is located on a thoroughbred farm in the heart of bluegrass country tucked into the rolling countryside, less than a mile from Keeneland.

Bourbon Balls

Wild Turkey Bourbon

2 c. (500 grams) fine vanilla
  wafer crumbs
1 c. (250 grams) finely
  chopped pecans
1 c. (250 grams)
  confectioners sugar, plus
  additional confectioners
  sugar for rolling

2 Tbsp. cocoa
2 Tbsp. light corn syrup
⅓ c. (6 Tbsp.) Wild Turkey
  bourbon

Mix all ingredients together. One at a time, take a teaspoon of mixture, roll it into a ball, and roll the ball in additional confectioners sugar. Store in a tightly closed container.

Wild Turkey Bourbon is America's best-selling, super-premium bourbon produced by Master Distiller Jimmy Russell. Carefully crafted in Lawrenceburg, Kentucky, Wild Turkey is produced by Austin, Nichols and Company and is one of America's favorites.

Mother Smith's Peanut Brittle

USEC

2 c. raw peanuts
1 c. white (refined) sugar
1 c. white corn syrup

1 tsp. salt
1 tsp. soda
butter

Pour sugar and syrup in heavy iron skillet and cook on medium-high heat until sugar is dissolved. Add raw peanuts; stir in and cook on medium heat (stirring occasionally) until peanuts are light brown and start to pop open. Taste to make sure peanuts are done. Remove skillet from heat; stir in salt and soda and mix thoroughly. Pour quickly into pan or platter lined with buttered aluminum foil. Break into appropriate size pieces when cool.

United States Enrichment Corp. located in Kevil, is the only facility in the U.S. to produce fuel for Nuclear Power Plants. Bob Smith, who shared his mother's recipe, worked on the Manhattan Project and was the manager of Technical Service Division for over 40 years.

Index of Recipes

Appetizers, Relishes & Pickles

Soups, Salads & Sauces

Meats & Main Dishes

Vegetables

Beverages, Microwave & Miscellaneous

Recipe   *Page Number*

J   NOTES

ORDER FORM

For additional copies of this fine cookbook, please complete and mail the order form to:

Celebrity Cooks
Attn: Pamela Whinnery
5754 Lovelaceville Rd.
Paducah, KY 42001

- -

Please mail me _____ copies of your Cookbook at $19.95 per copy plus $2.95 for shipping and handling per book.

Enclosed is my check or money order for $_____ .

Mail books to:

Name _____

Address _____

City _____ State _____ Zip _____

- -

Please mail me _____ copies of your Cookbook at $19.95 per copy plus $2.95 for shipping and handling per book.

Enclosed is my check or money order for $_____ .

Mail books to:

Name _____

Address _____

City _____ State _____ Zip _____

Cooking Hints & Tips

- Keep a recipe card upright by placing it in the tines of a fork and putting the fork handle in a glass.
- To keep a recipe book or card clean, place it under an upside-down glass pie plate. The curved bottom also magnifies the print.
- Use a photo album as a recipe book. Each time you cut a recipe out of a magazine, place it in one of the album's plastic sleeves.
- Glue an envelope to the inside of the front cover of your "favorite" cookbook to hold new recipe cards or recipe clippings.
- Before you start baking or cooking, keep a plastic bag handy to slip over your hand when the phone rings.
- If butter is used in place of vegetable shortening, the amount of butter should be at least 1/4 more than the amount of shortening.
- It is best to cream butter by itself before adding the sugar.
- When a chocolate cake requires greasing and flouring the pans, try using cocoa instead of flour. When the cake is done, there will be no white flour residue on your cake and it adds flavor.
- Before measuring honey or other sticky ingredients, dip your spoon in oil.
- Put cold oil in a hot pan so the food won't stick.
- Add a pinch of baking soda to your frosting and the frosting will stay moist and prevent cracking.
- When you boil water, place a lid on the pot and the water will come to a boil in a shorter period of time– saving at least 10 minutes.
- To keep dough from sticking to your rolling pin, cover it with a clean stockinette.
- For shiny pie crusts, brush the crust lightly with milk.
- For sugary pie crusts, moisten the crust lightly with water or beaten egg whites, then sprinkle with sugar.
- Never salt food to be fried–it will draw moisture to the surface and cause spattering in the hot oil.
- Before heating the fat when deep fat frying, add one tablespoon white vinegar to minimize the amount of fat absorbed by the frying food. The food will taste less greasy.
- Sugar can be powdered by pounding it in a large mortar or rolling it on a paste-board with a rolling pin. It should be made very fine and always sifted.

Cooking Hints & Tips

- No more slow cooker mess– Before you start the recipe, place a turkey size browning bag in your cooker and put the ingredients inside the bag. After serving your dinner, just take the bag out and throw it away.

- Here's a neat casserole trick: When you are baking a covered casserole, keep your dish and oven neat by propping the lid open just a bit with a toothpick. This will prevent the casserole from bubbling over.

- Use double-thick paper towels to place over cooling rack to keep the rack from making imprints into the cake while cooling.

- Use one 3" pan instead of 2" layer pans for a higher cake– more cake less work. Slice lengthwise for layers.

- To make any homemade or boxed chocolate cake recipe moist and fluffier, add a spoonful of vinegar to the dry ingredients. You'll be amazed at the difference.

- Dip your icing spatula in hot water and dry with a paper towel. The heat from the water will melt the oil in the icing making it smoother.

- When you need a cake cooled and out of the pan quickly, place a cold wet towel or paper towels under the pan.

- Out of icing for your cupcakes? Just pop a marshmallow on top of each cupcake for about a minute before they come out of the oven. It will make a delicious, instant gooey frosting.

- Use dental floss to cut cakes, especially delicate, sticky ones that tend to adhere to a knife.

- Extend the shelf life of your homemade or store-bought cakes, by storing a half apple with them.

- Store a few lumps of sugar with your cheese to prevent it from molding.

- Applesauce is a great fat substitute for low fat baking. Simply substitute half the fat in a recipe with an equal measure of applesauce.

- Disinfect your kitchen sponges by placing them in the microwave for 60 seconds.

- Peeling apples, pears and potatoes in cold, slightly salted water will help keep them from turning brown.

- If soup tastes very salty, a raw piece of potato placed in the pot will absorb the salt.

- You can cut a meringue pie cleanly by coating both sides of a knife lightly with butter.

Cooking Hints & Tips

MICROWAVE SHORTCUTS

TOASTING NUTS – Place 1/2 cup of nuts in a 2-cup measure. Micro-cook, uncovered, on 100% power about 3 minutes or until toasted, stirring frequently.

BLANCHING ALMONDS – In a small non-metal bowl, micro-cook 1 cup water, uncovered, on 100% power for 2-3 minutes or till boiling. Add 1/2 cup almonds to water. Micro-cook,uncovered, on 100% power for 1 1/2 minutes. Drain, rinse almonds with cold water. Slip off skins.

TOASTING COCONUT – Place flaked or shredded coconut in a 1-cup measure. Micro-cook, uncovered, on 100% power until light brown, stirring every 20 seconds. Allow 1 to 1 1/2 minutes for 1/4 cup and 1 1/2 to 2 minutes for 1/2 cup.

SOFTENING ICE CREAM – Micro-cook 1 pint solidly frozen ice cream, uncovered, on 100% power for about 15 seconds or until soft enough to serve.

PLUMPING DRIED FRUIT – In a 2-cup measure micro-cook 1 cup water, uncovered, on 100% power for 2-3 minutes or till boiling. Stir in 1/2 cup dried fruit. Let stand for 5-10 minutes.

SOFTENING BUTTER OR MARGARINE – Place unwrapped butter or margarine in a micro-safe dish. Micro-cook, uncovered, on 10% power, allowing about 25-30 seconds for 2 tablespoons or about 40 seconds for 1/4 cup butter or margarine.

SOFTENING CREAM CHEESE – Place an unwrapped 3-ounce package of cream cheese in a small micro-safe bowl. Micro-cook, uncovered on 30% power about 1 minute or until soft.

MELTING CHOCOLATE PIECES – In a glass measure micro-cook chocolate pieces, uncovered, on 100% power until melted, stirring once. Allow 1-1/2 minutes for 3-ounce or 1-1/2 to 2 minutes for a 6-ounce package.

MELTING CARAMEL – Place unwrapped caramel in a glass measure. Micro-cook, on 100% power stirring once. Allow 45 seconds to 1 minute for 14 caramels (about 1/2 cup) or 1 to 1 1/2 minutes for 28 (about a cup).

PEELING TOMATOES – In a 2-cup measure micro-cook 1 cup water, uncovered, on 100% power for 2-3 minutes or until boiling. Spear 1 tomato with a long tined fork. Submerge into hot water; hold about 12 seconds. Place tomato under cold water, slip off skin.

Cooking & Food Terms

AL DENTÉ – Describes foods, especially pasta, cooked only until soft enough to eat, but not overdone. The Italian translation is "to the teeth."

ADJUST SEASONING – To taste the dish before serving to determine the need for salt, herbs, or other seasonings.

BLACKEN – A method of cooking in which meat or fish is seasoned with a spicy mixture then fried in a hot skillet until blackened on both sides.

BLANCH – Blanching is a process in which food is briefly plunged in boiling water for a moment, then immediately transferred to ice water to stop the cooking process. Blanching tomatoes or peaches for about 20 seconds makes them easier to peel.

BRAISE – Braising involves cooking a food in a little fat to brown, usually on the stove top then covering and cooking slowly until done. This is particularly suited to less tender cuts of meat.

BROIL – To cook food directly under or over heat source, usually in the oven under the top broiling element or on the grill.

BROWN – To cook food quickly at a moderately high heat to brown the surface. May be done on the stove top or under the broiler in the oven.

BUTTERFLY – To cut a food down the center, but not quite through, leaving both halves attached, The food is then spread to resemble a butterfly.

CHUNKS – Usually bite-size pieces, about 1-inch or larger.

CLARIFIED BUTTER – Unsalted butter which has been melted and skimmed of milk solids.

CUBE – To cut into cubes, about 1/2 to 1-inch. Cube may also mean to tenderize meat with a tenderizing mallet or utensil which makes "cube" imprints.

CURE – To preserve food, usually meat or fish, by pickling, smoking, drying, salting, or storing in a brine.

CUT IN – To incorporate solid fat into dry ingredients using a pastry blender or knives.

DASH – Less than 1/8 teaspoon.

DEEP-FAT FRY – To cook in hot fat which is deep enough to completely cover the food.

DEGLAZE – To add liquid to the pan in which meat or other food was cooked. The liquid, usually broth or wine, is heated to loosen the browned bits left in the pan, and is often used as a base for sauce or gravy.

Cooking & Food Terms

DEGREASE – To remove melted fat from the surface of liquid, usually by skimming with a spoon, refrigerating to solidify the fat, or by using a cup or pitcher designed to separate the fat from the liquid.

DEHYDRATE – To remove moisture from food by drying it slowly in the oven or in an electric or manual dehydrator.

DEVEIN – To remove the vein from the back of shrimp or to remove the interior ribs from peppers.

DICE – To cut food into cubes about 1/8 to 3/4 inch in size.

DOLLOP – A spoonful of soft food, such as mashed potatoes or whipped cream. It may also mean a dash or "splash" of soda water, water, or other liquid if referring to liquid.

DOT – To scatter bits of an ingredient (usually butter) evenly over the surface of another food.

DOUGH – A mixture of flour, liquid, and other ingredients. Dough is too thick to pour but thick enough to roll out or work with hands.

DREDGE – To coat food with a dry mixture (usually seasoned flour or crumbs), either by sprinkling, rolling, or shaking the food in a bag with the flour or other ingredients.

DRIPPINGS – The juices or liquefied fats left in a pan after cooking meat or other food.

DRIZZLE – To pour a thin mixture, such as melted butter or thin icing, over food in a very fine stream.

DUMPLING – Large or small amounts of dough usually dropped into a liquid mixture such as broth, stew, or fruit. (2) A fruit or fruit mixture encased in sweet dough and baked.

EGG WASH – Egg yolk or white mixed with a small amount of water or liquid then brushed over baked goods to give color and sheen.

EN CROUTE – Food baked in a crust.

EVAPORATED MILK – A canned, unsweetened milk is homogenized milk from which 60% of the water has been removed. Whole evaporated milk contains at least 7.9 percent butterfat, while the skim version contains 1/2 percent or less.

EXTRACT – Concentrated flavors from various foods, usually derived from distillation or evaporation. Extracts, also called essences, may be solid or liquid.

Cooking & Food Terms

FILLET – A boneless piece of meat or fish.

FLAKE – To use a fork or other utensil to break off pieces or layers of food.

FLANK STEAK – A long, fibrous cut of beef which comes from an animal's lower hindquarters. Flank steak is usually tenderized by marinating, then boiled or grilled and cut thinly across the grain.

FLOUR – To lightly sprinkle or coat with flour.

FLUTE – To press a scalloped or decorative design into the edge of a pie crust.

FOLD – To incorporate a light mixture with a heavy mixture, such as beaten egg whites into batter or custard. The lighter mixture is placed on the heavier mixture, and a spatula is used to gently cut down and through the lighter mixture of the bottom of the bowl then up again. This procedure gently turns the mixtures over on top of each other, and is repeated until the two mixtures are combined.

FRENCH FRY – To deep-fry food, such as strips of potatoes.

FRICASSEE – To cook or stew pieces of sauteed meat in a sauce, usually with vegetables. Wine is often used as a flavoring.

FRIZZLE – To fry thin slices of meat or other food until the edges curl.

FROST – To apply sugar, frosting, glaze, or icing to fruit, cake, or other food.

FRY – To cook food in a fat over moderate to high heat.

GARNISH – To decorate food or the dish on which food is served.

GLAZE – A thin, glossy coating applied to the surface of a food. A glaze may also add flavor.

GRATE – To cut food into small shreds or particles, usually with a food grater.

GRATIN DISH – A shallow baking dish or pan, usually round or oval in shape.

GREASE – To spread fat (or non-stick cooking spray) on a cooking utensil or pan to prevent food from sticking. To grease and flour means to grease the pan then dust with flour. The flour is sprinkled into the greased pan then the pan is shaken to distribute evenly before inverting and discarding the excess.

GRILL – To cook on a rack directly over hot coals or other heat source.

Cooking & Food Terms

GRIND – To reduce food to small particles, as in ground coffee, ground beef, or ground spices. A variety of instruments may be used, including mortar and pestle, meat grinder, pepper mills, and food processor.

HALF AND HALF – A mixture of half cream, half milk. The fat content is between 10 and 12 percent.

INFUSE – To immerse tea, herbs, or other flavoring ingredients in a hot liquid in order to extract flavor.

JELL – To congeal, often with the addition of gelatin.

JIGGER – A liquid measure equal to 1-1/2 fluid ounces.

JULIENNE – To cut food into thin, matchstick strips. Julienne strips are usually about 1/8 inch thick, but the length varies.

KNEAD – A technique used to mix and work dough, usually using the hands. Dough is pressed with the heels of the hands, while stretching it out, then folded over itself.

LARD – Rendered and clarified pork fat. As a verb, to lard is to insert strips of fat into uncooked lean meat (such as venison) to tenderize and add flavor.

LEAVENER – An ingredient or agent used to lighten the texture and increase volume in baked goods. Baking powder, baking soda, and yeast are common leaveners.

LIQUEUR – Sweet alcoholic drink usually served after a meal. Liqueurs are usually flavored with aromatic ingredients such as nuts, fruits, flowers, or spices, and are frequently used in baked desserts and dessert sauces.

MARINATE – To let food soak in a seasoned liquid in order to flavor and tenderize.

MASH – To crush a food until smooth and evenly textured.

MEDALLION – A small, round cut of meat, usually pork, veal, or beef.

MELT – Heating a food (such as shortening, butter, or chocolate) until it becomes liquid.

MINCE – To chop food into small pieces, usually 1/8 inch or less.

MIX – To blend ingredients.

MOLD – To form a food into a shape by hand, or by placing or pouring into a decorative container (or mold) then refrigerating or cooking until firm enough to hold its shape.

MOUSSE – A sweet or savory dish, made with egg whites or whipped cream to give the light, airy texture.

Cooking & Food Terms

MULL – To flavor a beverage, such as cider or wine, by heating it with spices or other flavorings.

PARBOIL – To boil a food briefly, until partially done. A food might be parboiled before adding it to faster-cooking ingredients to insure all ingredients are evenly cooked.

PARE – To cut the skin from a food, usually with a short knife called a paring knife.

PASTEURIZE – To kill bacteria by heating liquids to moderately high temperatures only briefly. French scientist Louis Pasteur discovered the solution while he was researching the cause of beer and wine spoilage.

PASTRY BAG – A cone-shaped bag with openings at both ends. Food is placed into the large opening then squeezed out the small opening which may be fitted with a decorator tip. It has a variety of uses, including decorating cakes and cookies, forming pastries, or piping decorative edging. Bags may be made of cloth, plastic, or other materials.

PASTRY BLENDER – A kitchen utensil with several u-shaped wires attached to a handle. It's used to cut solid fat (like shortening or butter) into flour and other dry ingredients in order to evenly distribute the fat particles.

PASTRY BRUSH – A brush used to apply glaze or egg wash to breads and other baked goods either before or after baking.

PASTRY WHEEL – A utensil with a cutting wheel attached to a handle. It's used to mark and cut rolled-out dough, and may have a plain or decorative edge.

PIPE – To squeeze icing or other soft food through a pastry bag to make a design or decorative edible edging.

PIQUANT – A term which generally means tangy flavor.

PIT – To remove the seed or stone of a fruit or berry.

POACH – To cook in liquid at or just below the boiling point. For eggs, meat, or fish, the liquid is usually water or a seasoned stock; fruit is generally poached in a sugar syrup.

PREHEAT – To allow the oven or pan to get to a specified temperature before adding the food to be cooked.

PRESERVE – To prepare foods for long storage. Some ways to preserve foods are drying, freezing, canning, curing, pickling, and smoking.

PRICK – To make small holes in the surface of a food, usually using the tines of a fork. Pie crust is usually pricked.

Cooking & Food Terms

PULVERIZE – To reduce to a powder or dust by pounding, crushing or grinding.

PUREE – To blend, process, sieve, or mash a food until it's very smooth and has the consistency of baby food.

REDUCE – To boil a liquid until a portion of it has evaporated. Reducing intensifies the flavor and results in a thicker liquid.

RENDER – To extract the fat from meat by cooking over low heat. Rendered fat is strained of meat particles after cooking.

ROAST – To cook food in an open pan in the oven, with no added liquid.

ROLLING BOIL – A very fast boil that doesn't slow when stirred.

SAUTÉ – To cook quickly in a pan on top of the stove until the food is browned.

SCORE – To cut shallow slashes into ham or other food, to allow excess fat to drain, or to help tenderize.

SEAR – To brown meat quickly over high heat. Meat may be seared under a broiler or in a skillet on top of the stove.

SHRED – To cut food into narrow strips. A grater or food processor may be used to shred.

SIFT – To pass dry ingredients through a mesh sifter. Incorporates air, which makes food lighter.

SIMMER – To cook liquid at about 185° or just below boil. Tiny bubbles just beginning to break the surface.

SKIM – To remove a substance from the surface of a liquid.

SLIVER – To cut a food into thin strips or pieces.

STEEP – To soak, in order to extract flavor or soften.

STRAIN – To pour liquid through a strainer or colander to remove solid particles.

THICKEN – To make liquid more thick by reducing or adding a roux, starch, or eggs.

THIN – To dilute a mixture by adding more liquid.

TRUSS – To hold food together so it will retain its shape. Poultry and some roasts are often tied with twine or held together with skewers.

WATERBATH – To place a container of food in a large pan of warm water, which surrounds the food with heat.

WHIP – To beat ingredients with a whisk, or other utensil, which incorporates air into a mixture and changes the texture.

Ingredient Substitutions

INGREDIENT	AMOUNT	SUBSTITUTE
Allspice	1 tsp.	• 1/2 tsp. cinnamon and 1/2 tsp. ground cloves
Apple Pie Spice	1 tsp.	• 1/2 tsp. cinnamon, 1/4 tsp. nutmeg, and 1/8 tsp. cardamom
Arrowroot	1 1/2 tsp.	• 1 tsp flour • 1 1/2 tsp. cornstarch
Baking Powder	1 tsp.	• 1/3 tsp. baking soda and 1/2 tsp. cream of tartar • 1/4 tsp. baking soda and 1/2 cup sour milk or buttermilk (Decrease liquid called for in recipe by 1/2 cup.)
Bay Leaf	1 whole	• 1/8 to 1/4 tsp., crushed
Bread	1 slice dry 1 slice soft	• 1/3 cup dry bread crumbs • 3/4 cup bread crumbs
Broth, Beef or Chicken	1 cup	• 1 bouillon cube dissolved in 1 cup boiling water • 1 envelope powdered broth base dissolved in 1 cup boiling water • 1 1/2 tsp. powdered broth base dissolved in 1 cup boiling water
Butter	1 cup	• 7/8 to 1 cup hydrogenated fat and 1/2 tsp. salt • 7/8 cup lard plus 1/2 tsp. salt • 1 cup margarine
Buttermilk (sour milk)	1 cup	• 1 cup plain yogurt • 1 cup whole or skim milk plus 1 Tbsp. lemon juice or white vinegar • 1 cup milk plus 1 3/4 tsp. cream of tartar
Chili Sauce	1 cup	• 1 cup catsup, 1/4 tsp. cinnamon, dashes of ground cloves and allspice

Ingredient Substitutions

INGREDIENT	AMOUNT	SUBSTITUTE
Chives, Finely Chopped	2 tsp.	• 2 tsp. green onion tops finely chopped
Chocolate, Chips Semisweet	1 oz.	• 1 oz. sweet cooking chocolate
Chocolate, Semisweet	1 2/3 oz. 6 oz. pkg.	• 1 oz. unsweetened chocolate plus 4 tsp. sugar • 1 cup
Chocolate, Unsweetened	1 oz. sq.	• 3 Tbsp. cocoa plus 1 Tbsp. fat
Cocoa	1/4 cup or 4 Tbsp.	• 1 oz. sq. unsweetened chocolate (decrease fat called for in recipe by 1/2 Tbsp.)
Coconut Cream	1 cup	• 1 cup whipping cream
Coconut Milk	1 cup	• 1 cup whole or 2% milk
Corn	1 doz. ears	• 2 1/2 cups cooked
Cornmeal, Self-rising	1 cup	• 7/8 cup plain, 1 1/2 Tbsp. baking powder, and 1/2 tsp. salt
Corn Syrup, Dark	1 cup	• 3/4 cup light corn syrup and 1/4 cup light molasses
Cornstarch (for thickening)	1 Tbsp.	• 2 Tbsp. all purpose flour • 2 Tbsp. granular tapioca
Cracker Crumbs	3/4 cup	• 1 cup dry bread crumbs
Cream, Heavy (36% to 40% fat)	1 cup	• 3/4 cup milk and 1/3 cup butter or margarine (for use in cooking or baking)

Ingredient Substitutions

INGREDIENT	AMOUNT	SUBSTITUTE
Cream, Light (18% to 20% fat)	1 cup	• 3/4 cup milk and 3 Tbsp. butter or margarine (for use in cooking or baking) • 1 cup evaporated milk, undiluted
Cream, Whipped	2 tsp.	• Chill a 13 oz-can of evaporated milk until ice crystals form. Add 1 tsp. lemon juice. Whip until stiff.
Dates	1 lb.	• 2 1/2 cups pitted
Dill Plant, Fresh or Dried	3 heads	• 1 Tbsp. dill seed
Egg, Whole, Uncooked	1 large (3 Tbsp.)	• 3 Tbsp. and 1 tsp. thawed frozen egg • 2 1/2 Tbsp. sifted, dry whole egg powder and 2 1/2 Tbsp. lukewarm water • 2 yolks 1 Tbsp. water (in cookies) • 2 yolks (in custard, cream fillings, and similar mixture) • 2 whites as a thickening agent
Eggs, Uncooked	1 cup = ▸	• 5 large • 6 medium
Egg White	1 large (2 Tbsp.) 1 cup = ▸	• 2 Tbsp. sifted, dry egg white powder, and 2 Tbsp. lukewarm water • 8 large egg whites
Egg Yolk (1 1/2 Tbsp.)	1 yolk 1 cup = ▸	• 3 1/2 Tbsp. thawed frozen egg yolk • 2 Tbsp. sifted, dry egg yolk • 12 large egg yolks
Fines Herbes	1/3 cup	• 3 Tbsp. parsley flakes, 2 tsp. dried chervil, 2 tsp. dried chives, 1 tsp. dried tarragon

Ingredient Substitutions

INGREDIENT	AMOUNT	SUBSTITUTE
Flour, All-purpose thickening)	1 Tbsp.	• 1 1/2 tsp. cornstarch, arrowroot (for starch, potato starch, or rice starch • 1 tsp. waxy rice flour • 1 1/2 Tbsp. whole wheat flour • 1 tsp. quick-cooking tapioca
Flour, All-purpose	1 cup sifted	• 1 cup and 2 Tbsp. cake flour • 1 cup rolled oats, crushed
	1 lb.	• 4 cups sifted • 3 1/3 cups unsifted
Flour, Cake	1 lb.	• 4 3/4 cups
	1 cup sifted	• 1 cup minus 2 Tbsp. sifted all-purpose flour
Flour, Self-rising	1 cup	• 1 cup minus 2 tsp. all-purpose flour, 1 1/2 tsp. baking powder, and 1/2 tsp. salt

> **NOTE:** Substitutes for white flours added to most baked goods will result in a reduced volume and a heavier product. Substitute no more than 1/4 of white flour in a cake to ensure success. In other recipes, you can substitute whole wheat flour for 1/4 to 1/2 white flour.

Garlic	1 clove	• 1/8 tsp. garlic powder
Gelatin, Flavored	3 oz.	• 1 Tbsp. plain gelatin and 2 cups of fruit juice
Honey	1 cup	• 1 1/4 cup sugar and 1/4 cup water
Ketchup	1 cup	• 1 cup tomato sauce, 1/4 cup brown sugar, and 2 Tbsp. vinegar (for use in cooking)
Lemon Juice	1 tsp.	• 1/2 tsp. vinegar
Lemon Peel, Dried	1 tsp.	• 1 to 2 tsp. grated fresh lemon peel • 1/2 tsp. lemon extract

Ingredient Substitutions

INGREDIENT	AMOUNT	SUBSTITUTE
Marshmallows, Miniature	1 cup	• 8-10 regular
Mayonnaise	1 cup	• 1/2 cup yogurt and 1/2 cup mayonnaise • 1 cup of sour cream
Milk, Buttermilk	1 cup	• 1 cup sweet milk and 1 3/4 tsp. cream of tartar
Milk, Skim	1 cup	• 1/2 cup evaporated milk and 1/2 cup water
Milk, Sweetened	1 can (about 1 1/3 cups)	• Heat the following ingredients until sugar and butter are dissolved: 1/3 cup plus 2 tsp. evaporated milk, 1 cup sugar, and 3 Tbsp. butter or margarine
Milk, Whole	1 cup	• 1 cup reconstituted non-fat dry milk (Add 2 Tbsp. butter or margarine, if desired.) • 1/2 cup evaporated milk and 1/2 cup water
Mustard, Dry	1 tsp.	• 1 Tbsp. prepared mustard
Onion, Fresh	1 small	• Rehydrate 1 Tbsp. instant minced onion
Onion, Powdered	1 Tbsp.	• 1 medium onion • 4 Tbsp. fresh chopped
Onion	1 lb.	• 3 large onions • 2 to 2 1/2 cups chopped
Orange Peel, Dried	1 Tbsp.	• 2 to 3 Tbsp. grated orange peel
Parsley, Dried	1 tsp.	• 3 tsp. fresh parsley, chopped

Ingredient Substitutions

INGREDIENT	AMOUNT	SUBSTITUTE
Pumpkin Pie Spice	1 tsp.	• 1/2 tsp. cinnamon, 1/4 tsp. ginger, 1/8 tsp. allspice, and 1/8 tsp. nutmeg
Shortening, Melted	1 cup	• 1 cup cooking oil (Substitute only if recipe calls for melted shortening.)
Shortening, Solid (used in baking)	1 cup	• 1 1/8 cups butter (Decrease salt called for in recipe by 1/2 tsp.)
Sour Cream, Cultured	1 cup	• 1 cup plain yogurt • 3/4 cup milk, 3/4 tsp. lemon juice, and 1/3 cup butter or margarine
Sugar, Brown	1 cup firmly packed 1 lb. = ▶	• 1 cup granulated sugar • 2 1/4 cups firmly packed
Sugar, Granulated	1 lb. = ▶	• 2 1/4 cups
Sugar, Powdered	1 lb. = ▶	• 2 3/4 cups
Sugar, Granualted	1 tsp.	• 1/8 tsp. noncaloric sweetener solution or follow manufacturer's directions
Sugar, Granulated	1 cup	• 1 1/2 cups corn syrup (Decrease liquid called for in recipe by 1/4 cup.) • 1 cup of powdered sugar • 1 cup, brown sugar, firmly packed • 3/4 cup honey (Decrease liquid called for in recipe by 1/4 cup; for each cup of honey in baked goods, add 1/2 tsp. soda.)
Tomato Juice	1 cup	• 1 cup tomato sauce and 1/2 cup water
Yogurt, Plain	1 cup	• 1 cup of buttermilk • 1 cup of sour cream

Yields & Equivalents

FOOD	YOUR RECIPE STATES	YOU WILL NEED
Apples	▶ 1 cup sliced or chopped ▶ 1 lb.	◀ 1 medium (6 oz.) ◀ 3 medium
Apricots, Dried Halves	1 cup	5 oz.
Asparagus	16 to 20 stalks	1 lb.
Bacon	1/2 cup crumbled	8 slices, crisply cooked
Bananas	▶ 1 cup sliced ▶ 1 cup mashed	◀ 1 medium or 2 small ◀ 2 medium
Beans	5 to 6 cups cooked	1 lb. dried (2 1/4 cups)
Beans, Green or Wax	3 cups 1-inch pieces	1 lb.
Bread, White	▶ 12 slices (1/2 inch) ▶ 1 cup soft ▶ 1 cup dry	◀ 1-lb. loaf ◀ 1 1/2 slices ◀ 4 to 5 slices, oven-dried
Broccoli	2 cups flowerets, 1-inch pieces or chopped	6 oz.
Butter	1/2 cup	1 stick
Cabbage, Green Slaw (bag)	▶ 1 medium head ▶ 4 cups shredded	◀ 1 1/2 lb. ◀ 1 lb.
Carrots	▶ 1 medium ▶ 1 cup shredded ▶ 1 cup 1/4-inch slices	◀ 7 inches ◀ 1 1/2 medium ◀ 2 medium
Cauliflower	▶ 1 medium head ▶ 3 cups flowerets	◀ 2 lb. (with leaves) ◀ 1 lb.
Celery	▶ 1 medium bunch ▶ 1 cup thinly sliced or chopped	◀ 2 lb. (11 inches) ◀ 2 medium stalks

Yields & Equivalents

FOOD	YOUR RECIPE STATES	YOU WILL NEED
Cheese, Hard Cottage Cream	▶ 1 cup ▶ 2 cups ▶ 1 cup	◀ 4 oz. ◀ 16 oz. ◀ 8 oz.
Corn, Sweet	▶ 1 medium ear ▶ 1 cup kernels	◀ 8 oz. ◀ 2 medium ears
Cream, Sour Whipping (heavy)	▶ 1 cup ▶ 1 cup (2 cups whipped)	◀ 8 oz. ◀ 1/2 pt.
Crumbs, Finely Crushed Chocolate Wafer Cookie Graham Cracker Saltine Cracker Vanilla Wafer	▶ 1 1/2 cups ▶ 1 1/2 cups ▶ 1 cup ▶ 1 1/2 cups	◀ 27 cookies ◀ 21 squares ◀ 29 squares ◀ 38 cookies
Eggs, Large Whole	▶ 1 cup ▶ 1 egg	◀ 4 large ◀ 1/4 cup fat free egg product
Flour	3 1/2 cups	1 lb.
Garlic	1/2 tsp. finely chopped	1 medium clove
Lemons or Limes	▶ 1 1/2 to 3 tsp. grated peel ▶ 2 to 3 Tbsp. juice	◀ 1 medium ◀ 1 medium
Meat, Cooked Beef, Pork and Poultry	1 cup chopped or bite-size pieces	6 oz.
Mushrooms, Fresh	▶ 6 cups sliced ▶ 2 1/2 cups chopped	◀ 1 lb. ◀ 8 oz.
Canned	4-oz. can sliced, drained	◀ 2/3 cup fresh, sliced and cooked (5 oz. uncooked)

Yields & Equivalents

FOOD	YOUR RECIPE STATES	YOU WILL NEED
Nuts, (without shells) Chopped, Sliced or Slivered	▸ 1 cup	◂ 4 oz.
Whole or Halves	▸ 3 to 4 cups	◂ 1 lb.
Olives, Pimiento-stuffed Ripe, Pitted	▸ 1 cup sliced ▸ 1 cup sliced	◂ 24 large or 36 small ◂ 32 medium
Oranges	▸ 1 Tbsp. grated peel ▸ 1/3 to 1/2 cup juice	◂ 1 medium ◂ 1 medium
Pasta, Macaroni Noodles, egg Spaghetti	▸ 4 cups cooked ▸ 4 cups cooked ▸ 4 cups cooked	◂ 2 cups uncooked (6-7 oz.) ◂ 4 to 5 cups uncooked (7 oz.) ◂ 7 to 8 oz. uncooked
Peppers, Bell	▸ 1/2 cup chopped ▸ 1 cup chopped ▸ 1 1/2 cups chopped	◂ 1 small ◂ 1 medium ◂ 1 large
Rice, Brown Parboiled (converted) Precooked White Instant Regular Long Grain Wild	▸ 4 cups cooked ▸ 3 to 4 cups cooked ▸ 2 cups cooked ▸ 3 cups cooked ▸ 3 cups cooked	◂ 1 cup uncooked ◂ 1 cup uncooked ◂ 1 cup uncooked ◂ 1 cup uncooked ◂ 1 cup uncooked
Shrimp (uncooked, with shells) Jumbo Large Medium Small	▸ 1 lb. ▸ 1 lb. ▸ 1 lb. ▸ 1 lb.	◂ 21 to 25 count ◂ 31 to 35 count ◂ 41 to 45 count ◂ 51 to 60 count
Cooked (without shells)	▸ 1 lb.	◂ 1 1/3 lb. uncooked (with shells)

Yields & Equivalents

TEASPOONS	TABLESPOONS	CUPS	FLUID OZ.	MILLI-LITERS	OTHER
1/4 teaspoon				1 ml.	
1/2 teaspoon				2 ml.	
3/4 teaspoon	1/4 tablespoon			4 ml.	
1 teaspoon	1/3 tablespoon			5 ml.	
3 teaspoons	1 tablespoon	1/16 cup	1/2 oz.	15 ml.	
6 teaspoons	2 tablespoons	1/8 cup	1 oz.	30 ml.	
			1 1/2 oz.	44 ml.	1 jigger
12 teaspoons	4 tablespoons	1/4 cup	2 oz.	60 ml.	
16 teaspoons	5 1/3 tablespoons	1/3 cup	2 1/2 oz.	75 ml.	
18 teaspoons	6 tablespoons	3/8 cup	3 oz.	90 ml.	
24 teaspoons	8 tablespoons	1/2 cup	4 oz.	125 ml.	1/4 pint
32 teaspoons	10 2/3 tablespoons	2/3 cup	5 oz.	150 ml.	
36 teaspoons	12 tablespoons	3/4 cup	6 oz.	175 ml.	
48 teaspoons	16 tablespoons	1 cup	8 oz.	237 ml.	1/2 pint
		1 1/2 cups	12 oz.	355 ml.	
		2 cups	16 oz.	473 ml.	1 pint
		3 cups	24 oz.	710 ml.	1 1/2 pints
			25.6 oz.	757 ml.	1 fifth
		4 cups	32 oz.	946 ml.	1 quart or 1 liter
		8 cups	64 oz.		2 quarts
		16 cups	128 oz.		1 gallon

Dash or Pinch– Less than 1/8 tsp.

Firmly Packed– Tightly pressed ingredients in measuring cup.

Lightly Packed– Lightly pressed ingredients in measuring cup.

Even / Level– Precise measure. Discard any ingredients that rise above the rim of the measuring cup.

Rounded– Allow ingredients to pile above the rim measuring cup into a nice round shape.

Heaping– Pile as much of the ingredient on top of the measure as it can hold.

Sifted– Sift before measuring to ensure ingredient is not compacted.

General Oven Chart

Very Slow Oven ....250 to 300° F.
Slow Oven ....300 to 325° F.
Moderate Oven ....325 to 375° F.
Medium Hot Oven ....375 to 400° F.
Hot Oven ....400 to 450° F.
Very Hot Oven ....450 to 500° F.

BREADS

Baking Powder Biscuits	400° F.	12 - 15 min.
Muffins	400° - 425° F.	25 - 35 min.
Quick Breads	350° - 375° F.	25 - 35 min.
Yeast Breads	375° - 400° F.	45 - 60 min.
Yeast Rolls	400° F.	15 - 20 min.

CAKES

Butter Loaf Cakes	350° F.	45 - 60 min.
Butter Layer Cakes	350° - 375° F.	25 - 35 min.
Cupcakes	375° F.	20 - 23 min.
Chiffon Cakes	325° F.	60 min.
Sponge Cakes	325° F.	60 min.
Angel Food Cakes	325° F.	60 min.

COOKIES

Bar Cookies	350° F.	25 - 30 min.
Drop Cookies	350° - 375° F.	18 - 25 min.
Rolled Refrigerator Cookies	350° - 400° F.	8 - 12 min.

PASTRY

Meringue	350° F.	12 - 20 min.
Pie Shells	450° F.	12 - 15 min.
Filled Pies	450° F.	
	lower to 350° F.	8 - 12 min.

NOTES: These are just general temperatures and times, always use what is specified in the recipe.

Modern oven thermostats are adjustable, so it is necessary to periodically check the ACTUAL oven temperature with an accurate thermometer designed for the purpose and adjust the dial, or have your serviceman perform this service at least once a year.

Always follow HIGH ALTITUDE directions, temperature settings and times when appropriate to your locale.

Meats
Seasonings & Marinades

FLAVORING CHART

MEAT	SEASONINGS			
Beef	rosemary sage garlic dill	mushrooms dry mustard shallots paprika	chili peppers peppercorns berries tomatoes	beer red wine balsamic vinegar
Chicken or Turkey	lemon ginger tarragon sage	thyme oregano dill peppers	garlic apple cider dry mustard fruit juices	paprika red wine white wine
Fish	cilantro bay leaf basil fennel	lemon lime dill saffron	black pepper garlic sweet peppers tarragon	rosemary herbed vinegar
Lamb	garlic curry mint lemon	rosemary thyme sage ginger	saffron mustard seed	
Pork	apples garlic ginger lemon	cloves rosemary orange zest lemon zest	coriander unsweetened preserves dried fruits	Madeira or port wine
Veal	ginger oregano mustard marjoram	shallots mushrooms orange lemon	Marsala wine garlic thyme	
Veg.	garlic lemon dill vinegar	nuts parsley mint rosemary	basil allspice sweet peppers pepper flakes	marjoram chervil chives nutmeg

TIP: For added flavor, blend garlic and herbs (fresh or dried) into a dish ahead of time. At the last minute of cooking time, toss in. This gives an extra dimension in taste.

Meats
Doneness Chart

DESCRIPTION	DEGREES FAHRENHEIT
Ground Meat & Mixtures	
Turkey, Chicken	165° F.
Veal, Beef, Lamb, Pork	160° F.
Fresh Beef	
Medium Rare	145° F.
Medium	160° F.
Well Done	170° F.
Fresh Veal	
Medium Rare	145° F.
Medium	160° F.
Well Done	170° F.
Fresh Lamb	
Medium Rare	145° F.
Medium	160° F.
Well Done	170° F.
Pork	
Well Done	170° F.
Poultry	
Chicken, Whole	180° F.
Turkey, Whole	180° F.
Poultry Breasts, Roasted	170° F.
Poultry Thighs, Wings	180° F.
Duck & Goose	180° F.
Seafood	
Fin Fish	Cook until opaque and flakes easily.
Shrimp, Lobster, Crab	Shell should turn red Flesh pearly opaque.
Scallops	Flesh should turn milky white or opaque and firm.
Clams, Mussels, Oysters	Cook until shells open. Discard any unopened.

Candy Making Chart

Important tips to remember when making candy:
1. Dissolve sugar completely to keep large crystals from forming; wash down the sides of the saucepan by placing a cover over the saucepan for about 2-3 minutes.

2. Heavy, flat bottom saucepans will prevent candies from scorching.

3. A candy thermometer is essential for proper temperature.

4. Cool fudges to lukewarm before beating or shaping.

5. Butter, not margarine, should be used in most candy recipes to ensure the best textures and results.

Thread	begins at 230°	The syrup will make a 2" thread when dropped from a spoon.
Soft Ball	begins at 234°	A small amount of syrup dropped into chilled water forms a ball, but flattens when picked up with fingers.
Firm Ball	begins at 244°	The ball will hold its shape and flatten only when pressed.
Hard Ball	begins at 250°	The ball is more rigid but still pliable.
Soft Crack	begins at 270°	When a small amount of syrup is dropped into chilled water it will separate into threads which will bend when picked up.
Hard Crack	begins at 300°	The syrup separates into threads that are hard and brittle.
Caramelized	Sugar 310° to 338°	Between these temperatures the syrup will turn dark golden, but will turn black at 350°.

Herbs & Spices

ALLSPICE – Usually used in ground form, allspice has a flavor like a combination of cinnamon, nutmeg, and cloves. Allspice is used in both savory and sweet dishes.

ANISE SEED – Related to parsley, this spice has a mildly sweet licorice flavor.

BASIL – Most people are accustomed to using fresh basil in their favorite Italian dishes, but this licorice-like herb is equally at home in Thai coconut curry or a Provencal pistou. Dried basil tastes completely different from fresh, so if you want to add a shot of basil flavor try blending basil with olive oil and storing cubes in the freezer.

BAY LEAF – A pungent flavor. Available as whole leaf. Good in vegetable and fish soups, tomato sauces and juice. Remove before serving.

CARAWAY – Their slightly anise flavor works particularly well with rye breads as well with the kind of sweet and sour dishes favored in Central Europe such as pork and apples or braised red cabbage.

CARDAMOM – Whole cardamom pods can appear in pilaf rice, curries, or Scandinavian baked goods. Ground cardamom loses its flavor.

CAYENNE PEPPER – A touch of spicy cayenne can add a lot of heat to a dish without radically changing the flavor. It is a mixture of ground chili peppers and can be used in a wide variety of cuisines.

CELERY SEED – The wild celery plant these seeds are from are on more and more menus emphasizing regional and local cuisine. The seeds add their pungent flavor to anything from cocktails to coleslaw and can be used whole or ground.

CHIVES – Leaves are used in many ways. May be used in salads, cream cheese, sandwiches, omelets, soups, and fish dishes.

CILANTRO – This herb is truly a love it or hate it proposition. Stems are quite sweet and can be added raw along with the leaves while the roots are prized by Thai chefs for curry pastes.

CINNAMON – Cinnamon adds sweetness and heat to sweet and savory dishes alike. Cinnamon sticks are often added whole to coffee, stews, rice, curries, or tangines and removed before serving. It is a staple in baked goods–a sprinkle makes even a simple bowl of oatmeal smell and taste great.

CLOVE – Often paired with cinnamon and nutmeg, cloves are dried flower buds that are sold both ground and whole. They have a warm, sweet flavor that works great with sweet and savory, like clove studded ham. For a more potent flavor grind them yourself.

CUMIN – Can be experienced in all kinds of dishes from Mexico, India and the Middle East. The toasted seeds can be used whole in dishes and eaten as is, or be ground right before use. Pre-ground cumin loses potency quickly, but can be helped by toasting first in a dry skillet over medium-low heat.

Herbs & Spices

DILL – The feathery leaves of the dill plant add light anise flavor to seafood, soups, salads, and lots of other dishes. Dill is almost always added at the very last minute. Keep fresh in the refrigerator by storing it in a glass of water with a plastic bag placed over the top.

GINGER – There are many ways to use this peppery root from fresh to dried and ground to pickled or crystallized. Each of these preparations adds unique flavors and textures to everything from stir-fries to roasted meats to classic ginger snaps.

MINT – Commonly associated with sweet treats, mint lends its cooling, peppery bite to plenty of savory dishes, particularly from the Middle East and North Africa. Perfect for summer-fresh salads or to liven up a sauce, leftover fresh mint can also be used to brew a fragrant tea which is equally tasty served hot or cold.

MUSTARD – Mustard is great to have around to add heat and a piquant flavor in sauces, dressings, marinades, and entrees. Whole mustard seeds are often part of the pickling spices, but are also a key part of many Indian curries where they are toasted in oil first until they pop.

NUTMEG – An aromatic spice with a sweet and spicy flavor. Nutmeg adds warmth and depth to foods but doesn't overpower other ingredients.

OREGANO – A pungent herb primarily found in Mediterranean and Mexican cuisines, it is one of the few herbs that survives the drying process relatively unscathed. Use dried oregano for longer stewing or dry rubs, but make sure to use half as much dry as you would fresh since the flavor is so intense. Oregano can also be used as a substitute for its close cousin marjoram.

PAPRIKA – Paprika has too often been relegated to the role of garnish, mostly because of its beautiful rich color. There are all sorts of paprika that can add flavors from mild to hot.

PARSLEY – Formerly regulated to the role of garnish, fresh parsley is coming into its own for its fresh flavor and great health benefits, but dried parsley lacks both flavor and color.

PEPPERCORN – Along with salt, black pepper is half of a team that is so fundamental to cooking that they get called upon nearly every time you need to spice up a dish. There are all sorts of peppercorns that each offer their own flavors and degrees of heat.

RED PEPPER – Dried red chili pepper sold either ground or in flakes, red pepper works well either added early to dishes that are going to cook for a while or simply shaken on near the very end. Because they vary greatly in terms of heat, taste your red pepper to see just how hot it is.

ROSEMARY – Can be used fresh or dried for long cooking in soups, meats, stews and more. Use sparingly at first and more if needed.

Herbs & Spices

SAGE– Used fresh. May be used in poultry and meat stuffings; in sausage and practically all meat combinations; in cheese and vegetable combinations, or curry.

TARRAGON– Experimenting with this anise-like herb in classic French favorites such as bearnaise sauce, creamy tarragon chicken, or fresh vinaigrette can help you learn how to use tarragon to lift flavors without overpowering a dish.

THYME– One of the most popular herbs in American and European cooking, thyme can be paired with nearly any kind of meat, poultry, fish, or vegetable. To use fresh thyme, peel off as many of the leaves as you can from the woody stem by running your fingers along the stem.

VANILLA– An aromatic spice with a warm flavor, vanilla is the seed pod of an orchid. It's available dried or as an extract.

HERB AND SPICE TIPS

In contrast to herbs, spices are nearly always dried and are mostly ground before using. Pre-ground spices lose their potency quickly, so they should be stored in airtight containers in a cool, dark place and be replaced around every six months. Whole spices retain their flavor longer (for up to five years) and can be used as is or quickly ground with mortar and pestle or an inexpensive coffee grinder (reserve one for spices to avoid coffee flavor).

To get the best flavor from your spices, "toast" them in a dry skillet over low heat, stirring frequently, until they start to release their aromas. Even ground spices can perk up a bit after a quick toast in a skillet, but ones that are too old and faded are generally beyond repair.

FRESH SEASONINGS

- In recipes, cut salt in half and add more fresh herbs and spices.
- When doubling a recipe, herbs and spices should only be increased by one and a half times. Taste, and then add some if necessary.
- Add sage, bay leaf and garlic at the beginning of the cooking process as they have a strong flavor. Herbs with more subtle aroma such as basil, parsley, and fennel are best when added at the end of the cooking process to preserve their flavor.
- Delicate aromas can be lost due to overcooking.
- Cut or chop fresh herbs to expose more surface area. This will release more flavor.
- Here's a chart to convert dried herbs to fresh

1 tsp. dried herbs	=	1 Tbsp. fresh herbs
1/8 tsp. garlic powder	=	1 medium clove of garlic
1 tsp. onion powder	=	1 medium onion, finely chopped
1 tsp. ground ginger	=	1 tsp. grated fresh ginger

Cooking Vegetables

- Times on chart are for fresh, one pound vegetables.
- The cooking times are in minutes.
- NR = Not recommended.
- Steaming times begin when the water boils and creates steam.
- Vegetables are done when they are tender, but still crisp. (They should not be mushy.)

VEGETABLES	STEAM	MICRO.	BLANCH	BOIL	OTHER
Artichoke, whole	30-60	4-5 each	NR	25-40	NR
Artichoke, hearts	10-15	6-7	8-12	10-15	Stir-fry 10
Asparagus	8-10	4-6	2-3	5-12	Stir-fry pieces 5
Beans, green	5-15	6-12	4-5	10-20	Stir-fry 3-4
Beans, lima	10-20	8-12	5-10	20-30	NR
Beets	40-60	14-18	NR	30-60	Bake 60
Broccoli, spears	8-15	6-7	3-4	5-10	Blanch; Bake
Broccoli flowerets	5-6	4-5	2-3	4-5	Stir-fry 3-4
Brussels sprouts	6-12	7-8	4-5	5-10	Halve; Stir-fry 3-4
Cabbage, wedges	6-9	10-12	NR	10-15	
Carrots, whole	10-15	8-10	4-5	15-20	Bake 30-40
Carrots, sliced	4-5	4-7	3-4	5-10	Stir-fry 3-4
Cauliflower, whole	15-20	6-7	4-5	10-15	Blanch; Bake 20
Cauliflower, flowerets	6-10	3-5	3-4	5-8	Stir-fry 3-4
Corn, on cob	6-10	3-4	3-4	4-7	Soak 10; bake 375°
Corn, cut	4-6	2 per cup	2 12-4	3-4	Stir-fry 3-4
Eggplant, whole	15-30	7-10	10-15	10-15	Bake 30 at 400°
Eggplant, diced	5-6	5-6	3-4	5-10	Bake 10-15 425°
Greens, Collard, turnip	NR	18-20	8-15	30-60	Stir-fry 4-6
Greens, kale/beet	4-6	8-10	4-5	5-8	Stir-fry 2-3
Mushrooms	4-5	3-4	NR	3-4 /broth	Stir-fry or broil 4-5
Onions, whole	20-25	6-10	NR	20-30	Bake 60 at 325°
Onions, pearl	15-20	5-7	2-3	10-20	Braise 15-25
Parsnips	8-10	4-6	3-4	5-10	Bake 30 at 325°
Peas	3-5	5-7	1-2	8-12	Stir-fry 2-3
Peppers, bell	2-4	2-4	2-3	4-5	Stir-fry 2-3
Potatoes, whole	12-30	6-8	NR	20-30	Bake 40-60 at 400°
Potatoes, cut	10-12	8-10	NR	15-20	Bake 25-30 at 400°
Spinach	5-6	3-4	2-3	2-5	Stir-fry 2-3
Squash, sliced	5-10	3-6	2-3	5-10	NR
Squash, halves	15-40	6-10	NR	5-10	Bake 40-60 at 375°
Tomatoes	2-3	3-4	1-2	NR	Bake halves 8-15
Turnips, cubed	12-15	6-8	2-3	5-8	Stir-fry 2-3
Zucchini	5-10	3-6	2-3	5-10	Broil halves 5

Counting Calories

CANDIES, SNACKS & NUTS

Almonds	12 to 15	93
Cashews	6 to 8	88
Chocolate Bar (nut)	2 ounce bar	340
Coconut (shredded)	1 cup	344
English Toffee	1 piece	25
Fudge	1 ounce	115
Mints	5 very small	50
Peanuts (salted)	1 ounce	190
Peanuts (roasted)	1 cup	800
Pecans	6	104
Popcorn (plain)	1 cup	54
Potato Chips	10 medium chips	115
Pretzels	10 small sticks	35
Walnuts	8 to 10	100

DAIRY PRODUCTS

American Cheese	1 cube 1⅛ inch	100
Butter, margarine	1 level Tbsp.	100
Cheese (blue, cheddar, cream, Swiss)	1 ounce	105
Cottage Cheese (uncreamed)	1 ounce	25
Cream(light)	1 Tbsp.	30
Egg White	1	15
Egg Yolk	1	61
Eggs (boiled or poached)	2	160
Eggs (scrambled)	2	220
Eggs (fried)	1 medium	110
Yogurt (flavored)	4 ounces	60

DESSERTS

Cakes:

Angel Food Cake	2" piece	110
Cheesecake	2" piece	200
Chocolate Cake (iced)	2" piece	445
Fruit Cake	2" piece	115
Pound Cake	1 ounce piece	140
Sponge Cake	2" piece	120
Shortcake (with fruit)	1 avg. slice	300
Cupcake (iced)	1	185
Cupcake (plain)	1	145

Pudding:

Bread Pudding	½ cup	150
Flavored Pudding	½ cup	140

Pies:

Apple	1 piece	331
Blueberry	1 piece	290
Cherry	1 piece	355
Custard	1 piece	280

Counting Calories

Lemon Meringue	1 piece	305
Peach	1 piece	280
Pumpkin	1 piece	265
Rhubarb	1 piece	265

Ice Cream:

Chocolate Ice Cream	$\frac{1}{2}$ cup	200
Vanilla Ice Cream	$\frac{1}{2}$ cup	150

Miscellaneous:

Chocolate Eclair (custard)	1 small	250
Cookies (assorted)	1, 3-inch dia.	120
Cream Puff	1	296
Jello, all flavors	$\frac{1}{2}$ cup	78

BREADS & FLOUR FOODS

Baking Powder Biscuits	1 large or 2 small	129
Bran Muffin	1 medium	106
Corn Bread	1 small square	130
Dumpling	1 medium	70
Enriched White Bread	1 slice	60
French Bread	1 small slice	54
French Toast	1 slice	135
Macaroni and Cheese	1 cup	475
Melba Toast	1 slice	25
Noodles (cooked)	1 cup	200
Pancakes, wheat	1, 4-inch	60
Raisin Bread	1 slice	80
Rye Bread	1 slice	71
Saltines	1	17
Soda Crackers	1	23
Waffles	1	216
Whole Wheat Bread	1 slice	55

BREAKFAST CEREALS

Corn Flakes	1 cup	96
Cream of Wheat	1 cup	120
Oatmeal	1 cup	148
Rice Flakes	1 cup	105
Shredded Wheat	1 biscuit	100
Sugar Krisps	$\frac{3}{4}$ cup	110

FISH & FOWL

Bass	4 ounces	105
Brook Trout	4 ounces	130
Crabmeat (canned)	3 ounces	85
Fish Sticks	5 sticks or 4 ounces	200
Haddock (canned)	1 fillet	158
Haddock (broiled)	4 ounces (steak)	207

Counting Calories

FRUITS

Apple (raw)	1 small	70
Banana	1 medium	85
Blueberries (frozen/unsweetened)	½ cup	45
Cantaloupe Melon	½ melon large	60
Cherries, fresh/whole	½ cup	40
Cranberries (sauce)	1 cup	54
Grapes	1 cup	65
Dates	3 or 4	95
Grapefruit (unsweetened)	½	55
Orange	1 medium	70
Peach (fresh)	1	35
Plums	2	50
Tangerine (fresh)	1	40
Watermelon	1" slice	60

MEATS

Bacon (crisp)	2 slices	95
Frankfurter	1	155
Hamburger (avg. fat/broiled)	3 ounces	245
Hamburger (lean/broiled)	3 ounces	185
Ham (broiled/lean)	3 ounces	200
Ham (baked)	1 slice	100
Lamb Leg Roast	3 ounces	235
Lamb Chop (rib)	3 ounces	300
Liver (fried)	3 ½ ounces	210
Meat Loaf	1 slice	100
Pork Chop (medium)	3 ounces	340
Pork Sausage	3 ounces	405
Roasts (beef)		
Loin Roast	3 ½ ounces	340
Pot Roast (round)	3 ½ ounces	200
Rib Roast	3 ½ ounces	260
Rump Roast	3 ½ ounces	340
Spareribs	1 piece, 3 ribs	123
Swiss Steak	3 ½ ounces	300
Veal Chop (medium)	3 ounces	185
Veal Roast	3 ounces	230

SALADS & DRESSINGS

Chef Salad/mayonnaise	1 Tbsp.	125
Chef Salad/French, Roquefort	1 Tbsp.	105
Cole Slaw (no dressing)	½ cup	102
Fruit Gelatin	1 square	139
Potato Salad (no dressing)	½ cup	184
French Dressing	1 Tbsp.	60
Mayonnaise	1 Tbsp.	110

Napkin Folding

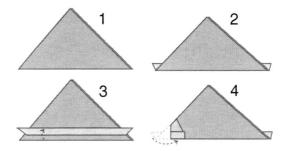

CANDLE

Candle Fold Instructions:
1. Fold into triangle, point at top.
2. Turn lower edge up about 1".
3. Turn over, folded edge down.
4. Roll tightly from left to right.
5. Tuck in corner. Stand upright.

DIAGONAL STRIPE

Diagonal Stripe Fold Instructions:
1. Fold edge A to edge B.
2. Fold edge A to edge B. Loose edges at top.
3. Roll down the top flap.
4. Roll down the second flap
5. Roll down the third flap
6. Fold sides back as pictured.

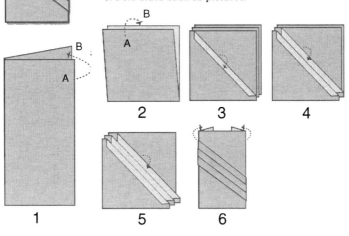

Table Settings

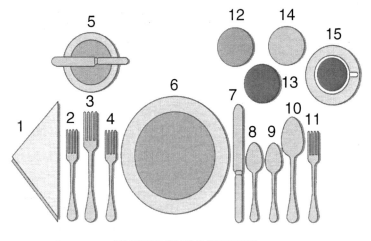

FORMAL TABLE SETTING

1. Napkin
2. Salad fork
3. Dinner fork
4. Dessert fork
5. Bread-and-butter plate, with spreader
6. Dinner plate
7. Dinner knife
8. Teaspoon
9. Teaspoon
10. Soup spoon
11. Cocktail fork
12. Water glass
13. Red-wine glass
14. White-wine glass
15. Coffee cup and saucer

GENERAL TABLE SETTING

1. Napkin
2. Salad fork
3. Dinner fork
4. Bread-and-butter plate
5. Salad plate
6. Dinner plate
7. Dinner knife
8. Teaspoon
9. Soup spoon
10. Water glass
11. Wine glass

- Don't put out utensils that won't ever be used.

- Bring the coffee cup and saucer to the table with the dessert.

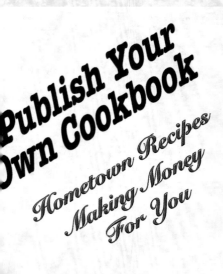

Publish Your Own Cookbook

Hometown Recipes Making Money For You

GRACIOUS GIFTS

FROM THE KITCHENS OF
SPRING RIVER BAPTIST WOMEN

Recipe For Success

very low price   67 days to pay!

No money down!

Delivery within 60 working days

*Raise $500 to $25,000 with
Our Guaranteed
Cookbook Fundraising Program*

Trading recipes has been a popular hobby for generations! Now you can turn this tradition into an exciting and profitable **Fundraising** Program that involves the entire community! Fundcraft helps you every step of the way with a proven plan that guarantees your success. Request your FREE copy of our Recipes For Success Publishing Guide that explains how easy it is to publish your own cookbook.

Hometown Recipes Making Money For You

Order Your Free Recipes For Success Publishing Guide Today!

THE
TASTEFUL
TABLE

CRYSTAL SPRINGS
UNITED METHODIST WOMEN

Organization _____

Name _____

Address _____

City _____ State _____ Zip _____

Home Phone _____

E-mail _____

"You collect the recipes...Fundcraft does the rest!"

We Have Your Recipe
for
Successful Fundraising

Cookbooks are proven fundraisers and perfect keepsakes. Preserve treasured recipes for your church, school, family or organization. We make it affordable, profitable and fun!

Creating your own unique cookbook with hometown recipes is an easy, enjoyable way for groups of all sizes to raise money. All over America, churches, schools and groups like yours are earning thousands of dollars selling their personalized cookbooks using the proven Fundcraft Cookbook Program.

Return the postage paid card today or visit us online at www.fundcraft.com

Satisfied Customers In All 50 States